DEVON AND CORNWALL RECORD SOCIETY

New Series, Volume 51

Painting of Thomas Hill by John Hales at the Pepys Library,
Magdalene College, Cambridge.

DEVON AND CORNWALL RECORD SOCIETY

New Series, Volume 51

THE LETTER BOOK OF THOMAS HILL 1660–1661
Westcountry mercantile affairs and the wider world

Edited by June Palmer

Exeter
2008

ISBN 978 0 901853 51 6

Designed and typeset by Kestrel Data, Exeter

Printed and bound in Great Britain by
Short Run Press, Exeter

CONTENTS

*To the memory of my husband, Donald,
who was a great encouragement to me.*

EDITORIAL NOTE

The script of this letter book is, on the whole, fairly clear and has been retained as far as possible. Capital letters have been kept but, occasionally, it is difficult to decide whether a capital was intended. Punctuation has been added where necessary and therefore some sentences have been shortened with extra capitals not in the original. Italics have been used for names of ships and also for parts of letters which have been translated from the Italian.

The format for sterling and dollars has been standardised and therefore differs in places from the original. The letters 'li' have been replaced by lb or £ as applicable. The letters themselves have been given numbers for ease of reference. This numbering is not in the original. To avoid repetition the closures of most of the letters have been omitted.

Many of the letters were written to merchants abroad who were using the New Style [abbreviated to NS in the text] of the calendar which, at this period, was ten days ahead of the Old Style [abbreviated to OS in the text] used in England. Sometimes this discrepancy is indicated in the letter by both dates being given. Where this has not been done and is necessary for the sense, it has been added in square brackets. In England the New Year was still regarded as starting on 25 March. Therefore in letters for the first part of the year have generally been given the double date e.g. (for 1661) of 1660/1661. Please note that Schellinks, in his journal throughout was writing in the New Style and this is not always clear. It becomes apparent when the dating of this letter book and Schellinks' journal is compared.

It has been difficult to decide what form of a surname to use. In some cases the variation is great, very often in the same letter, the surname 'Braems' being an example of this. In the text of the letter book I have kept the original. When referring to the names in the Introduction I have used what I consider to have been the most usual spelling at that time. Today the surname might well have changed e.g. the descendants of the 'Jennens' family now seem to call themselves 'Jennings'. Please note, in reference to William Jennens of Plymouth, that the authors of Schellinks' Journal transcribed it originally as 'Tennens' and then as 'Innes'.

The first letters of the book are in shorthand – for the editorial conventions which I have used for this section please see the beginning of the text.

The illustration on the front cover, 'The ship Royal Charles which brought Charles II back to England in May 1660' and those on pages xvii, xviii, xxi, xxii and xxv are from 175M86/P6 at the Hampshire Record Office and are used with their permission. Most of the drawings are not dated but are from 1660 and 1690 and would appear to be from the journal of Edward Barlow.

ABBREVIATIONS FREQUENTLY USED IN THE TEXT

BL Add. MS   Additional Manuscript, British Library

Boyd   Boyd's List of Londoners – in the Society of Genealogists

CRO   Cornwall Record Office

DNB   *Oxford Dictionary of National Biography* (Oxford 2004) eds. H.C.G. Matthew & Brian Harrison

DCNQ   Devon & Cornwall Notes & Queries

Evelyn   *The Diary of John Evelyn, Esq., F.R.S.* ed. William Bray (London 1818) reprint Chandos edition, not dated

Familiar Letters   *Familiar Letters which passed between Abraham Hill and several eminent and ingenious persons of the last century.* (London 1767) (copy in the library of the Royal Society)

Hutton   *The Restoration* Ronald Hutton (Oxford 1985)

Pepys [+ Vol.no]   *The Diary of Samuel Pepys* eds. Robert Latham & William Matthews (London 1970-1983)

Roseveare   *Markets and Merchants of the Late Seventeenth Century* ed. Henry Roseveare (Oxford 1987)

Schellinks   *The Journal of William Schellinks' Travels in England 1661–1663* trans from the Dutch and edited by Maurice Exwood and H.L. Lehman (London 1993)

Spalding   *Contemporaries of Bulstrode Whitelocke* Ruth Spalding (Oxford 1990)

Steckley   *The Letter Book of John Paige, London Merchant 1648* ed. George F. Steckley (London Record Society 1984)

TNA: PRO   The National Archives, Public Record Office

Woodhead   *The Rulers of London 1660–1689* J. R. Woodhead (London 1965)

ACKNOWLEDGEMENTS

The Thomas Hill Letter Book is at the Centre for Kentish Studies. I would like to thank the archivist and staff for their help in providing me with a microfilm of the document and for their permission to publish. With its many references to the Restoration of Charles II, to the members of the Royal Society and with the connection to Samuel Pepys I am surprised that no-one else preceded me, possibly the first pages, with what appears to be unintelligible shorthand, were off-putting. I discovered the document when visiting Kent on an expedition with my husband who was looking for ancestors from that county. I had found a reference to the Letter Book but had no idea that it would have any connection with Devon and Cornwall. I opened the book at a random page and discovered a letter to a 'Bryan Rogers', although no address was given. This was, however, a very familiar name to me having already worked on the history of Penryn & Falmouth. When I was able to study the full text I realised that about half the letters were written to people in Devon and Cornwall or who were connected with those counties.

The Kent connection is also of interest and I recall one very fortuitous and accidental encounter in Bridge when trying to obtain entry to a locked church in search of a Braems family monument. A gentleman came to our assistance, I believe Mr John Williamson, and we held his dog whilst he went to collect the key. He is one of the very few people in Kent who had researched the history of the Braems family and I am grateful for his help.

The staff of the Cornwall Record Office kindly allowed me to use their microfilm reader to study the document and I would like to thank them for this and for their help with my research over many years. I appreciate the kindness of the staff of several record offices including the Public Record Office, the Guildhall Library Manuscript Department, the British Library, the Royal Institution of Cornwall, the West Country Studies Library at Exeter and the Archives at Genoa, Livorno and Lucca. The Local Studies Library in Poole has also permitted me to use their microfilm reader and given up their time in helping me with the film. The staff of both the Royal Society and the Pepys Library at Magdalen College, Cambridge, have been very welcoming and have kindly allowed me to use a photograph of the painting of Abraham Hill at the Royal Society and one of the painting of Thomas Hill which is placed in a very prominent position in the Pepys Library. I am grateful too to the Kent Archaeological Society for their consent to reproducing an illustration from *Archaeologica Cantiana,* to the Hampshire Record Office for permission to use the drawings in their possession.

Two of my relatives, Steven and Petra Sheil, who live near Amsterdam, undertook the task of searching for documents relating to the Thierry family in the Gemeentearchief, Amsterdam and I appreciate the time they took in order to help me.

I have had to seek help to translate the Italian. I am indebted to several people but in particular I would like to thank David Dearlove of Penzance for his initial help at a time when I knew no Italian. Without his careful reading of the letters I would have found the transcription and translation very difficult. I would like to express my thanks to Oliver Padel for introducing Timothy Underwood of Cambridge to me. The latter was able to identify the type of shorthand used, which was necessary before any serious attempt could be made to transcribe it.

I am very appreciative of the help of Donald, my husband, who has accompanied me on our several expeditions to Kent, Hampshire, London, Genoa, Lucca and Livorno and has taken very useful notes.

In conclusion I am most grateful to the Devon & Cornwall Record Society for agreeing to publish this document. Margery Rowe was very encouraging when I first approached her and helped me considerably, Andrew Thorpe gave me much useful advice and finally Todd Gray has undertaken the preparation of the document for publication, a time consuming job. I would like to thank him for his kindness, patience, good humour and for his friendship for a period of over twenty years.

INTRODUCTION

OVERSEAS TRADE IN THE FIRST FOUR DECADES OF THE SEVENTEENTH CENTURY

Dramatic changes in the trading patterns of England took place at the beginning of the seventeenth century. Nicholas Canny has described this expansion of trade as 'spectacular' and attributes it to 'merchant investment in a series of new companies'.[1] The North Atlantic fisheries and the first successful colonial settlements in North America and the Caribbean increased the number of transatlantic voyages; the founding of the East India Company in 1600 heralded the English commitment to trade in that area whilst England came to replace the cities of northern Italy in the organisation of Mediterranean trade.[2] The Levant Company had been founded in 1582 and this was a direct challenge to Venetian interests previously dominant in that part of the world.[3] Italy became an important staging post for ships to the Levant, often goods were sold there in order to obtain the necessary currency for buying luxuries which wealthier people were now demanding. At the same time the Crown was becoming more dependent on the customs and other taxes levied on trade rather than the older sources of finance.

The West Country was in a unique position to take advantage of all these changes, its geographic position being the most important reason. Many of the ships leaving London for the New World, for the Mediterranean or the East Indies might well call at the Cornish and Devon ports on their way out, especially if weather conditions, new intelligence or lack of provisions demanded a safe haven. Many visits, where no goods were landed, were not entered in the port books. State Papers and High Court of Admiralty disputes, for example, often have references to ships coming in to Westcountry ports, which are not recorded elsewhere. In particular they might seek the sanctuary of the Fal estuary. Falmouth, as a town in its own right, did not in theory exist until it was granted a charter in 1661 but the advantages of its harbour were well known to mariners.[4] Similarly ships might call here on their return voyage not only after a long Atlantic crossing, but increasingly, as the century progressed on the even longer voyage from the East Indies. Westcountry mariners became accustomed to these long intercontinental voyages and the experience gave them greater advantage over their rivals.

Devon and Cornwall too were fortunate in their principal exports, cloth from Devon and tin and pilchards from Cornwall. By the beginning of the seventeenth century a considerable quantity of the nation's woollen cloth came from Devon. Since the end of the fifteenth century cloth expansion was centred on Exeter with most of the trade being with France.[5] In the seventeenth century the chief market was still France. Devon merchants had some problems with their London rivals in establishing their right to free trade in cloth but this dispute was settled in the 1630s.[6]

Cornish pilchards became a usual part of the cargo of ships visiting Spain and Italy and Cornish tin was in great demand in the Ottoman Empire. Tin too was an important element in the income of the monarch. As Mariko Mizui stated:'An annual rent for the patent of pre-emption, along with the coinage tax, became a stable and significant income for the Crown' and the regular payment received also gave the Crown the opportunity to increase its borrowings from the tin farmers.[7]

The long association between Westcountry merchants and those of Spain resumed when the long period of war between England and Spain ended in 1604. With peace finally signed, trade gradually increased. Many of the Westcountry merchants or their sons took their expertise in the Spanish trade to London. One such Devon man was John Paige who, as a very young man, was sent to Tenerife and then returned to London to be apprenticed to Gowen Paynter, another Devon man from a Dawlish family. John Steckley, in his introduction to John Paige's letters, describes Paige

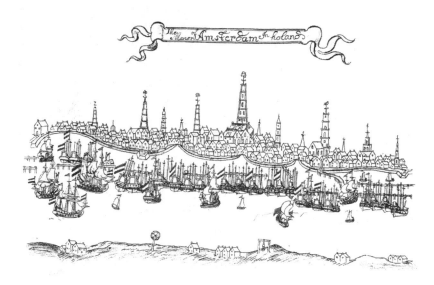

Amsterdam

as 'one instance in an established pattern of mobility which had had
consequences for London's trade...the Lants, Boones, Warrens and
other contemporaries of Paige had brought their knowledge of the
Spanish trade from Westcountry towns to London'.[8] The examples
quoted are from Devon but Cornish families were also involved.
Two brothers from the Enys family worked in Spain, Samuel Enys
was there in the 1620s to be followed later by his brother, Richard.
Other Westcountry merchants in London strengthened the trading
network by taking as apprentices young men from Devon and
Cornwall. William Cloberry, a haberdasher and Devon man, for
example, took as his apprentice Peter Kekewich of Cornwall in
1624.[9] Other relatives of these London merchants stayed behind:
John Paige had a cousin, also John Paige, working in Plymouth,
and so this network was further intertwined. In addition to these
new opportunities, the staple trade of the West Country with
France continued. French wines had long been a popular import.

The growing confidence, especially in the Devon ports of
Dartmouth, Plymouth, Barnstaple and Topsham (where goods
for Exeter were generally landed especially at times when Exeter's
canal was silted up) led to major new developments in these ports

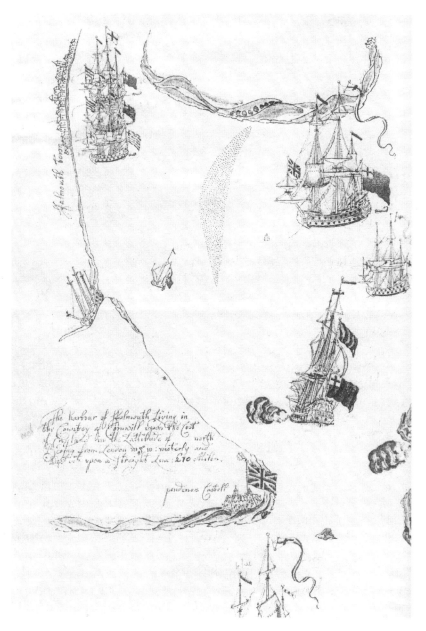

Falmouth

at the beginning of the century with many new public and private buildings being erected which reflected the growing prosperity of the Devon merchants.[10] The Cornish merchants on whole were less wealthy but the Rashleighs, originally from Devon, found their fortune in Fowey.

The movement of merchants westward also reflects the growing attraction of the Westcountry ports. Alison Grant mentions the Colmers who came from Birmingham to Plymouth.[11] Another Birmingham man, Abraham Jennens, who arrived in Plymouth at the beginning of the seventeenth century, married Judith Shere, the daughter of a Plymouth merchant, and became one of its leading merchants. Richard Hill and Francis Nosworthy, both from Devon, settled in Truro about the same time.

The importance of many of the Mediterranean countries was increasingly recognised as the seventeenth century progressed by leading families in Devon and Cornwall and many sons were sent as apprentices to merchants in London who were concerned with the Mediterranean trade. Three sons in the important Boscawen family from Truro went to Turkey: Edward was apprenticed in about 1648 to the grocer and Turkey merchant, Thomas Hodge in London. To the same master and at the same time went Joseph Carew from Antony.[12] Two of Edward's brothers died in Turkey[13] and other Carews were there in the 1660s. The Italian trade, used partly as a staging post to the Near East, also increased. Plymouth in particular had close connections with Italy.

The Cornish ports were less busy than their Devon counterparts. Apart from tin, pilchards and the other Cornish export, helling stones, no large quantities of local goods were exported from Cornwall, and the major imports were directly connected to the exports of tin and pilchards. The population of Cornwall was comparatively small; therefore household necessities and luxuries were needed in only small quantities. Goods from abroad that were landed in Cornwall were often sent on by coastal vessels to major centres of population such as London or Bristol. The two principal imports therefore were salt, preferably from France although also from Portugal, required for the fishing industry and timber used in both the fishing industry and the mines. Charcoal was also imported in increasing quantities by the end of the 1630s for tin smelting. Spanish iron was in demand particularly for use in the mines and canvas and coarse linen cloth were required for ships' sails as well as for clothing. The two major sources for timber were Ireland and Hampshire with the quantities from the Scandinavian countries increasing during the century, the trade with Norway began to flourish in the 1630s and 1640s.[14] Almost all the ports in Cornwall were involved in these trades but the ports themselves differed widely in their mode of operating.

The 'head port' for Cornwall, in terms of customs, was the Devon port of Plymouth. Plymouth therefore played an important part in Cornish trade. The parishes on the western side of the Tamar provided the largest number of seamen and ships in Cornwall according to the survey of about 1626.[15] More pilchards were exported from Plymouth in the sixteenth century and sometimes in the seventeenth century than were exported directly from Cornwall.[16] Many Plymouth merchants were heavily involved in Cornwall and their names were entered as merchants in the port books of Cornwall although they were not resident there.

Looe was greatly influenced by Plymouth: when trying to estimate the amount of salt imported and the number of pilchards exported for Looe no sensible ratio can be found and it can only be concluded that much of the salt was used for pilchards later to be exported from Plymouth.[17] The cargoes of Looe were very similar to its neighbour to the west, Fowey, although the latter was a busier port, the most important in Cornwall in the first part of the century.[18]

At the beginning of the century large quantities of Newfoundland fish came into both of these ports, most of which was re-exported to the continent. 100,000 fish were exported from Fowey in 1610 and double that quantity in 1611 (though this figure contains fish brought in at the end of 1610 and not sent out until 1611). Looe, in 1610, exported over 90,000. However, it was the connection with France that was paramount in both ports. The size of the ships, mostly around 15 to 25 tons, reflects this French trade and there were far more local boats involved than in the other Cornish ports. But ships left Fowey for other continental countries: Mr Napper of Plymouth sent the *Truelove* of London to Fowey to take in pilchards, from there she proceeded to Alicante, Valencia, Carthagena, Genoa, Naples, Majorca, back to Alicante, then to Lisbon, Dover and London.[19]

Penryn on the estuary of the Fal had an even greater international flavour, occasionally unsavoury. The charter of 1621 described

Naples

Barbados

it as a town which had 'much traffic in and upon the sea' but added because of 'the arrival of sailors and other unruly men there resorting together divers riots and routs but also very many great offences are there often committed'.[20] The large harbour entrance to the Fal meant many ships coming into Penryn were larger than at Fowey, but there were very few vessels described, in the first part of century, as belonging to Penryn or Falmouth. There were only three in the survey of about 1626. At the beginning of the century the trade of Penryn could not compare with that of Fowey.[21] By 1639, however, Penryn was overtaking Fowey and, in that year, more pilchards were exported from Penryn, (mostly through the Straits of Gibraltar), than from Fowey and more salt was imported. Much timber was also required for the pilchard hogsheads and for the mines. Penryn's imports from France included salt, wine, canvas and Caen stones. From Spain there came Malaga fruit, raisins, iron, and tobacco on a Dutch ship from Barbados. In 1639 cotton wool and indigo arrived from the West Indies. Penryn benefited from the American trade as did its mariners: Philip Luxon, master of the *Blessing* of Falmouth, was accused of drinking some of the goods on the outer voyage to James Town in Virginia.[22] The *Blessing* was unusual in being a local ship.

There has been some disagreement about the importance of the other port on the Fal River. There does not appear to be any evidence that Truro was declining as a port in the first part of the seventeenth century.[23] Merchants of the calibre of Richard and Jacob Daniell, Francis Nosworthy, Richard Hill and Robert White would not have stayed in a declining port. Truro was a Coinage Town and the centre of the tin mining industry. The data on the amount of tin produced varies over the years and no data exists for the years 1615 to 1624 or 1626 to 1637.[24] In those years where figures do survive about 10,000 cwt of tin was produced in Cornwall. Of this Truro regularly shipped out somewhere around 2,500 to 3,000 cwt. In the earlier part of the century most of the tin was taken to London on the tin boats for the tin farmers but increasingly some was shipped directly abroad: in 1639 Truro sent about 400 cwt overseas.

The other principal port for tin was Helston, with its port on the Helford River; in 1611 it sent out about 4,635 cwt (assuming a slab or block of tin was around 3 cwt at that time) as against

Truro 3,174 and Fowey 1,265. Unfortunately very few coastal port books survive for Helford until 1640 which makes it difficult to judge if this were the usual amount.[25] In 1639 the figure was 3,294 from Helford; but few other commodities came in or went out from the Helford river though the tin ships were also loaded with goatskins.

In the eighteenth century Mount's Bay, in the far west of Cornwall, with the communities of Marazion, Penzance, Newlyn and Mousehole, was one of the chief ports exporting pilchards.[26] In the first half of the seventeenth century the evidence is less clear. In 1635 around 500 hogsheads were dispatched abroad but we do not know how many were sent coastwards. Certainly both Mount's Bay and St Ives imported fairly large quantities of salt.[27] In 1638 2,000 sacks of charcoal were imported indicating the growing importance of the area for mining.

Irish cargoes were prominent at both ports, in 1635 and 1638, for example, over 600 Irish hides, both raw and tanned, came into Mount's Bay from Wexford. The Caribbean and North American ships often stopped at both St Ives and Mount's Bay with cargoes of tobacco, a commodity which increased through the seventeenth century. In 1628 about 16,000 lbs were imported into St Ives [28] and 5,000 lbs from the West Indies landed in Mount's Bay in 1638. Surprisingly, during the first half of the century, very few local boats were mentioned for either two ports: it was mostly the French who brought salt and left with pilchards or the Irish who brought timber.

Padstow was the nearest Cornish port to Ireland and not surprisingly it was also very much involved with Irish commodities.[29] By 1639 Padstow was to take over from Fowey as the principal port for the export of helling stones: in 1639 some 300,000 were exported, almost all to Ireland.

The Devon ports also varied greatly in their expertise and capacity. The fortunes of Plymouth were soaring by 1610[30] and about 350 shipments were recorded entering or leaving the port which was twice as many as thirty years before. A new fish market was built there in 1602.[31] Plymouth was blessed with a large harbour and enterprising merchants many of whom such as Robert Trelawny traded with or helped to settle the New World. Although France was Plymouth's main trading partner a fifth of its shipments went to the Mediterranean.

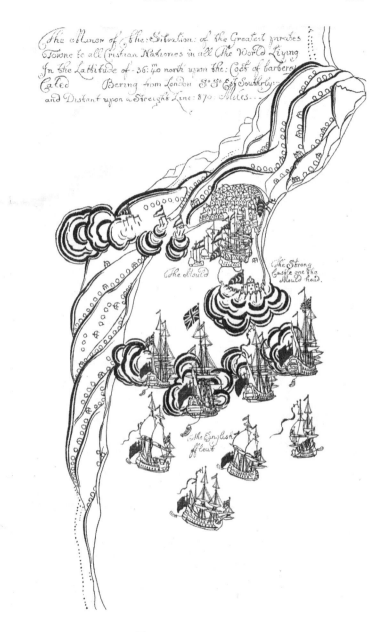

The Manor of the Situation of the Greatest pyrates Towne to all Cristian Nationes in all The World Lying In the Lattitude of 36:40 north upon the: Cost of barberey Caled   Bering from London   So So Est Southrly: and Distant upon a Streight Line: 870. Miles—

The Mould

The Strong Castle one the Mould head.

the English fleate

Pirate town

Dartmouth was an important port. It has been claimed that 'by the third quarter of the sixteenth century the trickle of ships going annually to Newfoundland was beginning to look like a fleet, especially those from Dartmouth.'[32] In the early seventeenth century it had the greatest number of ships of any port in Devon.[33] Totnes was silting up therefore Dartmouth took over some of its trade. Exeter had a similar problem at times when its canal was impassable to larger ships but it relied successfully on Topsham and as mentioned contained many prosperous merchants. During the war with Spain many prize cargoes had been brought into Exeter and, partly because of the levies on these, the total customs revenue for Exeter and its member ports in 1594 was the highest for any single provincial port in England.[34]

Of the north coast ports Barnstaple also suffered some silting up through the century but Bideford took over and enjoyed the increasing prosperity of the trading to New World especially in the import of tobacco. Both were trading partners with Bristol and with Ireland.

The amount of trade at all these ports varied from year to year, with some difficult years in the 1620s and 1630s. Wars with France and Spain were a hindrance, but above all it was the capture of many ships and seamen by the Barbary pirates which inhibited local trade.[35]

THE HILL DOCUMENTS

Richard Hill was one of the merchants who was raised and worked during this period. He was born in Devon in the 1590s, apprenticed in London as a cordwainer, possibly around 1620, and married Agnes Trewolla from Cornwall in the 1620s. He continued to work in London until his death in January 1660, his wife dying a few weeks later. Their second son Thomas, upon the loss of his parents, undertook the task of acting as administrator for their estates. In order to try and separate the affairs of his late father from current business Thomas started a new book in which to copy the letters concerning his late father and this letter book has survived in the Centre for Kentish Studies.[36] These letters contain other information not necessarily relating to his father's estate and provide many personal details of Thomas and his family. The letter book supplements other Hill papers in the British Library[37] which comprise a miscellany of public, private and business papers of the Hill family and which were used by one of the family's descendants, Richard Hill, in articles for *Devon and Cornwall Notes and Queries* and for *Archaeologica Cantiana*.[38] Some of these latter papers were transcribed and deposited in the Cornwall Record Office.[39]

The letters comprise one of the most significant collections of English merchants' papers for the seventeenth century even though many others between merchants are extant for this period. Upon receipt these would generally be kept as separate documents and not necessarily copied elsewhere. They may well be found fastened together in bundles with string[40] and it is not possible to ascertain whether some might have been mislaid and the bundle is incomplete. Those sent out by a merchant however were often copied in a volume bought specifically for the purpose and entered in sequence so that, provided the volume itself remains intact, individual letters were not lost.[41] The pages of the volume itself might well be numbered which provides a further safeguard that contents are complete. Sometimes pressure of time (for instance the need to catch the post) might prevent the full text being copied into the letter book but then the writer would generally insert a brief note to explain the contents and the reason for the omission. Therefore a merchant's letter book provides the opportunity for assessing the activities of a merchant over a specified period of time and in particular to trace all his trading connections. A letter book is especially valuable when some accounts also survive. With Thomas Hill there are a few accounts written at the back of the book (which have been reproduced in Appendix A). Accounts by themselves are valuable but can only give the statistics of a completed transaction. A letter book can show a more human side to an activity such as international trade where so many imponderables occur and the reasons for decisions or vacillation can be complex. One can follow the exasperations and frustrations of the writer or the joy at some unexpected successful transaction as well as pick up everyday gossip among friends. Compared with the letter book of Valentine Enys, that of Thomas Hill's is short and written for a specific purpose but is valuable in particular for the time span which it covers and also for the connections with other better-known published material such as the diary of Samuel Pepys and the journal of William Schellinks.

THE HILL FAMILY

The Hill family are of particular interest to historians in both Devon and Cornwall for Richard Hill was a Devon man who married a Cornish woman and who therefore had many connections in both counties. These connections are apparent from Thomas Hill's letter book, and almost half the letters relate to merchants in Devon and Cornwall. Richard Hill would seem, from the papers in the British Library, to have been a member of the Hill family from Shilston (near Chagford) in Devon and he used the Shilston arms. Several family members lived in Cornwall. One of these was Richard Hill, a wealthy merchant in Truro who died in 1640,[42] and for some time it was thought that the Devon Richard was his son but it has been shown that this was not so; Richard's son, aged 6 months in 1620, died before his father. The dates are wrong and moreover the Devon Richard Hill specifically mentions that his father was Thomas.[43]

Richard Hill was born in the 1590s, the son of Thomas Hill, a tanner of Moretonhampstead. From the Hill papers it would seem that Thomas was born about 1550 and lived, according to his descendants, to the great age of 98, dying in Moretonhampstead in 1648 or 1649. Richard was one of a numerous family. Of his brothers, three, John, Andrew and Hillary, remained in Devon but a younger brother, William, was apprenticed to Richard in 1632,[44] became a merchant, lived in London and took advantage of his brother's connections with Cromwell's government to obtain contracts for the supplying of victuals to the forces, herrings to Dublin and to indulge in land buying.[45] Richard was generous in helping out his many brothers and one of his son's problems as administrator of his father's estate was the retrieval of money lent to his uncles.

Upon his death Richard was described as a citizen of London and a cordwainer and it may well have been that the man to whom he was apprenticed was Ambrose Jennens, a cordwainer, and brother to Abraham Jennens a merchant of Plymouth with whom Richard was to have very close connections.[46] In the 1620s Richard married Agnes Trewolla of the Trewolla family, the daughter of Thomas Trewolla who had property near Mevagissey. Her mother's family were the Hallamores, an important merchant family in Penryn through much of the seventeenth century.

THE PRINCIPAL ASSOCIATES OF RICHARD HILL IN THE WEST COUNTRY

Because Richard Hill was a Devon man, he was well acquainted with the merchants of Plymouth. From later references made by his son, it would seem that his principal associate and friend in that port in the 1620s and 1630s was Abraham Jennens. It may be that, when a son was born to Richard and Agnes in 1635, they named him after Abraham for that is a name which seems rare in the Hill and Trewolla families.

There are many references to the activities of Abraham Jennens in Plymouth[47] and his name appears frequently in the port books in the 1630s. From Richard Hill's accounts of 1633 he worked closely with other well-known merchants such as Robert Trelawny and Justinian Peard. He is said to have welcomed the Pilgrim Fathers and entertained them in his house. [47]

When Abraham died in 1649 he left behind two daughters and six sons,[48] two of whom, Ambrose and William, feature prominently in the letter book. Ambrose worked in Plymouth as a merchant in the 1630s but by 1641 had moved to Seville, a favourite city for Westcountry merchants.[49] At least three members of the Upton family from Devon were in the area in the seventeenth century and Richard Enys from Cornwall was in partnership with another Richard Hill from Devon (no relation to the first) in the 1680s and 1690s. The will of Ambrose's father Abraham suggests he was not particularly successful there and was in a dispute with his father's friend, Richard Hill. When he returned to Plymouth from Seville in 1645 he was immediately arrested as a suspected Royalist but released after he protested his innocence and his absence during the war.[50] After this episode he rose in favour with the authorities: he was in Penzance for a short time but later moved to Penryn where he became Commissioner for Prizes in Falmouth and a customs official. He held both posts when the letter book began in February 1660. In Penzance with him was his particular friend, Bryan Rogers, the customs officer for the port, who had been a customs official in Plymouth during the Civil War. He died in 1652. Ambrose was mentioned in his will[51] and it would have given pleasure to Bryan Rogers to know that his son, also Bryan, married Ambrose's daughter, Joan, in Penryn. Both Ambrose and his son-in-law were living in Falmouth by 1662 but, as there is no reference to Bryan Rogers in the Hearth Tax list of that year, it is assumed that he and his wife were living with his father-in-law in the largest house in Falmouth. This building, which had 13 hearths, was in the area known as Mulberry Square, Bryan Rogers was to continue to occupy it on Ambrose's death in 1666 and from where he was to become one of the leading merchants in the west of England. At the change of regime in 1660 Ambrose's accounts became subject to scrutiny by the government commissioners. Bryan Rogers visited London to try and sort out the problems of his father-in-law and it was Thomas Hill who did his best to provide assistance. In return both Ambrose Jennens and Bryan Rogers attempted to help the Hills with their Cornish problems.

The principal correspondent of Thomas Hill among the Jennens brothers was William, the family's most important merchant. He was the fourth son but his father's will was very much biased in his favour, although it could be that Abraham had already made substantial settlements for his three eldest sons. Much of the property which Abraham had bought in Plymouth and elsewhere, including some in Dartmouth, was left to William.[52] In 1633 a William Jennens is mentioned in Richard Hill's account as dwelling in London but it is not known if he were the same man.

That he was difficult to deal with can be seen from some of Thomas Hill's letters: Thomas and his brother Abraham were the recipients of a curt letter from him criticising their treatment of Mr Eliot's representative in London to which Thomas had to write a diplomatic letter in reply. Others too found him difficult and quarrelsome. He entered into a dispute with the Plymouth Corporation over rights over the quay and was criticised over his part in the building of Charles Church. A revealing comment survives from the French merchant Robert Oursel of Rouen who quarrelled with Jennens over the latter's excessive charges on commission.[53] Oursel called Jennens '*un frippon et un francq coquin*', and added 'we are not at war with one another – why can't they give up this habit of pillage!' William Jennens was recognised as being one of Plymouth's leading merchants in the 1660s and 1670s and was described by Thomas Hill as the chief correspondent in England of the leading Amsterdam merchant, James Thierry, who figures so prominently in this letter book.

William married Elizabeth, the daughter of Robert Trelawny who was very much involved with settlement in North America.[54]

Robert Trelawny, Member of Parliament for Plymouth in the Short and Long Parliaments, was a Royalist who was imprisoned in London at the outbreak of the Civil War and died there in 1644. Of Elizabeth's surviving brothers, Samuel the eldest, a lawyer and Member of Parliament for Plymouth in 1660 and 1661, does not feature in the letter book but the names of Robert and John occur. Robert died in Oporto in about 1660 and from there a legacy was sent to Elizabeth by the hands of Thomas Hill. John Hallett, a London merchant with an estate at Killigarth in Cornwall,[55] agreed, after some hesitation, to accept Elizabeth's younger brother, John, as an apprentice. In the 1650s he was sent to Hallet's Italian correspondent, John Byam, in Naples. Byam later became a friend of Thomas Hill as can be seen from the letter book. John Trelawny's business activities are questionable: his accounts were so confused that they became subject of a court case in which John Hallett, John Byam and Peter Kekewich, another Cornish merchant, were involved.[56] The first reference to John Trelawny in the letter book is in shorthand and difficult to decipher but it would appear that he went to Venice and, on his return to London, and had problems with the law.[57]

The other principal merchant in Devon associated with Richard Hill was Bernard Sparke of Exeter. He was also a correspondent of James Thierry. The Sparkes were well known as a family not only in Exeter but also in Plymouth (Robert Trelawny the elder had married Judith Sparke). Sparkes also were merchants in London. Several had the name of John so it is not known whether the John Sparke in the letter book was a close relative of Bernard. Bernard's sister, Lucretia, married Peter Toller who lived in Fowey.[58] Peter Toller acted as host to Jacobi Thierry and William Schellinks, the illustrious Dutch traveller, when they visited Cornwall in 1662. Bernard Sparke was working as a merchant in Exeter as early as 1647 for he is mentioned in the port book of that year.[59]

Justinian Peard, a member of the well-known Barnstaple merchant family, had moved to Plymouth by 1633 when he is mentioned in the account that year. He was Mayor in 1644. His brother Charles also had business dealings with Richard Hill but died at the end of the 1650s owing about £6. Thomas Hill was to encounter a great deal of difficulty in recovering this from his widow Alice and the letters range from polite to threatening. Charles Peard's will was not proved until 1661 which may explain the delay and difficulty Alice had. Her son, Charles, died about the same time.[60]

Hugh Squier of South Molton is also mentioned. He was a friend of the whole Hill family, greatly beloved. That he was a generous and caring character is indicated by his founding a school in his native town and by his will.[61] This is an extraordinary document, very long, with bequests to charities in his home county and London and to many friends. In the twentieth century a bust of Hugh Squier was placed on the facade of the town hall of South Molton with the words 'Our great benefactor'.[62]

As a young man he went out to India, possibly on Richard Hill's ship *Society*. He was involved in a horrific shipwreck when a vessel overturned in the harbour at *Metchelepatam* [Masulipatam?] in the autumn of 1656. Many died, trapped in the vessel.[63] In 1657 he sent goods back to England for sale in the *Three Brothers* and asked for William Jennens' help when it reached Plymouth. On his return to England about 1657 he stayed some time with the Hills because of a leg injury. His mother wrote a letter of appreciation to her friends, Richard and Agnes, for their care of her son 'his great benefactors' and sent from Barnstaple a 'country dish' to show her thanks.[64] He was at the wedding of Abraham Hill and sent a description of it to Thomas in Italy.

Ephraim Skinner also appears in the letter book as the prospective partner of John Byam. He was from Barnstaple and was to become an important merchant connected with Italy. He later joined Thomas D'Aeth at Leghorn.[65]

THE 1633 ACCOUNT

Many Plymouth merchants occur in an account dated June 1633 which was drawn up by Richard Hill for his own information.[66] Although only a young man, he was already a prosperous merchant and engaged with the foremost trading partners. In consequence his business interests were diverse. In 1632 he had taken a lease of a house in Lime Street, in the parish of St Dionis in Backchurch (to be destroyed in Great Fire) at a rent of £30, a considerable sum.[67] His association with Maurice Thomson, the leading merchant in New World trade, had already begun. Thomson and his associates have been described by one historian as 'new-merchants' in contrast to the members of the older chartered companies.[68] These men were interested in trade with more recently discovered parts of the world. They took a leading part in the Newfoundland fish trade and also in the slave and sugar trades which were closely connected. They tried to avoid the restrictions placed upon trading by the old chartered companies who owed their privileges to the Crown. This attitude inevitably led to their hostility to the Crown. When a choice had to be made in the Civil War they became the leading supporters of Parliament in the merchant community of the City of London. Their experience in working together in many enterprises, including founding new colonies in America, led to their cooperation in supporting the government of Cromwell. Richard Hill was one of these 'new-merchants'. Maurice Thomson is mentioned in the 1633 account in connection with a large import of wine. The name of Roland Wilson, another well-known 'new merchant', also occurs.

The commodities were varied and Richard Hill's trading interests were world wide, as were those of his many associates in Devon. It is not surprising therefore to find several references to Newfoundland in his accounts. For example he had an 'adventure' with Edmund Holmewood (a London merchant) on an unnamed ship sailing to Newfoundland to catch fish and then returning, as many did, direct to Spain, in this case to Seville. From Newfoundland the *Alice Bonaventure* of Dartmouth sailed direct to Lisbon before returning to Dartmouth and London. Thomas Stower was the merchant concerned. Newfoundland fish oil (known as train oil) was a favourite commodity. A large consignment had been bought at Dartmouth by Mark Hawkings for Richard Hill in partnership with the Plymouth merchant, Thomas Wynsveare, and another consignment had been bought at Plymouth by Robert Gawd for himself, Wynsveare and Hill. Richard Hill also sold a parcel of pilchard train oil for Abraham Jennens. The name of the latter appears most frequently in the accounts in particular with reference to the importation of white sugar from the West Indies sometimes in partnership with Justinian Peard. Nicholas Bennet was another Plymouth merchant connected with this trade. Tobacco was also imported, that for Charles Duck had been delivered in January 1628/9 but the account had not been settled. Another debt, described surprisingly as 'doubtful', was the 14s 8d owed by the leading Plymouth merchant, Robert Trelawny, for the transport of tobacco. The Plymouth merchants imported wines of various types and from different countries often using local ships. The *Rebecca* of Milbrook, with Robert Hoskins as master, brought Malaga wine, the latter was also imported along with Xeres sack wine by Abraham Jennens and Justinian Peard on a Bristol ship. Hill sold 7 pipes of Canary wine on behalf of William Rowe of Stonehouse. It would seem that wine was the principal commodity dealt in by Richard Hill. The largest sum of money (£955.19.09) owed by him was to John Harvey, a merchant of Bordeaux, for French wines.

Several accounts were with merchants abroad but most of these also appear to be English: Isaac Ellis was at Amsterdam, John Smart at the Hague, William Clifton at Flushing, Thomas Colwell at Dunkirk, Peter Pole at St Malo and Edmund Doggat at Aveiro. The principal foreigner was Reynier Voet of Middleburg who traded in damask and table linen. The names of David Vanderheyden of Hamburg and Robert de Meyer of Bruges also occur.

Many Cornish merchants are mentioned and the commodities here reflect Cornish interests. The merchants of Fowey predominate: William Baker and Jonathan Rashleigh were involved with cargos of wheat, Henry Costen and John Mayow with Spanish iron, George Bird traded in Newfoundland train oil and barillas (soda plants) and William Bird in rosen (a form of resin). Spanish iron was favoured for use in the Cornish mines. Elis Hele of Plymouth and Tobias Browne of Marazion were both involved in this trade. At Saltash were William Stacey and at Looe was William Burrows. Further west Anthony Munday was an associate of Richard Hill.

The names of many London merchants are included, some with local connections in particular the Plymouth man, Gregory Clements, who was later to be executed as a regicide.

As part of his business Richard Hill arranged insurance premiums for his Westcountry correspondents, some of these list places visited by the ships; the *William* of Plymouth for example sailed from Plymouth to Cadiz, St Lucar and Seville, and the *Elizabeth* of Plymouth from Plymouth to Majorca, Barcelona and other ports before returning to Plymouth and London; the *Alice Bonaventure* of Dartmouth from Newfoundland to Lisbon and other ports and then back to Dartmouth and London. Aveiro in Portugal was a popular destination for Plymouth ships, returning presumably with salt for the fishing industry. Richard Hill himself was a ship owner and there is a reference to the building of a ship at Shoreham.

There is only one reference to trading with Guinea. This is a most intriguing reference to a reprisal voyage in association with James Gorant but no further details are given.

The whole account shows a man who traded in many commodities throughout the world. With its many references to the activities of the merchants of Plymouth, it also suggests that Plymouth itself was possibly not suffering a period of depression as has been suggested.[69]

THE CIVIL WAR AND INTERREGNUM

Were the two decades in the middle of the seventeenth century a disaster for English trade or were they the pivotal period for mercantile expansion which was to lead in the eighteenth century to the global spread of the British Empire? To try and continue to trade as a merchant during the period of war, and especially a civil war, was obviously difficult, and the difficulties increased for those living in ports that were under siege as was Plymouth, or one which changed hands as did Exeter. The merchants of Exeter must have welcomed the Restoration as bringing the possibility of calm after a period of upheaval. Alison Grant writes 'In spite of intervals of partial recovery, Devon traders, suffering from wars, taxation and uncertain trade, if not "utter ruin", could only hope that the change of government in 1660 would bring about the restoration of prosperity as well as the king'.[70]

On the other hand for some these were years of opportunity. The papers of Sir John Banks are also in the Centre for Kentish Studies. John Banks came of age in 1649 and his biographer wrote that 'his generation was... to find its years of opportunity during the Commonwealth and the Protectorate'.[71] The letters and associate documents of John Paige were edited by John Steckley in whose view they 'may well constitute the most complete documentation that is extant for any London merchant in the Interregnum'.[72] Paige was, it would seem, of Royalist tendencies but wisely stayed clear of politics and continued to trade throughout these years, on the whole successfully. He was primarily an importer of Canary wine. Steckley wrote significantly 'Londoners consumption of a luxury wine seems not to have been much affected by civil war

The Letter Book of Thomas Hill, 1660–1661

and political change', a remark which might well apply to other commodities.[73]

Richard Hill himself supported Parliament. There are occasional references to him in State Papers but very few family documents for the period of the war survive. It can be assumed that Richard Hill spent the war years in London where he continued as a merchant in London and it would seem likely there was a reasonable continuity in his pattern of trade. He was also in a position to benefit from his position as an 'insider'. As early as June 1643 he was appointed one of the four 'Treasurers and Receivers of all Monies as shall come in upon the Ordinance of Sequestrations'. This Committee sat at Goldsmith's Hall. It removed considerable sums from the estates of Royalist 'malignants'.[74] With William Pennoyer, another of the 'new merchants', he bought arms, ammunition and stores for the Army and, in 1644, reference is made in the Hill documents to an article of agreement between the Committee of Parliament for the Navy and Richard Hill and Richard Heaman, described as part-owners of the *Morning Star* of London, to transport men from Portsmouth to Cork.[75]

One of the few surviving Hill documents for the war period is the log of a ship which continued its voyage in spite of civil war at home. The *Richard Bonaventure* sailed with a cargo of lead from London in October 1642 on behalf of Captain Richard Crandley, Mr Richard Hill and Company. On 22 October it left the Isle of Wight and that night reached Plymouth Sound. On the 24th the captain conferred with Moses Goodyear and the following day in the Cattwater loaded 800 hogsheads of pilchards, a dozen calf skins and 87 rolls of tobacco. It left Plymouth on the 8 November, on the 25th entered the Straits and by the 29th had reached Carthagena in Spain where enquiries were made on the price of pilchards and a dispatch sent off to English merchants in Alicante, Mr Berkley and Mr Blunden. On the 30th some pilchards were unloaded and the ship reached Alicante on the 8th December. It left there on 24th December, returned to Carthagena where it loaded barillas and then continued to Venice, to Zante for currants and to other Mediterranean ports. It eventually returned to England in August 1643, reaching the Isle of Wight on August 22nd. The captain presumably had received some intelligence as to the ports which were not in the hands of the Royalist forces although he thought it prudent not to return to Plymouth.[76]

Many of Hill's family would seem to have been Parliamentary supporters but his relatives by marriage in Cornwall lived in an area controlled by the Royalists. One of Agnes Hill's brothers, Thomas Trewolla, became Mayor of Truro in 1653 during the Commonwealth. He was innkeeper of an inn situated in the very substantial building which stood on the site where Lloyds Bank and Lower Lemon Street are today.[77] His son, also Thomas, made a late but judicious marriage to the widow of the owner of the Bull Inn, the most famous inn in Truro of the time, and a few doors to the east of that occupied by his father and he therefore became the innkeeper there in the 1660s. The widow he married, Azias Osgood, was the sister of Thomas Oates, a mercer in Truro, who, because of his Parliamentary sympathies, had fled the town when its allegiance was given to the Royalist cause.[78] Agnes' mother's family, the Hallamores, were notable dissenters in Penryn, and it is possibly significant that Peter Hallamore is mentioned in Richard Hill's account of 1633 as the recipient of a Bible.

The allegiance of Richard Hill's chief correspondents in Plymouth, the Jennens family during the Civil War, however, is difficult to ascertain. Abraham's name appears in the Plymouth port book of 1643 when the town was under seige but his name does not seem to be included in 1644, although parts of the port book are difficult to decipher.[79] His eldest son, Abraham, was living in Saltash when he died in 1652. In his will[80] he favoured his brother Charles, with a legacy of £100 (as against £5 to the rest of his brothers). Colonel Charles Jennens may have been a Royalist for a man of that name was in Pendennis Castle when it surrendered in 1646.[81] The only legacy from the father to Charles was a collection of documents listing the debts owed by the King from the 1620s. Possibly his father thought he was the man most likely to retrieve these sums.[82] The Jennens had close connections with the Trelawny family and Robert was imprisoned in London and died there in 1644. Charles's cousin, Ambrose Jennens, the son of the Ambrose who had died in London in the 1620s, was certainly a Royalist. A Colonel in the Royalist army, he escaped to France after the Civil War. In the winter of 1646 to 1647 he acted as a second in a duel in which 'the seconds did so well pistol one another that a few hours after they died both'.[83] Ambrose Jennens, the son of Abraham, was living in Spain during much of the war. Willliam's whereabouts during the Civil War are not known but he was made Commissioner for Prizes in Plymouth 1660 and in 1662 was one of the first mayors for Plymouth after the Restoration, which would suggest he had had Royalist sympathies. How far Richard Hill continued to associate with members of the Jennens family during the war period is not known.

In spite of the war and the siege Plymouth's merchants continued to trade as is shown by the surviving port book for 1643 and a partial one for 1644/5. Trading was difficult but it continued wherever possible.

One port which benefited from the war was Falmouth which grew from its beginning as the village of Smithick: in the 1620s there were several houses in what is today the High Street but by 1640 other sites to the west along the shore had been developed in what is today Market Street.[84] Its importance to the Royalists during the war for the shipping of tin led to further expansion. Cornish tin was a valuable commodity for the Royalist forces. There was a shortage in London where the merchants were eager to obtain this valuable commodity. This may well explain the immigration into Cornwall of merchants at the end of the war. Some eventually settled in Falmouth. One was William Hill, the younger brother of Richard. He seems to have been in Truro shortly after the end of the war in 1646[85] but, by 1649, he was living near Falmouth where he was to marry, as his second wife Elizabeth Enys, the widow of John Enys, a merchant in Penryn. John was the brother of Samuel Enys for whom many accounts and letters survive for this period.[86]

That Cromwell's government were very concerned that the supply of tin should not be diverted to the Royalists is shown by a writ, dated October 1646, issued to arrest Oliver Sawle and John Robins in Cornwall because of 'their sending tin often beyond the seas covertly whereby the Commonwealth is defrauded.'[87]

1646 and 1647 were bad years for Cornwall; the county was plague stricken and little tin was produced; Pendennis and other strongholds were occupied by the Parliamentary forces and Cornwall was 'aflame with insurrection'.[88] In May 1648 there was a Royalist uprising in Penzance and the Lizard. Samuel Enys, who like Ambrose Jennens managed to stay out of Cornwall during the war, returned in June 1648 after these troubles were over and started to trade from Penryn. His letters to clients which survive from June 21 1648, hint at the problems of trading in unsettled times.[89] His client, John Sweeting, a pewterer in London (and also a Westcountryman) was desperate for tin but not only was production low in 1648 but there were serious problems with transport. The 'Revolt led ships', as Enys explained, (i.e. the fleet commanded by Prince Rupert) were stationed in the Downs attempting to block the entrance to the Thames and therefore to dispatch tin by sea was not sensible and to send it by land was a prolonged and arduous occupation even though the tin blocks themselves were now reduced in weight to around 1 cwt each where previously, before the war, the average had been nearer to 3 cwt.

But the end of 1648 was a turning point in European history, for the treaty was signed which ended the Thirty Years War. Although peace is generally beneficial for trade it also released many Dutch ships to compete with the English in America and the Mediterranean. The result was the Navigation Acts restricting colonial goods to English ships and the friction between the two countries led to war in 1652. By 1649 however the government was well aware of the need to strengthen the English fleet. Much of the proceeds from the Customs was used to build up this fleet and Professor Wheeler considers that 'the improvement in the technical expertise of the officers which had begun in the ship-money fleets, continued, providing England with one of the best navies in the world by 1649'.[90] With the abolition of the tin pre-emption and therefore a freer trade in tin, production increased by the early 1650s and by this period worries about tin going by sea had subsided. Samuel Enys, whose accounts exist for 1650, sent considerable quantities to London although none as far as is known to Hill. The latter, however, was very interested in tin as is seen by a note dated 1649: 'Ordered William Hill to send by every conveyance from Falmouth or Fowey to the value of £300 in tin for me and friends.'[91]

Trade in and from Cornwall would seem to have increased considerably in the early 1650s. We have evidence for this from the various customs accounts of the Cornish ports from 1650 to 1652[92] and from Samuel Enys's own accounts from June 1651 to October 1653. From one of these accounts we find Enys paying excise on about 1,000 cwt of tin from December 1650 to December 1651, which would seem to have been sent abroad. How much he smuggled is not known. One surviving invoice is for a consignment of tin sent to Leghorn on behalf of Mr John Nelson of London. Falmouth itself continued to prosper from this increase in trade in the 1650s and the village of Smithick was transformed by 1661 into the charter town of Falmouth and, by the time of the Hearth Tax list of 1662, it was of comparable size to Truro and to Penryn.

Tin was also the lubricant for Hill's trade with Italy and Turkey. By the 1650s this was one of his principal areas of operation and merchants in Leghorn were the Hills' principal correspondents. Leghorn was not only a vital staging post for the Near East but also a substantial market in its own right. It had been a free port since 1593 and it was not long after this that English merchants were well established there. Henry Roseveare believes that 'much of their commercial and naval power in the Mediterranean hinged upon this centre which, by the mid-seventeenth century, had outstripped its rivals to become Italy's chief port'.[93] Nine tenths of English imports to Italy went through Leghorn rather than making the much longer and tedious journey up the Adriatic to Venice. It was the pivotal port in the Mediterranean and Henry Roseveare adds that 'from Archangel and Newfoundland, from Ireland, England and Holland, vessels passed through on their way to Venice, Zante, Constantinople, Aleppo, Tunis, Tripoli and Messina'.[94] Thomas Dethick was one of the principal merchants mentioned by Hill. The Dethick family were among the leading London merchants and had close trading connections with the Banks family of Kent; John, later Sir John Banks, married the daughter of Sir John Dethick. Giles Lytcott, one of Thomas Hill's friends, was also closely connected to the Banks and both Thomas Dethick and Giles Lytcott appear in the Banks documents.[95] These documents show a similar pattern of trade to that pursued by the Hills; the principal commodities were tin, lead, some cloth, fish and pepper. Similar cargoes were sent out by the London merchant Charles Marescoe acting with the Lethieuillers and tin, bought from Bryan Rogers the Cornish merchant, made a profit of 21.9 per cent for Marescoe.[96]

English merchants stationed in Turkey might well pass through Italy on their journeys to the east. It was in Florence that Thomas Hill met Alexander Travell, one of his close friends, who was a merchant trading from Aleppo and who died in St John d'Acre Palestine. Trade with Turkey was of special interest to the West Country because of the demand for tin. Included in the Hill documents is a report, not dated but presumably sent to Richard Hill, which provides a useful description of the best commodities to be sent to Smyrna:

The next considerable commodity from England is tin which must be sent hither in small thin bars and it is requisite that every bar be stamped with the usual seal of the Rose and Crown. The softest metal and that which will run thinnest is the properest for the place where the chief and almost only expense is to tin over the copper pots, pans, spoons which they use for the dressing of their victuals. Only at Constantinople there is a great quantity consumed of casting of great ordinances. This market may require 3000 cwt per annum.[97]

The Mediterranean trade however suffered many setbacks during these years especially in the early 1650s. In December 1649 the Levant Company stated that eight of their vessels valued at £300,000 had been either taken or sunk by the French in the Straits. Nine months later the loss had reached 20 'great ships' and by 1652, when the first Dutch War began, another 21, worth £608,000, had been lost.[98] In March 1653 the English were defeated at the battle of Livorno by the Dutch who 'were able to station a strong force in the Straits and effectively shut the English out of the Mediterranean'.[99] But Admiral Blake's excursions into the Mediterranean in 1654 and the end of the Anglo-Dutch war brought relief, although there was still danger from Spain. Thomas Hill, in his letters, reported the loss of two large ships, the *Restoration* and the *Freetrade,* which were taken into Gibraltar as late as June 1660 (the month when the war with Spain officially ended). The increased expenditure and the more professional approach in the navy were having their effect not only in the Mediterranean but also in the West Indies where Jamaica was captured in 1655. Jonathan I.Israel writes, 'It first became evident to other European powers that England possessed outstanding advantages as a colonizing power, and that her Empire might soon outstrip all others, in the 1650s . . . the English Conquest of Jamaica from the Spaniards in 1655 caused as much alarm in Amsterdam, Hamburg, and Paris as in Madrid.'[100]

The West Indian trade became increasingly important to

Richard Hill in the 1650s. By this time he was working with Bernard Sparke of Exeter, William Jennens of Plymouth and James Thierry, an English merchant living in Amsterdam. They imported Barbados sugars and cottons: some of the sugars were taken direct to Thierry in Amsterdam although it is not known when this association started and whether it predated the First Dutch War in 1652.

James Thierry was an English merchant of Huguenot descent born in London about 1604[101] and a freeman of the Company of Weavers. He and his brother John were trading in London in the 1630s and suffered many financial lossess at that period. In a case brought before the High Court of Admiralty in 1637 Thierry supported his brother John in a bond to Bartholomew Nicholls of Plymouth for £1,900 and John owed his brother £3,000. At that time John was in prison facing bankruptcy but the brothers seem to have survived these problems.[102] James moved to Amsterdam and there married Maria van Rijn, the sister of the great Amsterdam merchant Pieter van Rijn, who had been left a fortune by her mother. By 1660 he was a prosperous merchant in Amsterdam, a prestigious client well worth cultivating. Much information has already been published about James Thierry and his family for it was his son, Jacobi or Jacobus, who came to England in 1661 accompanied by William Schellinks. The latter kept a journal of the son's travels including a visit to Devon and Cornwall and which has been translated from the Dutch.[103] Thomas Hill's letter book does much to enlarge on the references in that publication for Thomas took over the work of his father in providing the services in England required by Thierry and acting as the pivot for correspondence between Thierry's clients elsewhere in the country and Thierry himself.

Their trade would seem to have prospered but there were problems, some of which were still unsolved by the time of the letter book. The *Dolphin* was loaded in Barbados with sugars and other goods said to be worth £6,000 on behalf of James Thierry, Bernard Sparke, William Jennens and Richard Hill. On its way home it was seized by the *Robino* with a captain from Dunkirk working under a Swedish commission and the *Dolphin* may well have been taken to Sweden.[104] No compensation had been received when Richard Hill died although negotiations were taking place with the insurers of the ship. The ship is the subject of the first letter in the letter book and the dispute continued throughout the book. It is doubtful if anything more than part of the insurance was ever received although some of the cargo would seem to have been retrieved.

Thierry's ships sometimes went to Barbados via Guinea in West Africa to purchase African slaves. One such ship was the *Golden Dolphin* in which again Richard Hill and Bernard Sparke would also seem to have been involved. There is an unfortunate similarity between the names of these two ships which can not only confuse modern readers but also the participants themselves for on at least two occasions Thomas Hill wrote of the *Golden Dolphin* when it would seem he was referring to the *Dolphin*. In August 1661 Thierry gave evidence to the Admiralty Court in London that in 1657 he had sent this ship on a trading voyage to Guinea and then on to Barbados.[105] The ship got into distress and sailed to the Portuguese island of St Thomas to be repaired and have a new rudder fitted. The Governor at first entertained the crew so that the captain confidently unloaded his ship and put ashore 138 slaves and 'which goods were put into warehouses appointed by the said Governor there'. About 15 days later, in January 1658, the Governor seized the ship and took the crew prisoner. The captain was still a prisoner in 1660 when his wife was seeking urgent help. James Thierry estimated the losses suffered at £9,300 including £4,200 for the value of the slaves, £1,600 for the ship, £1,500 for loss of employment and freight and £2,000 for the crew and the loss of their goods. Again no evidence has been found for any compensation or for when the crew was freed. It was possibly this incident which made Thomas Hill wary of involvement in the Guinea trade.

Richard Hill was also by now involved in the East India trade and owned £2,000 of East India stock when he died in 1660 (valued at £1,000). From extant letters it would seem that Hugh Squier went out on one of Richard Hill's ships and possibly acted as Richard Hill's agent in India. In the East Indies the Dutch were the chief obstacles to the furtherance of the English trade. In November 1657 Thomas Hill reported to his brother Abraham from Genoa[106] information from Leghorn, a centre of gossip on the activities of the Dutch East India Company,[107] that the *Olive Branch*, of which Richard Hill owned a part, had been prevented from landing in Bantam by the Dutch who were at war with the local king. They tried Batavia but were refused entry so had to unload the goods on a small island on the coast of Sumatra called Pallagundi, a 'hot and unhealthy place', to which the goods from Bantam were brought stealthily by boats at night time. This delayed the ship, she lost the monsoon and was forced to winter at Mauritius leaving early in the spring and met with such 'prodigious' storms that when she came to the Cape of Good Hope she was almost a wreck. Thomas added 'we are much amazed what the Dutch can mean by this, as we have had a free trade and a factory there constantly from between forty and fifty years'. He then suggests to his brother very significantly that he should lay the whole matter before 'his highness; who I am sure will not suffer his subjects to be trampled on by any power on earth especially by the Hollanders'. This quotation is of particular interest because it shows the belief of Thomas that Cromwell, that is 'his Highness', had the interest of the merchants at heart and also that Thomas felt his father and brother might be able to exert influence on the government.

Richard Hill suffered other losses. The extent can be gleaned in a letter from his one-time partner Thomas Hollis, quoting his own losses (amounting to £9,970) but indicating that many were shared with Richard Hill.[108] The extent of his gains and losses may well have been typical of other merchants. The Interregnum was a volatile period in which to trade, there were opportunities and encouragement for success but many dangers and uncertainties beyond a merchant's control which could quite easily bring disaster.

However, Richard Hill did not have to depend solely on his trade as a merchant. In January 1649 he was appointed to a sixteen-man commission for the 'regulation of the navy and the customs', a commission which was 'entirely in the hands of Maurice Thomson and his new-merchant friends'.[109] In 1652 he was made a Commissioner with Samuel Wilson and Robert Turpin 'for the surveying, appraising and disposing of such goods, merchandise and commodities' taken in war. He held this office until his death and this necessitated many visits to Plymouth where ships taken as prizes might be brought in. Whilst in Plymouth in 1654 he received a letter from London of a rumour that 'King Charles is in town, came in disguise & a design in hand to cut off the Lord Protector and Lambert'. The work that Richard undertook had the potential for producing large profits and after his death claims were made that his estate owed considerable sums to the government.[110]

It would seem that he was able to provide his eldest son, Abraham, with a considerable fortune when, in 1657, he married Anne, the daughter of one of the leading Parliamentarians of the time, Sir Bulstrode Whitelocke. Abraham would never seem to have been short of money, much of which may well have come from his father. Later, however, Whitelocke himself was unsure of the true extent of Richard's wealth for he wrote that Hill 'was esteemed a more wealthy man, than he appeared to be at his death'.[111]

Richard Hill may have been ill during the last few years of his life which could have depleted his fortune. In 1654 he was chosen as Alderman of Candlewick Ward and then two years later one of the Aldermen for securing the peace of the City, but two days afterwards he was discharged on the payment of a fine of £400, no doubt partly due to ill health. However in 1656 he became Master of the Company of Cordwainers and presented them with a piece of plate later sold to help to cover the expenses of the Great Fire.[112]

His brief will was written in February 1659[113] and he left to his wife £2,000, the Cornish land leased by John Pasco for her lifetime, all his plate, pewter, brass, jewels, household and goods 'giving to my children what she thinks good'. She was also granted the lease of the house in Lime Street, which she could dispose of if she wished, for her own use. Thomas was bequeathed £2,000 and Samuel £1,000. Abraham was made the executor and the residual legatee. Agnes who died a few weeks after her husband does not appear to have left a will but merely a signed note giving instructions for the disposal of individual items including her clothes to her friends and her daughter-in-law, Anne. Samuel was given a 'cypress carved cabinet' and Thomas the chest in her chamber. Mention is also made of her Venetian ring which possibly Thomas had brought back from Italy.[114]

An inventory was made of Richard's house in Lime Street on 25 February 1660[115] before the death of Agnes. The house and contents reveal a wealthy and prosperous merchant. There were nine bedrooms, two garrets, two dining rooms, a gallery, a parlour and a counting house. The furnishings show his connections with many parts of the world. In the Painted Chamber and in Mrs Hill's Chamber were valances of green and blue perpetuana presumably from his native Devon. In the Green Chamber the head cloth to the bed was red serge lined with calico, the counterpane of fine East India stuff was lined with calico, the hangings of red serge had gilded leather and there were four red serge chairs and one which was green. The Tapestry Chamber was named after the old tapestries and there were also five pairs of tapestry hangings in the principal dining room with three Spanish tables, a little table, a Turkey carpet, one green perpetuana [table]carpet, 12 high chairs and six low chairs all of Turkey work. There was also a billiard table.[116] The parlour also contained two Spanish tables, a turkey carpet, a round table with a green cover, fifteen chairs of green perpetuana, a looking glass and a `coat of Arms in a frame'. Richard's son Thomas slept in a French bedstead with curtains of 'white dimitry wrought'. In his chamber were also one couch and six chairs, an escritoire and a large looking glass. It could have been here that Thomas worked and wrote the letters copied into the letter book. The whole inventory, including clothing, plate and the lease of the house and an adjacent tenement worth £450, came to £1,073.1s.0d. A few weeks earlier, possibly shortly after Richard's death, a list of his assets had been drawn up, which includes a figure for household stuff which is slightly less than that in the inventory. It mentions £600 in cash, stock in the East India Company, shares in various ships and adventures, and the lease of a tenement at Mevagissey. The total, £7,811.16s.0d, also includes a sum of £990 owing on the mortgage of Trelevan and no mention is made of Richard Hill's own debts. Debts owing to Richard Hill are mostly listed and it became Thomas Hill's task to try and recover these.

THE RESTORATION

Thomas returned home to England in 1659 a few months before his father's death. He had been sent by his father to Italy in 1657 to learn the language, acquire a knowledge of trading conditions and make useful contacts. How old Thomas was in 1657 is not known. Abraham had been baptised in 1635[117] and Samuel, the youngest brother, in 1646 but no reference has been found to the date of Thomas's birth. It was possibly around 1637.[118] Certainly by the 'elderly-brother tone' he took with young Samuel there was some age difference between them. Thomas had left England in the summer of 1657 and travelled to Marseilles via Paris to stay with Thomas Dethick in Leghorn. He also spent time in Genoa, Venice, Rome and Florence and with Signor Baldinotte, a Senator in Lucca. His enjoyment and enthusiasm for Italy remained with him and he had very fond memories especially of his stay in Lucca.[119] The letters to his Italian friends are somewhat exaggerated but even so give a feeling of his love for Italy. The contrast with Puritan London, especially for a young man brought up in a Puritan household, must have been great. It could be that these surroundings full of music, colour and religious devotion of a kind he had not known helped change his mind in favour of the Restoration of the king. Although close to Leghorn, which was in the Grand Duchy of Tuscany, Lucca was an independent state. It still has its formidable but attractive city walls which were apparently only completed shortly before Thomas Hill's arrival. In the middle ages it had been a foremost silk producing town but by the middle of the seventeenth century this industry was less important.

Some letters survive which were written from Thomas to Abraham before the letter book. One was quoted in a book containing what are called the *'Familiar Letters'* of Abraham Hill.[120] This letter is dated from Lucca on October 1 1657 shortly after his arrival:

> *I am here at the home of one of the Senators Signior Baldinotti, it is pleasantly situated, about a mile from the city, amongst the mountains, which makes it very agreeable; and as most of the gentry have left the city and come into these parts, it is still more so, by the friendly visits they are continually making to one another.*

He adds:

> *Since my arrival in Italy, I have missed few opportunities of hearing what music has been publicly performed, especially in the churches . . . What they excel in so much is in the eunuchs, whose voices are very rare and delightful and not to be compared but with one another, the other voices not so good as we have in England. The instrumental music*

is much better than I expected. The organ and violin they
are masters of . . . I am using my endeavours to collect
music for a single or two or three voices on which I have
had good success. [121]

While there Thomas was entrusted with landing and selling the
cargoes sent by his father from England. He made many friends,
especially Giles Lytcott and Benjamin Childe, and their influence
is possibly another reason why his loyalties began to change from
support for Cromwell's government to an enthusiasm for the
Restoration of Charles II. Information on the exiled King's Court
and the movement of his supporters was available in Italy. Thomas
reported to Abraham in October 1657 that Sir Theodore Gilbye
had arrived at Leghorn from England and was going 'to serve the
king of Scots'. This information was passed on to him by Giles
Lytcott.

Richard died on January 15 1660. Four days before this General
George Monck had reached York on his way down to London. That
the intervention of Monck would lead the way to the restoration of
the King was by no means clear at the time though some suspected
it. Bulstrode Whitelocke, Abraham's father-in-law, was one.[122]

The demand for a freely elected Parliament was growing and
the City of London greeted with delight the dissolution of the
old Rump, an event described by Ronald Hutton as 'possibly
the greatest expression of popular rejoicing London has ever
known'.[123]

The gradual realisation of the trend of these events can be
followed in the letter book. The first reference to national affairs
is the note (in short hand) dated 13 February 1660 revealing
that Thomas sent a copy of a letter of Monck to his friend Giles
Lytcott. This was presumably that sent to the Corporation of the
City of London, copies of which were being distributed elsewhere
in the country.[124] In the shorthand letter sent by Thomas eleven
days later there is a reference to a vote in Parliament and in the
letter to Signor Gioseppe Baldinotti he refers to the assembling
of a new parliament the following month 'and there is great hope
for the King who is already in Flanders'. On 16 March the act for
the dissolution of parliament had been passed and preparations
were being made for new elections. Thomas reported that Sir
Thomas Myddleton (the father of a friend, Richard Myddleton)

had returned and was gone to Wales to prepare for elections. Sir Thomas Myddleton had been involved in the Royalist rising of 1659.

On 4 April the Declaration of Breda, the statement of terms by which Charles II was prepared to return, was signed by the King. By April it was apparent that there was a definite movement to the Restoration and this is shown by the preparations being made by Thomas's Royalist merchant friends for a return to England but, by 12 April, there were worries of a setback when it was learnt that the leading Republican soldier, Lambert, had escaped from the Tower and there were fears of disturbances. By the 20 April, however, the excitement was rising 'The news is great expectation from the party at Breda, who is here expected suddenly' and on the 28 April Thomas reported to William Jennens in Plymouth that 'the Parliament have adjourned until Tuesday morning, when 'tis supposed they will enter on that which is termed the great work'. A few days later Thomas expressed the feeling of many that 'the present affaires give a general satisfaction to the nation' and he wrote of the 'universal *allegrezza* of the people at return of the King'. The enthusiasm of this son of a strong Parliamentary supporter is astonishing. The attire he and his associates wore at Barham Downs is described in detail and reference made to the motto of his troupe, 'Forever Loyal' which would seem most inappropriate for this bevy of young men, many the sons of supporters of Parliament. The King's entry into the City and, in the following year, the Coronation itself, are recounted in a similar exuberant tone.

THE MANAGEMENT OF THE ESTATE OF HIS FATHER BY THOMAS HILL FEBRUARY 1660 TO DECEMBER 1661

In the midst of this growing excitement Thomas Hill had undertaken the formidable task of settling his parents' estates. It was possibly realised that the management would be time consuming and more fitting for a younger son with no other responsibilities although Abraham, the elder brother, was frequently consulted.

Some of the more difficult and embarrassing problems for Thomas involved immediate family. Richard Hill's brothers and sisters seem to have been disappointed in the contents of the will of their brother. Aunt Elizabeth Moreton in Cornwall was sent one of Agnes Hill's gowns and a saddle was dispatched to cousin Betty but this was all. No rings were left by Richard as a memento to his relatives, a usual bequest, and this was resented. Moreover he did not release his brothers from debts which they owed him. Thomas therefore was under a legal obligation to try and get the debts repaid. One of the more frustrating tasks was to obtain the £26 owed by Uncle Hillary. Polite letters containing family news deteriorated into veiled legal threats but all was useless. Uncle Hillary apparently offered to pay the debt in a few months time. When this elapsed there was no sign of payment and Hillary stopped replying to Thomas' letters therefore another uncle had to be approached for help. It was not until much later that Hillary considered repaying the debt as he half promised in a letter to Abraham; whether he succeeded is unknown.[125]

But these sums were small compared with the £800 owing for Trelevan near Mevagissey. At the end of the 1640s, the Trewolla family of Trelevan had been in financial difficulties and Richard Hill had agreed to lend his wife's father, Thomas, and John, believed to be her nephew, £550 secured on a mortgage of Trelevan at a high interest rate of eight per cent. John Trewolla sold the property to a leading Truro lawyer, Walter Vincent, possibly without disclosing the mortgage. By 1658 £990 was owed. In 1659 it would seem to have been agreed, after a Chancery Case, that Walter Vincent should pay £800 to obtain a clear title and at this point the deeds would be handed over. This had not been paid by 1660. To retrieve this from Walter Vincent, an able and slippery Truro lawyer, well practised in exploiting the law for his own ends, proved very difficult. Thomas enlisted the support of his friends in Falmouth, Ambrose Jennens and Bryan Rogers, but they too failed and suggested that the compromise put forward by Vincent that half would be paid and the deeds handed over with the other half owing on a bond from Vincent and John Trewolla, should be accepted. The Hills were reluctant to agree for they realised the second £400 would never appear and had no faith in their cousin John. The dispute continued beyond the scope of the letter book. Further cases in Chancery followed but it may be some compromise was reached for Walter Vincent's ownership of Trelevan is described by Polsue as beginning in about 1667.[126]

The relationship with Richard Hill's younger brother, William, was particularly difficult. From the account of debts drawn up on Richard Hill's death it appears William owed his brother £234.14s.3d. What happened to this money is not known for, surprisingly, it is not mentioned in the letter book. Thomas was trying to develop his own career as a merchant and he hoped, optimistically, that his uncle William, by this time a merchant in Falmouth, would help to cultivate a successful trade between there and London. It was not long before he realised that his uncle was both lazy and incompetent. William was slow to answer letters and to adjust accounts and above all, much to Thomas' surprise, showed complete heartlessness towards his elder son William, who was at this time a guest in the Hill's house in London learning to become a merchant. Thomas had to plead with his uncle for money to provide clothes and other necessaries for his young cousin and was astonished that his uncle should declare a preference for his younger son Peter. The letters from Thomas, a young man, to his older uncle, are extraordinary. It is not surprising therefore that Thomas made no further attempt to trade with William and relied instead on the Hills' friend, Bryan Rogers, who was himself to become one of the most prominent merchants in the south-west.

Thomas was more successful in reclaiming other debts. The £6 owed by Mrs Alice Peard of Barnstaple was eventually paid. That owed by the Yarmouth merchants to Richard Hill and James Thierry was obtained after only a short delay. Settling accounts at this period was inevitably a long process and it was some time before merchandize in other hands was sold. In the days before modern taxation merchants did not at this period necessarily make an annual review of their business and the last time, for example, that William Jennens and Richard Hill had balanced their accounts was in 1657. Thomas, as he frequently pointed out, required quick settlements so that the estate could be wound up.

Some merchants were ready to take advantage of Thomas' inexperience; Justinian Peard, in Plymouth, added over £100 to his account for which Thomas could find no justification. William Jennens, in spite of the friendship between the two families, refused to pay £20 commission owing whereas he himself had charged for such commission in similar circumstances. The Jackson brothers claimed £40 which they said had been owing from 1639 although they had not thought to mention it during the whole intervening period whilst Richard was alive. It was fortunate that Richard had, it would appear, kept his accounts meticulously so that Thomas was able to peruse through past papers to try and ascertain the truth of these claims. The dispute with John Lane, referring back to business transacted also in 1639, would seem to have been settled amicably.

Thomas had also to deal with insurance claims on ships which had foundered. Some merchants specialised as insurers and it was generally, it would appear, not too difficult to insure a ship and cargo at fairly reasonable rates. Thomas Hill pointed out to Bryan Rogers, who questioned whether Amsterdam was not the preferred place for insurance, that James Thierry, in Amsterdam, often insured in London. Some of the amounts quoted for insurance, considering the dangers, seem very reasonable and it is surprising that Bryan Rogers was able to insure his *Providence*, when it might well have already sailed from Barbados. The problems lay in persuading the insurers to settle when they had admitted liability. They procrastinated and Thomas had to waste much time walking round to their homes to persuade them to pay. One insurer on the *Dolphin*, Gifford Bale, went bankrupt which was again not unusual.

1660 was a year of transition between two regimes. This added to Thomas's problems. The money used in Cromwell's time was withdrawn from circulation and caused difficulties over payment; laws of the old regime were abrogated and others introduced and above all new men came to power. It was necessary to be able to identify who were or would be the inner circle of the new administration. One of the vital services Thomas could provide for his friends both at home and abroad was to let them know the names of the winners and the losers. The latter consisted principally of those who had acted as judges at the execution of King Charles the First. Some were known to Thomas for they had been colleagues of his late father. For instance, Gregory Clements was a Plymouth man who had earlier traded with Richard Hill but Thomas expresses no emotion when reporting Clements' capture to his friends. Nor is there any mention of anxiety in the Hill household over the fate of Sir Bulstrode Whitelocke, Abraham's father-in-law, one of the leading supporters of Cromwell's regime and whose position in the early period of the Restoration was at one time in doubt. It was Heneage Finch who tried to exclude him from the Pardon.[127]

The Hill, Jennens and Sparke partnership was fortunate in

the winners. Some were Westcountrymen well known to them. William Morrice, who became Secretary of State in June 1660, had bought Werrington in 1651 and was described as a personal friend of William Jennens. Sir Richard Ford was a Devon man and Thomas Killigrew, who was to enjoy considerable influence with the King, was from the Cornish family. Thomas Hill referred to him as a friend but whether that was true or an expression used to impress others is not known. In any case, he was able to use him to help James Thierry, although a bribe of £60 was handed over, and later Thomas was asked by some apparently unknown aristocrat for help in influencing Thomas Killigrew to approach the king to obtain a peerage. Killigrew was later employed in arranging for the naturalisation of James Thierry's son.

THE NAVIGATION ACT OF 1660 AND THE VISIT OF THE THIERRYS TO ENGLAND

James Thierry required considerable help and information from Thomas Hill when the new Navigation Act was introduced. Thierry was of English nationality but, because he worked from Amsterdam, he was greatly affected by the terms of the Act. An earlier act had been introduced by Cromwell and the 1660 Act was an extension of it. The details are laboriously explained in the letter book to Thierry. It was the Barbados trade which was most at risk from the Navigation Act. In order to comply with the terms of the act, which required an English merchant to swear an oath in person to an English customs officer that the owners of the ships and also the ships themselves were English, James Thierry had to make a personal visit to Dover; from there he continued on to London in the autumn of 1661. He brought with him his thirteen-year old son, named after his father but generally given the Dutch form of his name Jacobi or Jacobus, and his companion, William Schellinks.

The arrest at Dover of the *Robino*, the ship responsible for the capture of the *Dolphin;* the Thierry's stay at Bridge near Canterbury with Sir Arnold Braems; James Thierry's departure from England, taking with him Thomas' younger brother, Samuel; and the stay of Jacobi and Schellinks in the Hill's home in London are all mentioned in Schellinks' Journal. Thomas had to organise suitable clothing for his young guest and arrange lessons in English and dancing. Thomas by this time regarded himself as an expert in handling the younger generation as can be seen from the rather pompous letters to his young brother in the Netherlands extolling the virtues of concentration and hard work.

THOMAS HILL AND MARRIAGE

Thomas was a sociable person with many friends, but his father's untimely death prevented any immediate possibility of marriage. That some suitable bride would be found for him on his return from Italy is evident from the asides in letters to John Byam and the Baldinotti. Richard Hill was regarded as a wealthy man who would be prepared to make a suitable settlement on his younger son. Richard's death ended this possibility. Thomas, however, rejoiced in his friends' successes in this field and in particular that of Giles Lytcott marrying the wealthy Devon heiress Sarah Culling. The speed of the courtship would suggest some prior discussions before Giles return to England. It could be that Giles sister, Ursula, who was married to John Upton of Lupton, alerted her brother to the possibility after Richard Culling's death. In his will written in July 1659, and proved April 1660,[128] Culling left the bulk of his estate to his only daughter, Sarah, a girl not then 16. This estate included much property in Devon. The value of Sarah's inheritance was thought by Thomas to be £7,000. Richard Culling had been born at Woodland but at the time of his death was living in Exeter with John Yeo 'in whose house I now table', as he noted in his will.

THE ROYAL SOCIETY

Many of the letters also give some hints to the involvement of Thomas and above all of his brother Abraham in the then growing interest in scientific research. Abraham for example, asked for some lodestones from Italy for his experiments.

Abraham Hill, who has been described as a 'scientist of some distinction', was the first Treasurer of the Royal Society in 1663.[129] The Royal Society evolved partly out of meetings held at Gresham College, which Thomas mentions as a frequent meeting place for his friends. Gresham College was founded under Sir Thomas Gresham's will of 1596 and was on the site of his mansion between

(Old) Broad Street and Bishopgate Street. 'Its emphasis was on the practical uses of knowledge and it provided (as it still does) lectures on Divinity, Civil Law, Physic, Astronomy, Geometry, Rhetoric and Music'.[130] After a lecture there on 28 November 1660, which Abraham attended, the first steps were taken for founding what was to become the Royal Society in 1663. Hill was therefore a founder member. Thomas Hill's own involvement is less clear. There are no references to him in the early journals of the Society in the 1660s. He was however very concerned in obtaining for '*certi virtuosi*' (as he describes his brother's colleagues) not only scientific books from Italy but also occasionally materials required for research. He continued this in the 1670s and at that time there are at least two letters from Thomas, whilst he was working as a merchant in Lisbon, to the Society providing and offering to obtain information.[131] There has been some discussion on the involvement of merchants in the Society. It must not be forgotten that, at this period, Abraham himself was working as a merchant and this letter book would seem to suggest that both he and Thomas were making a valuable contribution. The contribution of another merchant, Robert Balle, has been examined elsewhere. Balle was not only a contemporary of the Hills and a Devon man but also a merchant trading with Italy.[132] How far other friends of Thomas were involved is not clear but Alexander Travell, for example, is mentioned in the *Familiar Letters* of Abraham Hill as an admirer.[133]

TRADE AT THE RESTORATION

But the most interesting references in the letter book are to trade and especially to that in Cornish tin and pilchards. No overseas port books survive for Cornwall between 1642-1660 and it is difficult with the available evidence to estimate the quantity of goods set out from the ports. This is particularly true of Penryn and its neighbour Falmouth which was growing rapidly during this period. For these two ports there is only a partial port book for 1660, no commodities are given and only the second half of the year is covered but the list of ports and areas with which Penryn traded is impressive including Norway, Leghorn, Venice, Genoa, Alicante, Cadiz, Madeira, the Caribbean and North America.[134]

In the 1660 port book some of the trading activities of Bryan

Rogers can be followed. However the letter book supplements this with information on tin and pilchards sent to London and to the Mediterranean. The quantities quoted for Bryan Rogers in the letter book appear negligible compared with his trade in 1677 when he exported 2,249 cwt.[135] It is noticeable that the tin he sent to London was not on commission, with no prior buyer in mind and Thomas Hill acted as his factor. The price was rising at this time. Tin was a favourite export to the Mediterranean and it was this which Thomas Hill asked his uncle William to buy for him with the proceeds of the hops and iron. The possibility of a farm of the tin is mentioned in the letter book. Samuel Enys, together with Christopher Bellott, were granted the farm of the coinage duty on tin in Devon and Cornwall at Christmas 1660. With the Restoration coinage duty was restored, the coinage halls themselves had to be repaired after so many years of disuse; 'coinage halls are unserviceable and both beams and weights wanting' the coinage hall at Lostwithiel, in particular, 'being ready to fall into the pit', it was reported in February 1661.[136]

The Hill brothers continued to investigate sending pilchards to the Mediterranean. The markets for different varieties of fish were interdependent. A poor fishing season for the Dutch off Newfoundland and the loss of their ships suggested there would be a good trade in the Mediterranean for Cornish pilchards. However, 1661 was a poor year and Thomas and his friends did not feel it prudent to pay out the high price of 12s per thousand pilchards especially when they learnt that a hogshead had sold in Leghorn for only eleven dollars.[137] Thomas' instructions to Bryan Rogers for large well-preserved fish in tight casks were to be mirrored by other merchants who had genuine worries about the keeping qualities of Cornish pilchards if inadequately salted and packed. Peter Hill, William's son, was to receive similar letters from Thomas D'Aeth in 1700 and it was a constant theme in the correspondence of Valentine Enys early in the next century.[138] However Thomas Hill obviously showed some reluctance to repeat the instructions of his associates to Bryan Rogers who was experienced enough by that time to know what was required.

Tin and pilchards were only two of the commodities in which Rogers specialised. He imported much timber from the Baltic and his increasing correspondence with James Thierry would suggest a great interest in the West Indies. His factor in Barbados would seem to have been his brother-in-law, the Plymouth merchant George Thompson, who had married his sister Mary in 1642. Their son, Bryan, became a merchant in Penryn. After the death of his first wife, the daughter of Ambrose Jennens, Bryan Rogers married Jane, the daughter of John Tregeagle. This brought him important London connections with the Lethieuilliers and other leading merchants because John Tregeagle had married the daughter of Alderman Sir William Hooker and this enhanced Bryan Rogers' status as the greatest merchant in the West Country.

For William Jennens in Plymouth and Bernard Sparke in Exeter the partnership with Thierry was possibly their major concern. It was for this reason that they wished to know the progress of Thomas' investigations into the new Navigation Acts which could seriously affect that trade. Bernard Sparke was also interested in the rumour that a monopoly was being sought on the African trade.[139] Bernard Sparke's concern with the Guinea/Barbados trade is shown by a case in 1661 concerning the *Paragon*.[140] The *Paragon* was built in Bristol on account of Bernard Sparke and John Cooke of Exeter. Also in the partnership were John Sparke and John Bawden who were described as English merchants at Barbados. The ship was loaded with sugar at Topsham about August 1661 and sailed for Guinea with John Bawden on board where the sugar was exchanged for African slaves. A Dutch ship from Amsterdam forbad them to trade, taking their ship and their cargo. As the ship was thought to be worth about £1,100 and the slaves would have yielded, it was estimated, at least £9,740 this would have been a serious catastrophe for Bernard Sparke if no restitution were obtained. The evidence for this does not appear to have survived.

Trading in cloth was also important but there is little reference to Devon serges in the letter book. The Hills' agents in Leghorn had difficulty in selling some cloth, called 'hounscotts', which had been sent there earlier. However, Thomas' account of the problems of dyeing cloth in the winter time could have relevance for Devon. The import of silks from the Orient was a major concern and the profits obtained from exports to Italy were sent from Italy to Constantinople and Smyrna to buy silks and galls the other commodity in demand from there. Trade with the eastern Mediterranean was extensive as can be seen in the report of the sinking of Captain Haddock's ship *Hannibal* with its cargo of silk and of currants from Zante which was worth a reported

£50,000. The Italian trade was however somewhat unbalanced as far as the Hills were concerned. Thomas Hill could suggest little of substance to his friends there to send to England. His laborious attempt to sell lute strings met with little success, since London was apparently awash with that commodity (although the watch strings were disposed of by personal selling) and he had to discourage his Lucca friends from sending Lucca and Florence silks which were not so saleable as those from the east. Apart from olive oil and wine Roman gloves were in demand but it is interesting that Thomas' Italian friends were eager to have their boots made in England of English leather.

DANGERS TO TRADE

Merchants abroad, and especially in the Mediterranean, were always concerned at the possibility of war. John Byam suffered in 1655 when he had to remove himself hastily from Naples with the possible loss of his trading books. War with Spain, which occurred in 1658, ended officially in June 1660 but rumours of another conflict spread when King Charles announced he was to marry a Portuguese rather than a Spanish princess. Rivalry between other nations also caused concern. Thomas describes the pitched battle between the French and Spanish ambassadors' entourages over precedence when welcoming the Swedish ambassador. This ended with several deaths. The Spaniards won the contest by shooting the coachman and the horses of the coach of the French ambassador. Samuel Pepys describes how the City rejoiced that the French had lost. The possibility of ships falling into the hands of 'Turkish' or rather North African pirates was endemic through the century. The danger increased in 1661 necessitating English warships in the Mediterranean.[141]

Almost the last letter in the letter book recalls an earlier conflict. Imprisoned in Pendennis Castle in 1661 was Colonel Edmund Harvey. Bryan Rogers was approached for help. Bryan Rogers may well have shown some hesitation for Harvey, a draper with 'an unsavoury reputation', had been earlier imprisoned in the Tower accused of defrauding Cromwell's government of £30,000. However, Harvey was the father of Abraham Hill's brother-in-law, Samuel, who also married a daughter of Sir Bulstrode Whitelocke.[142]

THOMAS' ACCOUNTS

By the end of 1661 Thomas felt himself in a position to exhibit the accounts and produced a final statement on 13 January 1662, two years after his father's death.[143] The total amount received was £4,191.11s.11d. which included £2,074.17s.7d recovered by June 1660. The debts owing by the deceased together with the funeral expenses amounted to £3,030.19s.11d leaving a balance of £1,160.12s.0d of which Thomas and Samuel together inherited a third. These figures however did not include the estate which Richard Hill left to his wife. This second account amounted to some £3,000 exclusive of some expenses and the remainder used to pay Thomas and Samuel the bulk of their inheritance of £2,000 and £1,000 left to them by their father. Putting together these two accounts it would seem that the value of Richard Hill's estate was a little over £4,000. This is not as high as might have been expected. Abraham himself acquired around £1,000. This again suggests that he had been given a substantial settlement by his father on marriage.

Comparing the accounts drawn up in January 1660 with the references in Thomas Hill's letters, it is realised that many of the people cited as debtors do not appear in the letter book. It is possible that these debts were collected easily but it is puzzling that there is no reference to them. Of the ships mentioned then some but not all occur in the letter book. Their cargoes presumably were sold and the amounts added to the final statement of January 1662. However, Thomas Hill reached his target of around £4,000. As we know that some of the debts quoted, including the major sum regarding the mortgage of Trelevan and that of Thomas Hollis were not realised by 1662, the amount must have been made up with increased profits from the commodities. Possibly the tin sent to Smyrna brought in a large sum.

LIVES AFTER THE LETTER BOOK

A few letters survive in the Hill papers for the period after 1661. A letter from William Hill to Thomas dated 10 July 1663 concerning his son William, who had left the Hill household but not told his father where, is signed by 'loving Uncle W. Hill' suggesting the ill-feeling between Thomas and William had ended.[144] With this letter

is another, dated seven years later, but this time from Dublin. His
second wife, Elizabeth, had died and William had decided to try
his luck in Dublin. 'Sometime after my coming over I married a
widow that had no children, with whom I live very comfortable.'
Nothing more is heard from uncle William and what happened to
son William is not known. However, there are two letters from
William's son, Peter. He stayed in Falmouth, married a local girl,
and became a prosperous and respected merchant. He died about
1722.[145] He also became a customs officer in Falmouth.

Jacobi Thierry and William Schellinks stayed with the Hill
family during the winter of 1661 to 1662. On 13 February[146] 1662
Schellinks reported 'we moved from Mr Thomas Hill's where we
had been staying so long, to our newly hired accommodation in
Fleet Street.' On 24 March he mentions they went on to the *Black
Horse* which had arrived from Barbados. In June he and Jacobi
visited the West Country where they stayed with Bernard Sparke
in Exeter, William Jennens in Plymouth, Bernard Sparke's brother-
in-law, Peter Toller, in Fowey and Bryan Rogers in Falmouth. They
also visited Penzance. Thomas Hill continued to assist them whilst
they stayed in England, in particular in trying to arrange for the
naturalisation of Jacobi as an English citizen.

By 1677 William Jennens was feeling so old and tired that he
excused himself from taking up the office of Sheriff of Cornwall.[147]
His shrewdness deserted him when it came to choosing a husband
for his daughter Anne. She married Edward Norsworthy of
Ince. By this time Edward Norsworthy was in serious financial
difficulties and Edward was unable to pay his part of the marriage
settlement resulting in a Chancery Case initiated by his father-in-
law. The final eclipse of the family was due to Edward's support
for James II, following him into exile.[148] William Jennens died in
1688 leaving his wife Elizabeth to try and sort out the affairs of
their daughter.

When Bryan Rogers died in 1692 his financial affairs were in
complete disarray due mostly, it would seem, from his attempt to
arrange a farm of tin in 1688, he himself pledged a sum of £8,000
being one eighths of the whole. The timing was unfortunate for
the whole scheme was disrupted by the overthrow of James II and
Bryan Rogers it would appear lost a considerable amount of money.
After his death his widow had several chancery cases to endure
initiated by angry creditors, one of whom was under the illusion

that Bryan Rogers on his death had been worth £40,000.[149]

Bernard Sparke died in 1668. He asked that the Dean of Exeter should conduct his funeral service at the Cathedral taking the text from Job: 'Man is borne to sorrow as the Sparks fly upwards'. He would seem to have been a wealthy man, leaving much property, a coach with four horses and an annuity of £200 to his wife. He had no children therefore his nephew and nieces and young cousins were remembered generously.[150]

Giles Lytcott prospered in the succeeding years and became Controller General of Accounts. He died in 1696 mentioning 'his loveing wife Sarah'. His eldest son, also Giles, predeceased his father and died in the East Indies and the second son, John, so displeased his father that he was virtually omitted from the will. He was to die the following year. Two daughters lived to marry.

Samuel Hill, who was left £1,000 by his father, did not live long to enjoy his inheritance. Two letters of his written from Holland survive, one for 22 August and the other 12 September 1664.[151] Both these letters record the large number of deaths from the plague. Samuel himself was to die the following year at the age of 19 and was buried in Amsterdam.

SAMUEL PEPYS AND THOMAS HILL

From the letter book Thomas Hill emerges as likeable, friendly and a very sociable young man. This view is verified in the writings of a man who was to become one of his greatest friends. It was on 11 January 1664 that Samuel Pepys first met Thomas Hill, 'a young gentleman I suppose a merchant, his name Mr Hill, that hath travelled and I perceive is a master in most sorts of Musique and other things'.[152] Two months later they met again in a coffee house 'and there very fine discourse with Mr Hill the merchant, a pretty gentile, young, and sober man'.[153] On 15 April 1664 Pepys wrote 'At noon to the Change, where I met with Mr Hill the little merchant, with whom I perceive I shall contact a musical acquaintance' but he then added 'But I will make it as little troublesome as I can'. The friendship which developed was anything but 'troublesome'.[154] Pepys soon succumbed to Hill's charms and their mutual love of music and interest in Italy bound the two friends together. Thomas's letters to Italy reveal his especial enjoyment of Italian music and Pepys, partly through

Thomas's influence, came to acquire a similar taste. Later Pepys was to describe Thomas as 'my friend, the merchant that loves musique and comes to me a-Sundays, a most ingenious and sweet-natured and highly accomplished person'.[155]

By 22 July 1664 they were meeting more regularly. Hill, with his friend Thomas Andrew, went to Pepys' house to listen to an Italian singer: '*Seignor* Pedro who sings Italian songs to the Theorbo most neatly; and they spent the whole evening in singing the best piece of musicque, counted of all hands in the world, made by Seignor Charissimi the famous master in Rome. Fine it was indeed, and too fine for me to judge of'.[156] Later in that year they spent another evening together – `with Mr Andrews and Hill 'we sung with my boy Ravenscrofts four-part psalms, most admirable music. Then (Andrews not staying) we to supper; and after supper fell into the rarest discourse with Mr Hill about Rome and Italy, the most pleasant that I ever had in my life. At it very late and then to bed.'[157]

In January 1665 Thomas told his friend that was to be made Assistant to the Secretary of the Prize Office, Sir Ellis Langton, which was to be held at Sir Richard Ford's. Pepys was disappointed for he felt that Thomas deserved a more important office. He had had the idea of marrying Thomas to Elizabeth Pickering, the niece of the Earl of Sandwich who was described as 'comely but very fat'. However he had second thoughts, as he realised that his friend was not sufficiently wealthy for such an alliance. In 1668 she married Pepys' rival at the Admiralty, John Creed.[157]

By 1665 Thomas' greatest friends were the members of the Houblon family. Reference had been made in letters to parties attended by Mrs 'Hubland' in 1661. Of the five Houblon brothers, all merchants, Thomas was particularly friendly with James and his wife Sarah. Later James Houblon was also to become one of Pepys' closest friends.

The Houblons also enjoyed these musical evenings. Pepys wrote of one on 31 January 1665 when James Houblon was present. On the 12 February speaking of Thomas he wrote 'we spent the evening very finely, singing, supping and discoursing'. On 26 February 'Hill stayed and supped with me; and very good discourse of Italy, where he was, which is always to me very agreeable'. On 22 March he and Thomas were invited to the Houblon's home; 'After dinner Mr Hill took me with Mrs Hubland, who is a fine gentlewoman – into another room, and there made her sing; which she doth very well – to my great content.'¹⁵⁸

Thomas Hill would appear to have left London during the plague. By 1665 negotiations between his brother Abraham and Thomas Hollis to buy St. Johns, Sutton-at-Hone in Kent were completed and they may have then vacated the Lime Street house and moved there. Thomas was at Woolwich on 10 September 'he and I all the morning at Musique and a song he hath set, of three parts; methinks very good'.¹⁵⁹ On 29 October Pepys describes how they met at Greenwich and then 'To supper and discourse of Musique, and so to bed, I lying with him, talking till midnight about Berchenshaws music rules which I did to his great satisfaction inform him on.'¹⁶⁰ On 1 November he writes 'Lay very long in bed, discoursing with Mr Hill of most things of a man's life, and how little merit doth prevail in the world, but only favour'.¹⁶¹

In 1666 Pepys lost the company of his friend. On the 9 February he records an entertainment, where he dined with Thomas Hill and the five Houblon brothers. 'A fine sight it is to see these five brothers, thus loving one to another and all industrious merchants. Mr Hill going for them to Portugall was the occasion of the entertainment'. Because he was leaving England Thomas Hill arranged to have his portrait painted. February 14 *St Valentine's day*. 'This morning called up by Mr Hill, who my wife thought had been come to be her Valentine, she it seems having drawn him last night, but it proved not; however, calling him up to our bedside, my wife challenged him.' They then went out by coach to Lord Sandwich's, on to the Lord Chancellor's new house and after that to Mr Hales 'who is drawing his picture – which will be mighty like him, and pleased me, so that I am resolved presently to have my wife's and mine done by him, he having a very masterly hand.'

Thomas came on the 2 March to say goodbye to his friend before going to Portugal. In May Pepys records going to Mr Hales to collect his own picture for which he paid £14 (plus 25s for the frame) and also paid £7 for a copy of Thomas Hill's painting (5s for the frame).¹⁶²

Thomas continued to keep in touch with Pepys. In the Pepys Library is an extract from a letter written by Thomas from Lisbon in April 1673 in which he begged Pepys for any music he could send out to him: 'we have a little Consert among us, which gives us entertainment, wee have five Hands for Viols & Violins three of us use both , and all except me, the Violl but the want of Music in this Country obliges us to play over and over againe'. In the same letter Thomas mentions a young man (Cesare Morelli) who was born in Flanders but brought up in Rome and had 'a most admirable Voyce & Sings rarely to his Theorba, and with great skill'. Thomas arranged for him to come to England in 1674.[163]

THE LATER YEARS IN THE LIVES OF THOMAS AND ABRAHAM HILL

Thomas Hill, for the last years of his life, acted as a factor for the Houblons in Oporto and Lisbon. When James Houblon and Sarah had a daughter, named after her mother, Thomas became godfather. Thomas died in Lisbon in 1675, under forty years of age. In his will he left two sums of £100 to Mrs Jane Maskelyne and Mrs Dorothy Hubert, £100 to James Houblon and Sarah to buy a ring 'in memory of our friendship' and half of the remainder of his estate went to his goddaughter, Sarah Houblon, as 'an acknowledgement of my Gratitude to my best and closest friends, her parents' the other half of the estate was divided between his nephew and niece, Richard and Frances Hill, the son and daughter of his brother Abraham. The value of the estate is not known.[164]

Of the three brothers Abraham lived the longest. He continued

St John's, Sutton-at-Home. The home of Abraham Hill from the article by R.H. Ernest Hill, *Archaelogica Cantiana*, Vol. xxiv, by kind permission of the Kent Archaelogical Society.

Painting of Abraham Hill, artist unknown, at the Royal Society, London.
Ref P/0064. © By kind permission of the Royal Society.
The painting is on permanent loan from the Hill family.

to trade as a merchant after his father's death but, in 1665, bought
the estate of St. John's, Jerusalem at Sutton-at-Hone in Kent
from Thomas Hollis who it would seem still owed Abraham a
considerable sum of money. Abraham lived the life of a leisured
but learned gentleman. He continued his association with the
Royal Society being an original Fellow and their Treasurer from
1663 to 1666 and again from 1677 to 1699. He was also secretary
from December 1673 to November 1675 and a Member of Council
from 1663 to 1666 and again from 1672 to 1721.[165] There are
references to him in the diaries of both Pepys and Evelyn. He was
later, in 1691, Comptroller to Archbishop Tillotson of Canterbury
and in the reign of William and Mary was Commissioner of Trade
and Plantations from 1696 to 1702 and, as the work became
more onerous, he was made responsible for matters concerning

New England, Newfoundland and New York. A ten volume of his commonplace books survive and he became sufficiently well known to warrant a place in the *Dictionary of National Biography*. Whilst at Sutton-at-Hone he conducted an experiment to introduce Devon cider into Kent, planting many orchard trees obtained from Herefordshire and Devon but this was apparently not a success.[166] As Thomas had mentioned in the letter book, Abraham's first wife, Anne, died in 1661 leaving behind two young children Richard and Frances. In 1662 Abraham married again, this time to Elizabeth, the daughter of another merchant, Michael Pratt, but she also died in 1672. Abraham himself lived until 1721, Richard, his son, died a short time afterwards leaving no heirs. Frances never married. When she died in 1736 she left as her principal heir William Hill of Carwythinick, her second cousin from Falmouth, the grandson of Thomas's uncle, William.

THE YEARS AFTER THE RESTORATION

Richard Hill was a merchant of some importance who lived and worked through much of the first 60 years of the seventeenth century. The West Indies, the East Indies, Africa and above all the Mediterranean were the chief spheres of his operations and the surviving papers of the Hill family do much to illuminate the extent of these activities. As a Westcountry man he could appreciate the possibilities more than most. In the next fifty years these trends continued and accelerated and other merchants from Devon and Cornwall were not slow to take up the various challenges, many of them doing so by living and working overseas.

The close trading ties with Spain continued until the War of the Spanish Succession put an end to Westcountry merchants settling in Spain. Up to that time many of the leading merchant families had sons in Spain or in the Canaries. Valentine Enys from Penryn remained in the Canaries until just before the outbreak of war, his brother, Richard, was in Cadiz at the beginning of the 1690s in partnership there with Matthias Aldington and another Richard Hill (also from Devon but no relation to the first). Their firm was of some importance as they were the principal correspondents of the London merchant Charles Peers.[167] Cadiz and Malaga were the bases of the two Upton brothers, Ambrose and Arthur. Near by, at Port St Mary, another Penryn man, John Munday, the son of Peter Munday whose travel accounts exist for the first part of the century, died there in 1697 professing the Catholic faith.[168] The close connections between Cornwall and Spain were enhanced when the packet ship service was started from Falmouth to Corunna in 1689. (When war broke out in 1702 the destination was changed to Lisbon and thereby increasing the Portuguese connections which had grown in the 1690s from a greater demand for Portuguese salt after war broke out with France in 1689).

The Mediterranean countries and especially Italy continued to appreciate Cornish pilchards. Increasingly many larger ships of 100 tons or more left Mount's Bay and passed through the Straits to Malaga, Alicante, Genoa, Leghorn and Naples and sometimes on to Venice. They would frequently return from Zante with the currants so loved by the English. Even there an occasional Westcountry merchant could be found; but the misfortunes of the Cornishman, James Praed, highlight the problems merchants had to face when living in a foreign country. He complained of being threatened with death and had to return hurriedly to England.[169] Other Westcountry merchants however spent many years of their lives in Italy, Ephraim Skinner, who has already been mentioned, was in Leghorn for several years; Giles, Charles and Robert Balle lived in Genoa, Messina and Leghorn.

The Italian merchant whose activities are best documented is Francis Arundell the youngest son of William Arundell, a merchant who settled in Falmouth during the Interregnum. Francis Arundell first went to Leghorn about 1690 and he stayed there until shortly before his death in 1712. Letters to him and accounts exist from 1704. These letters and accounts, written by his Plymouth-born correspondent, Arthur Martyn, provide a detailed picture of English trade with Italy, which involved West Country merchants such as Robert Corker the leading Falmouth merchant and successor of Bryan Rogers. Francis Arundell arranged that his nephew, Peter Champion from St Columb, should succeed him in Italy and named him as one of his principal heirs. The mother of Arthur Martyn was an Upton from Devon, therefore he also was born into a family with important trading connections, his partner at one time being William Upton.[170] Peter Hill from Falmouth also traded with Italy. Thomas D'Aeth of Italy and later London corresponded with him in the early 1700s. Thomas D'Aeth was also in correspondence with the Exeter merchant, Edward Mann;

in February 1699, for example, he negotiated for the export of 180 pieces of long ells to Italy.[171]

Some of the proceeds of the fish, cloth and tin sold in Italy were sent to Constantinople, Smyrna or Aleppo to be invested in silks or galls. Tin continued to be a profitable export and West Country merchants can be found in that region too: members of the Carew family were still there in the 1660s and Richard Hoblyn was in Smyrna in the 1680s.

In the late 1650s Richard Hill's principal correspondent was James Thierry in Amsterdam. From the 1660s the trade between the West Country and the Netherlands increased considerably although, because of the Navigation Acts, the emphasis was to change. Richard Hill and James Thierry had been partners in exporting sugar from the West Indies to Amsterdam. This direct trade was illegal after 1660. Sugar and tobacco had to be unloaded and re-exported. By 1678 the re-export of tobacco was an important factor in West Country trade and for Falmouth in particular.[172] Bryan Rogers was very much involved in this, possibly in cooperation with James Thierry. The latter's name appears in a port book for Falmouth for 1678. Other commodities re-exported to the Netherlands included furs of every description.[173]

The Dutch connection with Devon also increased considerably with an interest in Devon cloth. The mixed worsteds from Tiverton were especially favoured as were later a great variety of the new draperies. In return came linens from the Haarlem bleacheries and duck (a heavy fabric of plain weave) for sail cloth.[174]

Richard Hill and Bernard Sparke had both been interested in West Africa but the involvement of West Country merchants increased during the century. Thomas Corker, the brother of Robert mentioned above, spent several years in Africa acting for the Royal Africa Company.[175] After his death, his associate, Stephen Jackson, came to Falmouth and an occasional reference can be found in the Falmouth port books to trade with Guinea.

With an increasing production of tin, more timber was required for the mines. Much of the smaller timber came from the New Forest area. The port books of Southampton show Cornwall was the principal destination of timber sent from there together with charcoal for the blowing houses. Timber was also in demand for making the containers for fish and other exports and also for ship repairs. Some also came from Ireland but increasingly by the end of the century large amounts of the larger balks, masts and many deals came from Norway chiefly in Dutch ships. Occasionally, and more frequently by the next century, timber was brought in from North America.

The quantity of tin had indeed increased substantially compared with the 1630s figures From Truro in 1667 over 15,000 cwt of tin was dispatched. A similar increase can be seen in other commodities: in 1668 almost 12,000 sacks of charcoal were imported into Penryn, the figure for 1636 had been about 3,500. In 1668 the quantity of salt imported into the county had increased by about 50% from the pre-war period. In 1668 Falmouth imported over 500 cwt of raisins from Alicante, in 1638 3 cwt came into Penryn and very little elsewhere. In 1639 29,500 helling stones went from Padstow, by 1668 the number was 746,000.

From the late 1660s a similar increase can be found for the Devon ports. Stephen Fisher wrote that, 'In the period from 1680 to the 1720s Devon's economy was amongst the most thriving and advanced in the nation'. He put this down to several factors including Devon's location, the increased production of woollen cloths and the consequently prosperous towns and the establishment of the Plymouth dockyard in the 1690s.[176]

There were periods of stagnation especially after the war with France broke out in 1689. The Cornish port books especially show the downturn in trade. But with peace in 1697 came recovery and, although the merchants had to face many problems when war recurred in 1702, the loss of trade was not as great.

Many of the trends, which were to make Great Britain one of the greatest trading nations in the eighteenth century can be discerned in the documents left by Richard Hill and in the letter book kept by his son in 1660. The details also reveal the impact on ordinary lives and the importance of individuals' efforts in creating a mercantile empire.

THE SHORTHAND

The shorthand used in the Hill letter book is that of Thomas Shelton. He invented two distinct forms of shorthand. The first which he published as *Short Writing* in 1626 (later, in 1635,he named it *Tachygraphy*) is the best known and was, at the time, very popular.[1] This was used by Samuel Pepys. It was based, to a large extent, on the earlier works of John and Edmond Willis. The second system, which he invented and published in 1649 as *Zeiglographia,* is less well known and is very different from the first. Further editions of the latter were published, one of which is dated 1659 and a copy is in the British Library. 1659 is the year when Thomas Hill returned from Italy. If I am right in assuming that Thomas Hill himself wrote the first twenty four letters which are in shorthand, possibly he learnt it from this edition on his arrival in England.

I had problems trying to decide the system of shorthand being used. When I started to transcribe these documents I knew nothing about shorthand in the seventeenth century. I compared Thomas Hill's script with that of Pepys but it did not appear to be the same.[2] However, I was able, through comparing the pattern of symbols and words used by Thomas Hill in the first lines of his letters and also the position of the date given in longhand for the letter to which he was replying, to discover most of the signs for the consonants. Timothy Underhill of Cambridge was able to recognise the form of shorthand used. The British Library edition of 1659 provided clues to the more complicated structures and also the many abbreviations used.

However, even with this help, it has not been possible to decipher every word of these letters. There are many problems: illegibility and fading of the document in places and the uncertainty as to whether a mark is part of the paper or a shorthand symbol are two. Many abbreviations are used which, if not known, can cause difficulties: for example the symbols for M and S together make the word 'instruments' and M and T 'information' both of which would be difficult to guess. I have found the symbol for B to mean 'be' or 'but' or 'by'; that for S 'as','is' or 'so' that for F with an L attached (which is not always apparent) can mean 'follow' or 'flesh' or 'fall' or 'fully'. If there are several of these ambiguous words together then it is difficult to guess the meaning of the sentence. There are separate symbols for vowels, which are normally used at the beginning of a word only, at other times the vowel has to be guessed from the position of the surrounding consonants. If a writer is careful, as apparently Pepys was,[3] then this can be ascertained, if the writer is in a hurry, as Thomas Hill would appear to have been at times, then the consonants are not positioned sufficiently carefully for this to be deduced. The writer also, in haste, might write the three down-strokes N, T and D without bothering about their different directions. The system is mostly phonetic but not completely: for instance the silent 'K' is often included for example in the word 'know' K and N are both used. There are two separate symbols for C and K although the sound is the same and often used indiscriminately without reference to the spelling.

Thomas Hill's own construction of sentences and use of words is frequently different from what would be common today. By comparing the shorthand letters with those in longhand I have tried to follow his structure to interpret a sentence but sometimes, even when the shorthand appears clear, the meaning itself is not obvious.

I therefore apologise for any mistakes or omissions but I felt that it was better to include my own transcription of these letters rather than to leave them out or give only a brief summary. The writer did not continue the use of shorthand after the first 23 letters. The next letter is in a different hand therefore it is possible this was written by a clerk who did not know shorthand and longhand was used hereafter although the writing changes back to the original. It could also be that Thomas Hill found that, although writing shorthand was quicker than longhand, reading it later was more tedious and decided to discontinue using it.

I myself am disappointed that these shorthand letters, not read for three and a half centuries, have failed to produce more interesting information. It is of interest, however, to consider that Thomas Hill and Samuel Pepys, who were later to become such special friends, should have left behind documents in shorthand, invented by the same man, which began within a few weeks of each other.

Notes

1. Nicholas Canny, 'The Origins of Empire: an Introduction' in *The Origins of Empire* ed. Nicholas Canny (Oxford 1998) p.4
2. Gigliola Pagano de Divitiis, *English Merchants in Seventeenth-Century Italy* (Cambridge 1997) xliii
3. Divitiis, *Engllish Merchants* xiii
4. The word Falmouth is used in documents of the period in particular the port books and at this time referred to the whole area around the estuary of the Fal including the town of Penryn.
5. Wendy R. Childs, 'Devon's Overseas Trade in the Late Middle Ages' in *The New Maritime History of Devon* Vol. 1 ed. Michael Duffy et al (London 1992) p.79
6. Alison Grant, 'Devon Shipping, Trade and Ports, 1600–1689' in *The New Maritime History of Devon* Vol. 1, p.132
7. Mariko Mizui, The Interest Groups of the Tin Industry in England c 1580–1640. Thesis, University of Exeter 1999
8. George F. Steckley, ed *The Letters of John Paige, London Merchant 1648–58* (London Record Society 1984) p.x
9. Guildhall Library MS 15860 Apprentice lists for the Haberdashers' Company
10. Alison Grant, 'Devon Shipping, Trade, and Ports' in *The New Maritime History of Devon* Vol. 1, p.130
11. Alison Grant, 'Devon Shipping, Trade, and Ports' in *The New Maritime History of Devon* Vol. 1, p.120
12. Guildhall Library MS 11593/1 Apprentice Lists of the Grocers' Company
13. T[he]N[ational] A[rchives]:P[ublic] R[ecord] O[ffice] C 108/67
14. Hermann Kellenbenz, 'The Organisation of Industrial Production' in *The Cambridge Economic History of Europe* Vol. V eds E.E. Rich and C.H. Wilson (Cambridge 1977) p.533
15. Todd Gray, ed. *Early Stuart Mariners and Shipping* (Devon & Cornwall Record Society NS Vol. 33)

16. John Scantlebury, 'The Development of the Export Trade in Pilchards from Cornwall during the Sixteenth Century' in the *Journal of the Royal Institution of Cornwall* 1989 NS Vol. 10, pt. 3, pp.330-59

17. Looe port books consulted include TNA: PRO E 190/1023/12, E 190/1023/15, E 190/1025/1, E 190/1035/14, E 190/1036/1. I would like to express my thanks to James Whetter for placing in the C[ornwall] R[ecord] O[ffice] his notes on many seventeenth century port books which I have used as well as looking at the originals. CRO AD 479/2

18. Fowey port books consulted include TNA: PRO E 190/1023/14, E 190/1024/23, E 190/1024/5, E 190/ 1031/7, E 190/1034/14, E 190/1035/11, E 190/1036/6

19. Dorothy O Shilton & Richard Holsworthy, eds. *H[igh] C[ourt of]A[dmiralty] Examinations 1637-8* (London 1932) ref. CA554

20. Roland J. Roddis, *Penryn The History of an Ancient Cornish Borough* (Truro 1964) p.23

21. Penryn port books consulted include TNA: PRO E 190/1024/4, E 190/1024/19, E 190/1031/19, E 190/1036/8, E 190/1036/4

22. Shilton & Holdsworthy, *HCA Examinations* ref. M290

23. Truro port books consulted include TNA: PRO E 190/1024/13, E 190/1024/18, E 190/1025/4, E 190/1025/3, E 190/1036/5, E 190/1036/15

24. G.R. Lewis, *The Stannaries* (reprinted Truro 1965) p.255

25. Helford (or Helston) port books consulted include TNA: PRO E 190/1021/5, E 190/1024/7, E 190/1025/2, E 190/1025/9, E 190/1028/5, E 190/1033/3, E 190/1035/7, E 190/1036/13

26. Mount's Bay port books consulted include TNA: PRO E 190/1023/5, E 190/1023/6, E 190/1036/9

27. St Ives port books consulted include TNA: PRO E 190/1625/7, E 190/1034/15, E 190/1036/3

28. TNA: PRO E 190/22/8

29. Padstow port books consulted include TNA: PRO E 190/1024/10, E 190/1035/2, E 190/1035/3, E 190/1036/2

30. Peter Cornford, 'Seafaring and Maritime Trade in Sixteenth-Century Devon' in *The New Maritime History of Devon*, Vol. 1, p.105

31. Todd Gray, 'Devon's Fisheries and Early-Stuart northern New England' in *The New Maritime History of Devon*, Vol. 1 p.143

32. Introduction to *The New Maritime History of Devon* Vol. 1, p.13

33. Todd Gray, 'Devon's Fisheries and Early-Stuart northern New England' in *The New Maritime History of Devon*, Vol. 1, p.142

34. Peter E. Cornford, 'Seafaring and Maritime Trade in Sixteenth-Century Devon' in *The New Maritime History of Devon,* Vol. 1, p.104
35. In the Hill papers at the British Library there is a list of ships taken into Algiers from 1638 to about 1646. Included in the list is the *Bonnebesse* of Plymouth, the *Senturion* and *Endeavour* of Milbrook, The *Virtue* of Dartmouth and the *Diligrence* of Barnstaple. BL Add. MS 5501
36. Centre for Kentish Studies U 145 C1
37. BL Add. MSS 5488, 5489, 5501, 5497
38. Richard Ernest Hill, *D[evon and] C[ornwall] N[otes and] Q[ueries]* Vol. iv 1906-7 pt. V pp.49 & 145; Richard Ernest Hill, *Archaeologica Cantiana* Vol. xxiv (1906) p.227 & Vol. xx1x (1911) p.268
39. CRO F3/786
40. Henry Roseveare, *Markets and Merchants of the Late Seventeenth Century* (Oxford 1987) p.14
41. The two most interesting and complete letter books for the West Country during the Stuart period are those of Valentine Enys (CRO 698) and Arthur Martyn (North Devon Record Office B69/38 & B69 add 3/1) In both of these the pages are numbered although in that of Valentine Enys there is a mistake by the author in numbering the pages.
42. CRO probate documents H1048
43. The Shilston pedigree is given in BL Add MS 5488 f. 74 but there would seem to be a problem in fitting Richard Hill and his father Thomas into it. Richard Ernest Hill, who was a genealogist, never succeeded in doing so.
44. Richard Ernest Hill, *DCNQ* Vol. iv, p.50
45. BL Add. MSS 5497 f. 164
46. The lists of apprentices in the Cordwainers' Company, Guildhall Library MSS 7351/1-2 have been searched but no record could be found for Richard Hill. Presumably Richard Ernest Hill failed to do so too for he does not mention one, although a reference to William, Richard's brother, is given.
47. For example R.N. Worth, *History of Plymouth* (Plymouth 1890) p.83
48. will of Abraham Jennens senior TNA: PRO PROB 11/ 212 dated 1650
49. TNA: PRO C 5/499/65
50. TNA: H[istorical] M[anuscripts] C[ommission] *Portland MSS* Vol. iii, p.150
51. TNA: PRO PROB 11/221 proved 13 April 1652

52. The details of this property can be followed in Abraham's will of 1650 together with three documents at the CRO i.e. CF3207, 3210 and 3211. Together they provide interesting information on many sites and streets in Plymouth in the seventeenth century.

53. Henry Roseveare, *Markets and Merchants* p.143

54. James Phinney Baxter, ed. *Documentary History of the State of Maine* (Maine Historical Society 1884) 2nd Series Vol. 111 contain the Trelawny Papers.

55. For information on John Hallett see the many references in James Derriman, *Killigarth* (Morden 1994)

56. re John Trelawny see TNA: PRO C 9/130/142

57. see Letter 6. Trelawny was involved in several Chancery cases including TNA: PRO C 5/425/68, C 9/23/112, C 9/411/188

58. CRO R253 post nuptial marriage settlement dated February 1661/2

59. TNA: PRO E 190/952/1 1646-7

60. Charles Peard's will was proved 11 February, 1661 TNA: PRO PROB 11/303

61. TNA: PRO: PROB 11/515. see BL Add. MS 5489 f. 75 re list of goods loaded on the *Society*

62. see John Cock, *Records of the Ancient Borough of South Molton in Ye County of Devon* (South Molton 1893) and records re Hugh Squier in the NoDRO e.g. B366/Box1/Section A3,5

63. The letter describing this is in BL Add. MS 5488

64. Letter of Joan Squier CRO FS3/786 no 11

65. There are many references in Henry Roseveare, *Markets and Merchants*

66. BL Add. MS 5488 p. 105

67. Close by was the Pewterers' Hall, one wonders if this was a reason for the choice of location.

68. Robert Brenner, *Merchants and revolutions: commercial change, political conflict, and London traders* (Cambridge 1993)

69. W.B. Stephens, 'Foreign Trade of Plymouth in the early Seventeenth Century' in *Reports & Transactions of the Devonshire Association* 1969 pp.127-137

70. Alison Grant, 'Devon Shipping, Trades and Ports, 1660–1689' in *The New Maritime History of Devon* Vol.1, p.136

71. D.C. Coleman, *Sir John Banks, Baronet and Businessman* (Oxford 1963) p.4

72. George F. Steckley, ed.. *Letters of John Paige 1648–1658* (London Record Society 1984) p.ix

73. Steckley, *Letters* xiv

74. Richard Ernest Hill, *DCNQ* Vol. iv p.50
75. BL Add. MS 5501 f. 23
76. BL Add. MS 5489 f. 49
77. June Palmer, *Truro in the Seventeenth Century* (Truro 1989) pp.20, 47, 48. TNA: PRO:C 7/590/60 (Th. Gregor v. Th. Trewolla) is of interest for the history of the Bull Inn.
78. TNA: PRO C 9/11/66
79. Plymouth port books 1642-3 TNA: PRO E 190/1036/18 and 190/1643/4 PRO:E 190/1036/23
80. TNA: PRO: PROB 11/224
81. Mary Coate, *Cornwall during the Great Civil War and Interregnum* (Truro 1963) p.267
82. These are mentioned in the letter book when Charles Jennens' wife or possibly widow paid a visit to Thomas Hill to try and retrieve them.
83. TNA: HMC *Portland Mss* Vol. III p.150
84. It is possible to follow the development of many of the sites in Falmouth from the rentals (CRO) of the Killigrew family who owned much of the land on which the town was built. A summary of the history of these sites has been placed in the Royal Institution of Cornwall by Alan Pearson and myself.
85. BL Add. Ms 5497 f. 164
86. CRO EN 1039
87. CRO CF 3492
88. Mary Coate, *Cornwall in the Great Civil War* p.267
89. CRO EN 1039
90. James Scott Wheeler, *The Making of a World Power* (Stroud 1999) p.41
91. CRO FS 3/786 no 2
92. See TNA: PRO E 122/230/13,14,15. PRO E 122/230/15 is described as a Plymouth customs book (Plymouth was the head port for Cornwall). It contains, however, the custom accounts for Mount's Bay, St Ives and Truro. Truro is not named in the document but can be recognised from the names of the merchants concerned and the destination of the cargoes. It is a very useful document.
93. Henry Roseveare, *Markets and Merchants* p.100
94. Henry Roseveare, *Markets and Merchants* p.103
95. The Centre for Kentish Studies U234. Gigliola Pagano de Divitiis has used these documents extensively in *English Merchants in Seventeenth Century Italy* (Cambridge 1997)
96. Henry Roseveare, *Markets and Merchants* p.102
97. BL Add. MS 5489 f. 11

98.   A.C. Wood, *A History of the Levant Company* (London 1935) p.54
99.   Jonathan I. Israel 'Empire: the Continental Perspective' in *The Origins of Empire* p.425
100. Jonathan I. Israel 'Empire . . .' p.423
101. TNA: PRO HCA3/49 f. 230 Although he died in the Netherlands his will is in the National Archives TNA: PRO PROB 11/446 dated 9 June 1698

      My relatives, Steven & Petra Sheil, very kindly visited the *Gemeentearchief Amsterdam* for me. They found references to three brothers, Jaques (i.e.James), Jean & Steffano Thierrij. Jaques was described as a merchant of Amsterdam, Jean of London or Rouen? and Steffano of Naples. Most of the contracts relating to freight were between the years 1634 to 1670 and most of the contracts of Jaques concerned trade with Naples, Genoa, Seville, Rouen, Port a Port, Rio de Janeiro and Lisbon. No references to the trade described in the Hill Letter Book were found.
102. Shilton & Holworthy *HCA Examinations*
103. Maurice Exwood and H.L.Lehman, eds. and trans. *The Journal of William Schellinks' Travels in England, 1661–1663*, (London Camden Society, 5th ser. 1993)
104. TNA: PRO HCA 3/49 f. 230
105. TNA: PRO HCA 3/49 fo. 231
106. CRO F3/786/11
107. Henry Roseveare, *Markets and Merchants* p.103
108. BL Add MS 5488 f. 6
109. Robert Brenner, *Merchants and Revolutions* p.553
110. BL Add. MS 5488 f. 115
111. Ruth Spalding, *Contemporaries of Bulstrode Whitelocke 1605–1675* (OUP, New York, 1990) p.120
112. Richard Ernest Hill *DCNQ* Vol. V p.51
113. TNA: PRO PROB 11/297
114. BL Add. MS 5488 f. 81
115. BL Add. MS 5488 f.115
116. This is one of the earliest references to a billiard table.
117. There is a discrepancy over the date of his birth. In the *Familiar Letters which passed between Abraham Hill and several eminent and ingenious persons of the last century* (London 1767 – copy in the library of the Royal Society) 1633 is given. There may also have been an eldest son, Richard who in 1646 married a lady called Tryphenia but who died in 1650. She remarried a John Jekyll and there was a dispute between Jekyll and his wife and Richard Hill over money owing to Francis, possibly her son.

118. Please note that in the Companion volume to *The Diary of Samuel Pepys* eds. Robert Latham and William Matthews (London 1970-1983) (quoted henceforth as Pepys X) some of the information given on Thomas Hill is wrong. Thomas was certainly not born as early as 1630 and he joined the Prize Office about the time of the 2nd Dutch War, not the first.
119. My husband and I spent a few days in Lucca and immediately fell under the charm of its situation, its buildings and its people. We too enjoyed the music which today is in particular that of Puccini who was born in the city.
120. *Familiar Letters which passed between Abraham Hill and several eminent and ingenious persons of the last century* London 1767. (copy in the library of the Royal Society).
121. *Familiar Letters* Letter VI p.16
122. Ruth Spalding, *The Improbable Puritan. A Life of Bulstrode Whitelocke 1605–1675* (London, 1975) p.218
123. Ronald Hutton, *The Restoration* (Oxford 1985) p.93
124. Hutton, *The Restoration* p.88
125. BL Add. MS 5488 f. 170
126. Joseph Polsue, *Lake's Parochial History of the County of Cornwall* Vol. iii p.333 (reprinted 1974)
127. Spalding *Contemporaries* p.91
128. Richard Culling's will TNA: PRO: PROB 11/297 proved 1660
129. Spalding, *Contemporaries* p.119
130. Pepys X p.161
131. The Royal Society LBC.4.458 and LBC.7.99. The interests of Abraham Hill and his colleagues can be ascertained from the titles of the books and the material they required to be sent from Italy by Thomas' friends there. The music sent was possibly mostly for Thomas himself but it could be that Abraham and his friends of the Royal Society also shared Thomas' interest in Italian music.
132. N.R.R. Fisher 'Robert Balle Merchant of Leghorn and Fellow of the Royal Society' in the *Journal of the Royal Society* Vol. 55 No 3/September 22, 2001. She quotes the observation of Thomas Sprat (the author of the *History of the Royal Society* dated 1667) on the participation of merchants :
    'They have contributed their labours: they have help'd their correspondence, they have employ'd their factors abroad to answer their inquiries, they have laid out in all countries for observations; they have bestowed many considerable gifts on their Treasury and Repository.'p.351
    Abraham and Thomas Hill would seem to be examples of this.
133. *Familiar Letters* For an account of Abraham Hill see the chapter

on Abraham Hill F.R.S. by R.E.W. Maddison in *The Royal Society Its Origins and Founders* ed. Sir Harold Hartley (Royal Society, London 1960) and also the eulogy at the beginning of *Familiar Letters*.

134. TNA: PRO E 190/1037/2
135. James Whetter's article on Bryan Rogers in *Old Cornwall* Vol. VI No 8 (1963) pp.347-52
136. *C[alendar) of S(tate) P(apers) D(omestic) 1660* p.211
137. The number of fish in a hogshead could vary, depending on the size of the fish. William Schellinks in 1662 on his visit to Cornwall mentions as many as 7,000. Thomas himself suggested a hogshead of large fish would amount to 5,000.
138. D'Aeth Letter Book Guildhall Library Ms 9563; Valentine Enys CRO 698 extracts from which are printed in June Palmer *Cornwall, the Canaries and the Atlantic – The Letter Book of Valentine Enys 1704–1719* Institute of Cornish Studies, 1997
139. The Royal Africa Company was reconstituted in 1671.
140. TNA: PRO CO 388/1 f 20
141. Todd Gray 'Turks, Moors and the Cornish Fishermen: Piracy in the Early Seventeenth Century' in the *Journal of the Royal Institution of Cornwall* 1990 part 4
142. Spalding *Contemporaries . . .* p.114
143. BL Add. MS 5488 f.123
144. BL Add. MS 5488 f.170
145. TNA: PROB 11/583 3 Feb 1722
146. The dates are given in the New Style, ten days after the Old Style i.e. February 3
147. *CSPD* 1677-8 p.480
148. TNA:PRO C 6/250/62 & C 5/169/13 William Jennens will was proved 15 May 1688 TNA: PRO PROB 11/391
149. TNA: PRO: C7/264/36
150. TNA: PRO: PROB 11/121 proved 1668
151. BL Add. MS 5489 ff. 35 & 36
152. Pepys Vol. V 1664 p.12
153. Pepys V 1664 p.83
154. Pepys V 1664 p.124
155. Pepys VI 1665 p.18
156. Pepys V 1664 p.217 & p.332
157. Pepys IV 1663 p 308; Pepys V1 1665 p.18
158. Pepys VI 1665 pp.27,44,64
159. Pepys VI 1665 p.219
160. Pepys VI 1665 p.282
161. Pepys VI 1665 p.285

162. Pepys VII 1666 p.42
163. Pepys Library, Magdalen College, Cambridge Mornamont papers Vol, II p.1281
164. TNA: PRO PROB 11/350 proved 10 May 1676
165. R.E.W. Madison *The Royal Society* p.174
    Abraham's judgement on financial matters was not always correct. In 1681 he advised Evelyn to sell his East India stock. Evelyn ignored the advice for several months by which time his £250 had trebled in value. He transferred the money to the Royal Society. Gillian Darley *John Evelyn, Living for Ingenuity* (Yale 2006) p.255
166. Pepys VI p.336; BL Sloane MSS 2891-2901; *DNB* Vol 27 p 103
167. Guildhall Library MSS 10187,10188,10188a
168. Will of John Munday TNA: PRO PROB 11/438
169. CRO X507/173
170. North Devon Record Office B 69 /38 and B 69 add 3/1. see article June Palmer 'Letters from London to Leghorn, 1704–1705' in *Nuovi Studi Livornesi* Vol.XIV 2007
171. Letters from Thomas D'Aeth to Peter Hill are included in the D'Aeth letter book Guildhall Library MS 9563.
172. Reference to the Hill interest in tobacco can be found in a letter dated 23 August 1655 from William Hill in Falmouth to his nephew, Abraham, in London 'if tobacco be a commodity for the Straits I can buy a parcel cheap of St Kitts.' CRO FS3/786
173. TNA: PRO E 190/1043/16
174. Charles Wilson, *Anglo-Dutch Commerce and Finance in the eighteenth century* (Cambridge 1941) p.36
175. see TNA: PRO C 9/177/8
176. Stephen Fisher, 'Devon's Maritime Trade and Fishing' in *The New Maritime History of Devon* Vol. 1 p.232

Shorthand references

1. see William J. Carlton *Bibliotheca Pepysiana: A Descriptive Catalogue of the Library of Samuel Pepys. Part IV Shorthand Books* (London, 1940) pp.42-6
2. Pepys 1 Some copies of the original are given e.g. opposite p.cii
3. Pepys 1 p.cii

The Letter Book

1. James Thierry Amster[dam] London 3 Feb 1659/60

My last was of the 20th past advising the needful since which I have yours of the 30th ditto & concerning your [request?] I herewith send you a copy of Mr Woodrof's[1] bond, at due time the money shall be demanded and when in cash shall advise you, till when pray forbear to draw any money to provide [expenses?] which possibly [.you.] may for they may not be punctual .in paying. as happily you expected. In my last I've prayed to have speedy accounts from you which do please [send off] and most earnestly press you to it and so much the rather because of my father's death and the great requirement to settle his estate which pray consider and dispatch them with all the speed may be.

This week we had a meeting with your insurers on the _Dolphin_, Mr Fowk, Mr Ellis (Mr Bale[2] who was the other you have been already advised was retired) all the particulars were shown them and appraised which satisfied [.them.] clearly that both ships, they agree, were condemned. But they say it plainly appears by the copy in the condemnation that they were condemned as belonging to Dutchmen and they assured to you as an English man. To this they had answer of your being an Englishman which we assured them we recall some other discourses past. In conclusion we agreed it.

[_The whole business is proving very difficult, the insurers are reluctant to pay and require more papers as proof._] They desire to know your lowest demand which if you please to advise in answer to this and give me promptly some letter of agreement or other authority [with reference to the amount?] I shall acquaint them with it and return you their answer promptly [.upon.] receipt.

Sir, since above was written on the other side I have yours of the 6th Curr[en]t to which no other answer is needful but what is on the other side to which refer you. For your agreement about making a demand on the assurers I suppose between 50 and 55 p[er] c[ent] you keeping to yourself the right of [recovery[3]] what may be something possible, they might be willing to concur [.to.] doing the like. Much time might be spent and what it may come to in the end may be difficult and this is my advice however shall act for you [.and.] shall give account. Herewith you have letter from Mr B Rogers.

1. John Woodroffe was a Yarmouth merchant who traded with Thierry and supplied herrings.
2. Mr Thomas Fowke. Mr Robert Ellis and Mr Bale all provided insurance for the *Dolphin*. Ald. Thomas Fowke see Henry Roseveare *Markets and Merchants of the Late Seventeenth Century* (Oxford 1987) p 582. Gifford Bale had gone bankrupt.
3. right of recovery – this possibly means that Thierry would keep the right to try to retain any goods that he might be able to recover.

2. Bernard Spark Exon 7th detto

I have not any of yours to answer, the present solely for advice that I have paid to the Com [ission] [for] Excise your bill £110.16 10½ which shall be passed to account. Mr Jennens advises that the *Swan* was at Dartm[outh] and loading fish to send herewith. Captain Hen[ry] Hatsel[1] is at present here in London whom I entreated that we might have a convoy. He hath told me he promises to write this day to Capt[ain] Heaton at Ply[mouth] and if it can be conveniently done we shall have it which will be well [in our interests?] The Court for proving of wills is now settling [as I am informed]. I hope to acquaint you what I promised in my last concerning our approved business.

[NB At the side there are some extra notes difficult to read concerning Mr Thierry's cargo in the Swan, the freight and the loading of fish.]

1. Captain Henry Hatsell. For a detailed account see J.D. Davies 'The Naval Agents at Plymouth, 1652–88' in *The New Maritime History of Devon* Vol. 1 eds. Michael Duffy et al (London 1992) p 179

3. Wil[liam] Jennens Plym[outh] detto

Yours of the 3rd I have received, with enclosed papers came bill being credited to yourself [.this.] shall be carefully kept and at your disposal your [-] shall be made out per its receipt. I perceive the ship *Swan* is at Dartmouth loading fish. God send her well.

I spoke yesterday with Capt[ain] Hatsell persistently pressing him to get me an [agreement?] for a convoy to sail with the *Swan* to which he answered that he would make business [.to.] write Pli[mouth] by today with promise that he would write [effectually] by this post to Capt[ain] Heaton if it can't be done or is not convenient should [.know it.] by return. I pressed for the letter that I might have perused it but he told me must write about other business I hope that will prevail [correspondingly] for you. Send to me word of both. Mr Croker[1] is here and we have spoken with him. The court for probate for the will is [satisfactorily] settled which hath been some hindrance to our private business but I hope will hath all been done that we may go on to settle all accounts with [creditors].

1. Mr Croker possibly Hugh a London lawyer. There was a well-known Croker family in Devon.

4. **Bernard Spark** Exon 11th ditto

Since my last on the 7th I have yours of the 8th advising the *Swan's* departure for Plymouth with 1100 q[uin]t[als][1] of fish I hope she hath [.arrived.] in safety. I understand that they may send her onward to Aviero.[2] Capt[ain] Hatsell told me yesterday that he had written to Capt[ain] Heaton at Plymouth about a convoy for the *Swan* that would write him again tonight so hope may obtain it. On the 9th C[urrent] I answered a letter to you from Mr Butson[3]. Pray when you write him the fish that went on the [– ?] he hath another re per the *Swan*. I thank you for the favour you promise being in the bill, this may probably do.

1. quintal a weight sometimes variable but generally around 100 or 112 lbs but see Roseveare p 203 where says about 3½ cwt.
2. Aveiro in Portugal was renowned for its salt much of which was imported into the West Country for the salting of pilchards.
3. A John Butson was an Exeter merchant and brother-in-law of Bernard Spark.

5. Th Trewolla Jnr [1] Truro d[it]to

Concerning the contents of his letter to my mother. That we were in sorrow for the death of my dear father, respects etc.

1. Thomas Trewolla junior, the son of Thomas Trewolla senior, was a cousin of Thomas Hill. The Trewollas were well known in Truro as innkeepers and Thomas Trewolla junior later kept the best known inn in Truro, The Bull.

6. Benja[min] Child[1] Leg[o]r[n]e London 13th Feb[ruary] 1659 [1660]

I confess I have been too remiss in answering your courteous letter of the 5th Dec[emb]re but the occasion you [are?] informed owed to duty and not your [fault?]. It hath pleased God to visit our family with very much sickness which proved mortal to my dear father to our great grief and disturbance for myself, in particular it hath intruded in more than ordinary business, being an administrator to his will which takes my own time being so put [about].

My articles are dispatched and think should be by you early on if [weather permits?] I am [delighted] that Mr Dethicks has confirmed you of my loss on the sea and provided the [title to you on a ring ?]. My letter by Mr Eliot[2] I expect came to hand and your favoured me in [deferring] the enclosed I must not expect answer. I wrote to discuss [about] M. Doucre and a letter from my P[at]rons gives an amount of [-?].

Mr Trelawny we are advised is arrived by mount to [Venice] and the [excellency] there did speak with him there and at the [-] although [seems] he may be certainly fined at the Poultry Court of London with the amount on the first being but for the value of $90 for I am informed Jona[than] Parker hath been to visit him, it is a bad sad business. I hope your cousin honest Mr Foot[3] is not a sufferer although it was reported that Mr Trelawny had forged his name to some small sum.

I am glad to hear you have so good a commission for Rob[ert] Foot I hope may settle it so I wish you both much joy and prosperity to which [if] in anything I may act pray formally command me. I demanded of Mr Parker if he had thought of returning to Leg[horn] for I had such advice from another hand he said not and that he would [.not?.] change whatever should be the [trend] of such a question.

I am intimately acquainted with <u>Mr Miles</u> here [-] we often discuss on you and make many great wishes among ourselves that you would take a journey and do it soon. If quickly done, Mr <u>Lytcott</u> is to commence and may possibly [.have.] planned on such a design, yes Sir, and writes you should be welcome on it.

Re the account [.I.] myself do work on it.

1. It would seem possible that Benjamin Child was either a relative of Josiah (later Sir Josiah) Child or of Francis Child, a banker and Lord Mayor of London but I can find no evidence for this. It would be interesting to know his exact provenance especially in relation to Thomas Hill's later comment in Letter No. 154 that Benjamin Child was in someway connected with the Restoration of Charles II.
2. Mr Eliot was a merchant in Leghorn.
3. Mr Foote possibly Samuel but several Footes were merchants. Jonathan Parker had been a merchant in Italy. Who Mr Miles was is not known.

7. Giles Lytcott [1] Detto

Sent him the letter of Monck and what news there was etc.

1. General Monck was in London by February 3. Pepys Feb 3 writes re Whitehall (Robert Latham and William Matthews eds. *The Diary of Samuel Pepys* Vol. 1 London 1979 p 39) 'whither General Monke was newly come and we saw all his forces march by in very good plight and stout officers'. Giles Lytcott was a Royalist and therefore would have been interested in the letter written by George Monck and his chief officers to Parliament on February 11. 'I heard the news of a letter from Monke, who was now in the City again and did resolve to stand for the sudden filling up of the House; and it was very strange how the countenance of men in the Hall was all changed with joy in half an hour's time'. (Pepys 1 p 50 Feb 11)

  Monck instructed the MPs of the Rump Parliament to issue writs for new elections within a week, bring back the secluded members and to dissolve altogether once this had been done. 'There followed the night of 'the Roasting of the Rump' possibly the greatest expression of popular rejoicing London has ever known'. (Ronald Hutton *The Restoration* (Oxford 1985) p 93).

8. Be[rnard] Spark Exon 14 Detto

Yours of the 11th C[urrent] have received. The invoice of the *Swan's* cargo I shall expect in your next. The bill you have passed on me for £120 at 15 days sight payable to the account of Jerom Stone I have accepted and at due day shall discharge it taking it to be on account of ¼ part of the fish aboard the *Swan* and God send her safe on her departure.

I take notice you have sold 10 pipes of oil at £38 at 4 months (to which I consent) lately being assured you will do for the best.

They [want a conveyance quickly ?] It would be better ready, may be loaded to you. I hope Mr Jenens will advise the *Swan* is departed with a convoy for I had Capt[ain] Hatsell's promise to write effectually Captain Heaton about it.

9. Francis Selwyn [1] Ven[ice] 17th D[it]to

I have not written you of late chiefly not having any of yours to answer. The enclosed bill you had concerned the cargo of the *Lewis* and which [.is.] here and [.the.] things you favoured me to place aboard her. The pieces of silk for yourself the captain, being my friend, brings them, assures that he [alone?] has them [with him ?]. Your brother Mr Ed[ward] Selwyn might [go there] to fetch them, I suppose before this may have done it. For my things I leave it to the Captain to convey them to me; for the books, being very troublesome to clear at the customs, so he takes them home as his own. You [must deduct?] my[account] to provide for you anything [before] Torrigno's departure in 4 days [-----?] I have bought the other thing[s] [- ?]. You mentioned Mr Gayer & possibly this may be for him himself he may be settling with you [- ?] & convey them hither. The [- ?] I have forebore to provide however shall deliver it to the boat *Hannibal*[2] which may depart in March for [Genoa, Leghorn ?] & such parts. [I hope you will employ to me for some other accounts ?].

You may possibly have heard of my father's decease. Pray buy a book of [arias?] of Loreta which will cost £5 and send them [me] home carefully.

---

1. Francis Selwyn, a merchant in Venice, was from Friston in Sussex. His brother, Edward, who is also mentioned, became an MP.
2. The *Hannibal* at this time was captained by William Haddock whose

son, Richard, later became an Admiral. *Oxford D[ictionary] of N[ational] B[iography] 2003 edition* Vol. 24. William Haddock commanded the *Hannibal* against the Dutch in 1653 and Richard served under him.

10. James Thierry Amster[dam] 17th Feb. 1659 /[1660][1]

Yours of the 20th C[urrent] I have received with the 2 enclosed papers [acknowledged] which I know are very well. The post arrived late and the letters not delivered till afternoon hath scarce the time to deliver to you any account of proceeding any further in your business, only that I have spoken with one of the assurers who saith that it is not an [unusual?] thing for the assurers to have [persons acting for them ?] they being so far distant from the policy where the business is to be followed & must act [.as.] a second person but the power [.to.] settle resting in you for (.in.) principle the business may be followed although I think this not very likely to be expected. Before my next I shall have a meeting with them and be able to advise you more fully. I shall be very careful to act for you to the uttermost and a fair full compromise in my opinion would be the most agreeable result [.for.] it will [otherwise] prove tedious and chargeable. Therefore pray consider on the proposals you had in my last to yourself and I have to hope on [*to receive*] your directions, I shall observe them from you absolutely. We've thought on 50 p[er] c[ent]. Pray say what you would be willing to agree for a speedier conclusion. I shall expect an account per next from you. The ship *Gust[avus] Adolphus* I hope is with you so that business may likewise find a speedy disposal.

1. It would seem from this letter that the insurers are suggesting appointing arbitrators to try and settle the dispute over the insurance for the Dolphin. Thierry is asked how much he would be prepared to accept. Hill suggests 50%.

11. Wm. Jennens Ply[mouth] 18 D[it[to

Yours of the 14th C[urrent] I have received the *Swan* I perceive is with you in safety. Captain Hatsell did write to Captain Heaton as he told me but [he] told me that he feared they would not do so for want of victuals. We wrote the insurer [*about some other insurance matter, of which the details are not given.*]

If Mr Tho[mas] Andrews[1] brings me the bond you mention I

shall keep it safe for your disposal and advise you. The convoy which goes for Portugall is now in the Downs and about to sail with the fish forthwith.

1. Which Thomas Andrews is not known. There was a Thomas Andrews who held a contract for the victualling of Tangier. (Pepys X p 8)

12. Amb[rose] Jennens[1] Penryn D[it]to

Yours of the 13th C[urrent] received I returning you thanks for your response to bring to [conclusion]. We desire to confirm your desire concerning the tin sent to Leg[horn]. In brief the business stands thus: the tin [found] in the 2 barrels and subsequently received per the *Hopewell* was $325[?] which sum we confirmed you in the bill as you noted. The tin in 3 barrels received by the *Defence* and *Dover Merchant* as by the word sent was $361.4.9 but it is sold too in the interim.

On my reminding you that the [bursar?] on the [-] did by your invoice value himself on me for $500.0.6 all which I consider to have confirmed & for the advice in my [enclosures] to you and the [debit?] on this being $138.15.3[2] is for a Cr[edit] in my father's account, and in yours with him you will likewise be charged with the said sum this I hope will give you a clear [insight] how the accounts were passed.

1. Note that in February 1660 Ambrose Jennens was still apparently living in Penryn and had not moved to Falmouth where he can be found in the Hearth Tax of 1662.
2. The figures are given in longhand but are not clear. There would seem to be some discrepancy here.

13. James Thierry Amst[erdam] 24th ditto

Yours of the 27th C[urrent] I have received with several accounts which on perusal finding right shall note accordingly. With the assurers on the *Dolphin* I have had a meeting the principal discussion will [sic] be at length the advice about the sum on a bill which thing appears very doubtful to agree and proofs to be made concerning to the [settlement?] withal would be tedious and chargeable. Therefore for not doing this they have an article inserted. They undertake to refer the whole business to the arbitrators. On the above request I sent mine on for each party concerned to choose. Forthwith they will [*and they expect the same from you which cannot reasonably be refused and it is for your benefit.*] If you have any proofs to further clear the business pray send them. Herewith is enclosed a letter of yours received from Mr Kenton.[1]

1. Which Mr Kenton is not known. A Francis Kenton was a goldsmith and banker see J.R. Woodhead *The Rulers of London 1660-1689* (London 1965) p 102.

14. Fran[cis] Selwyn Ven[i]ce ditto

Since my last of the 17th C[urrent] I have not received any of yours. The book and [stilettos ?[1]] you put aboard Capt[ain] Browne have received [in good condition thanks] for you care therein and [let me?] may know the pieces of silk likewise recommended to me for your sister they have not detailed them, and most have no [labels?] on them and you charge me in your account as [given?] to have been [already?] received according to yours of the 24 Oct past.

[*The next line is not clear.*]

I have sent a letter of yours to Mr Robinson[2] I now think [.he.] pays only a [little] and [is] not to pay anything at all for the [transport]. Thus I shall forbear to demand it for the [freight?] nor strictly have I spoken anything as yet of it only accidentally in discussion with your brother Richards. However I am [like to avoid it by the delay in this case?]. I know not any [article?] with you to request anything. The *Hannibal* may depart before I can have another of mine landed here. I shall take care to send you anything further desired.

1. The consonants in this word appear to be st, l, t.
2. A George Robinson is mentioned later in Letter no 84 to Francis Selwyn. There is also a reference to a G. Robinson in C[ornwall] R[ecord] O[ffice] EN1032 f. 9.

15. Giles Lytcott ditto

Answered [own note] with a book on the votes of parliament enclosed.[1]

1. Presumably details of the proceedings of parliament after the readmission of the secluded members on February 21. (Hutton p 96)

16. Bernard Spark Exon London 25th Feb.1659[/1660]

Sent him several [writings] on the *Dolphin* received from Mr Thierry.

1. Note that Bernard Sparke and William Jennens were also concerned with the *Dolphin*.

17 John Woodroffe Yarmouth 3d March 1659[/1660]

I have lately [discovered?] from Mr Tho[mas] King[1] that you asked him to pay the bond of £336 from yourself to me [to settle?] further payment due the 25 Current which if done shall be well. I shall deliver up the bond by writing [and desire] that you would [coordinate it?] with him or some other way that it may accordingly be performed at the day of account. [This is the last of instalments which have been paid at several times ?] Your payment, let this be [the last?] Sum demanded, Sir, [.and.] I request some such payment which I hope will be no great inconvenience to you.

1. A Thomas King is mentioned by Earle as a goldsmith. (Peter Earle *The Making of the English Middle Classes* (London 1989) p 161

18. B. Spark Exon ditto

Yours of the 29th past I have received with the ones of Mr Thierry [will be?] sent when Mr Jennens [returns]. We shall present them together. The abstract of our account with you I have received. The bill you passed for my payment to the account of Mr Jerome Stone being £120 I have paid and shall debit accordingly and we rest assured you will do the utmost you can disposing the *Swan's* oil to our advantage.

19. **James Thierry** Amst[erdam] 9th d[itt]o

Yours of the 12 C[urrent] I have received with the enclosed which shall be answered. Herewith are two for you. The writings you have given me too concern your business of the *Dolphin*, the instructions shall observe. I have spoken with the assurer we are earnest in our endeavouring to ingage him [rightly?] for you. I have thought for to interest Mr Tim Crusoe[1] who I suppose is well known to you for assistance in well advancing such business. [I] have as yet only spoken with him as of today, [.but.] may do it [according to a message sent on by his father ?] will do you the favour as desired. The next thing [for consultation] is the bond to send to the arbitrator which shall do.[–]I hope to give you some other [service?] I shall do my uttermost for your most advantage.

On the *Seven Stars*[2] business it will, in conclusion, be thus: the policy made upon the ship at & from Barbados to Amsterdam [they will indeed insure her direct there?] but when she sets sail from thence towards Guinney that will prove a deviation for the assurers.

[the next two lines are not clear – for this matter refer to letter no 47. This letter ends with]
I have spoken with Mr Crusoe who hath promised to see to this business for you.
[at side] Barbados to Amsterdam

1. Timothy Crusoe was an insurance expert.
2. The policy on the *Seven Stars* had been made assuming she would return direct from Barbados to Amsterdam. Thierry now wished the ship to be diverted to West Africa.

20. **Bern[ard] Spark** Exon 16th D[it]to

[This letter is not clear. It refers to the cargoes on the Swan and the invoice connected with them. It ends with Hill asking Sparke to continue disposing of the oil 'to the most advantage']

21. **James Thierry** Amst[erdam] 16   Di[tt]o

Upon the 9th C[urrent] I wrote in detail since which I have yours of the 19t[h ditto concerning the letter. Since my last I have [consulted] with Messrs Th[omas] Fouk, Rob Ellis for that referring to the

Dolphin business, the arbitrators formally acting are Mr Rd Holworthy, Tim Crusoe and Rd Skinner to whom proposed our giving a bond for your part. Messrs Ellis & Fouke sent away to the [scrivener?] to have such a [sealing] bond to the same effect. The time limited to the arbitrators to finish your business is by 2[n]d of April at the furthest when I hope we shall make an end to your content, my endeavour shall be what possible for your most advantage.

Of the 7 Stars' business I wrote you it loaded last week to which refer you. The bill of exchange you had [passed?] on me for £40 payable to Cap[tain] Will Bray inclosed the copy for payment [and?] we suppose gone. [*The next two lines concern insurance and are not clear.*]

About the *Dolphin* voyage especially as concerned Mr Spark, I have sent to him other writings, [.he.] may have advised you what error he hath observed such is the one with which Mr Jennens is concerned. He will give his suggestions upon which shall be returned as I think finished.

22. W[illia]m Vincent[1] Botus Fleming   17th D[it]to

Concerning the [news] of our loss in the death of my mother.

1. The William Vincent here must not be confused with the Vincent family of Truro. This William Vincent had married a sister of Richard Hill.

23. Eliza[beth] Mo[o?]reton sent to Mr Trewolla

Concerning the [news] of my mother's death and that I had a gown for her [which I will send her ?]

1. Elizabeth Moreton, who lived in or near Truro, was a relative of Agnes Hill who left her a gown.

[This is the end of the letters in shorthand. Please note that in the following letters occasional words or phrases translated from Italian have been put into italics.]

24. Dr Duncon[1] dit[to] 27th

S[i]r,

This Worthy person, Mr Gerald Angier[2] my intimate freind, whose affaires drawing him into Italie I make use of the opp[or] tunitie to present you my Respects and humble Service, with a new edition of the Common prayre booke[3], of itts usefullnesse w[i]th you I am already acquainted and hope itt may bee shortly soe w[i] th us – I have heard some speech of yo[u]r speedy intentions for England w[hi]ch if w[i]th yo[u]r convenience I should Gladly see many of yo[u]r [freinds x out] friends, strangers from home some yeares, are Lately returned, no doubt but quickly all may, thinges going on soe well that in all reasonable expectations nothing under heaven cann hinder itt. The exit Tyrsannis etc. upon the exchange[4] was publiquely expunged but by what authoritie is not said. Yo[u]r good Counsell to this Gentleman will bee kindly accepted by him and acknowledged by mee as an extraordinary Favour unto hi[m].

London March 1659

1. Dr Duncan was a merchant in Italy. Note that he, like Giles Lytcott, was already considering returning to England.
2. Gerald Angier. A Gerald Aungier died at Surat, *c.* 1682
3. The use of the common prayer book had been banned in England during the Interregnum but was apparently still being used in Italy when Thomas Hill was there. Evelyn writes in 1649 'I heard the Common Prayer (a rare thing in these days) in St Peter's at Paul's Wharf, London'. (*The Diary of John Evelyn Esq* William Bray (ed.) (London 1818 reprinted in the Chandos Classics – date not given) p 199
4. On the 16th March the act for the dissolution of the Long Parliament (over nineteen years since it first met) was finally passed and arrangements made for a new election. 'The previous evening an unknown man had drawn a premature conclusion from events by climbing a ladder outside the Exchange and painting out the inscription Exit Tyrannus, *Regum ultimus*, which had replaced the statue of Charles I at the Revolution. The watching crowd kindled bonfires and drank royalist roasts, and the incident featured as prominently in news-letters as the dissolution itself.' (Hutton p 104)

25. Mr Benj[ami]n Childe Detto

S[i]r,

The [word x out] worthy person, that does mee the honour to bee the bearer hereof, is Mr Gerald Angier; his affairs as a Merchant draw him for some few moneths into Italie and because I would demonstrate [?] the high respect & esteeme I have for him I take this occasion to make his vertues acquainted w[i]th yo[u]r well knowne Civilitys. I neede not or [word x out] engage you by a better motive than that constant readinesse (w[hi]ch I have experienced) to obleidge yo[u]r freinds I therefore most earnestly intreat you to afford him (as my freind of more then ordanarie inimacye) all the Counsell & assistance you know may doe him service ['I' x out] and I am Confident of yo[u]r satisfaction in bestowing this favour on a suject soe nobly qualified. By him I have sent a dozen bottles Canary whereof pray drinke w[i]th Mr Jo[hn] Kent[1] *With many thanks with my love* Deare hart.

1. John Kent. See Woodhead p 101 (J.R. Woodhead *The Rulers of London 1660–1689* London 1965)

26. Mr W[illia]m Mico[1] the d[it]to

S[i]r,

To make amends for my neglect in not adviseing you of the various affaires of England I finde my selfe suplied by the small peece, w[h]ich I herew[i]th present you; the bearer is an intimate freind [Mr Gerald Algier inserted at side] to whome if you please to afford yo[u]r Councell and assistance as his affairs may require you will ad a waighty obligacon to the very many you already have upon.

1. Both Samuel and William Mico were merchants connected with Italy. William Mico was in Livorno.

27. (in Italian) Sig[nor]e Jacopo Baldinotti Lucca D[it]to [1]

Since your last very welcome [letter] that I had in Venice I have not received any words of friends in Lucca although I wrote to you. It may be it is not strange that illustrious people like you should take any notice of an ordinary mortal like me. Anyway I would hope always to receive the dear letters of my Signor Jacopo but it

could be that you are married and your lady wife wants you all
to herself and [does not allow you to remember your servant who
is far away?] Be it as you wish but I shall not cease but to weary
you with my letters declaring always my very many obligations
towards you both which require that, to be fair, I should bear
witness to the extent of your kindness which I no way deserve.

However to encourage you a little I am sending to Signor
Gioseppe a piece of Holland cloth which I would wish that the
nuns would make into a 'half' shirt like those which were made
for you a little time ago, for which reason I have written to Signor
Gioseppe and I mention to you only so as to make a quick dispatch
and send to Messrs Lytcott & Gascoigne[2] at Livorno for all the
costs. I believe that you are the purse holder of the nuns who will
buy me the lace. I hope there is nothing but looking after these
expenses for you to do, and I would dearly like you to do this at
your leisure. With ever greater affection I would like to make you
a present of a ribbon of silver hair which you must accept with
my love towards you, dear master. Signor Piccini [is being sent?] a
small gift accompanied by a letter which I would be obliged if you
would ask him to receive at the same time as you kiss his hand on
the part of Hill and it may be that or he will give you some music
as I asked for in my letter and if this is done it will be the better for
dispatching it with the shirt and other things such as the [printed?]
books [and ?] those works of Penna[3] which were asked for, they
altogether can be sent to the aforesaid Lytcott & Gascoigne which
will be very useful because we correspond regularly.

1. When Thomas Hill was in Lucca he would seem to have stayed with
   both Signori Jacopo and Gioseppi Baldinotti (possibly brothers) and
   Signor Piccini. He greatly enjoyed his stay there.
   Evelyn gives a very good description of Lucca.
   'The next day [22 May 1645] I came to Lucca, a small but pretty territorie
   and state of itselfe.- The Citty is neate and well fortified, with noble and
   pleasant walkes of trees on the workes, where the gentry and ladies
   use to take the aire. 'Tis situate on an ample plaine by the river Serchio,
   yet the country about it is hilly. The Senate-house is magnificent. . . .
   The inhabitants are exceedingly civill to strangers, above all places in
   Italy, and they speake the purest Italian. 'Tis also cheape living, which
   causes travellers to set up their rest here more than in Florence, tho'
   a more celebrated Citty; besides the ladys here are very conversable,
   and the religious women not at all reserv'd; of these we bought gloves

and embroidered stomachers generally worn by gentlemen in these countries. The circuit of this state is but two easy days journey, and lies mixed with the Duke of Tuscany's, but having Spain for a Protector (tho' the least bigoted of all Roman Catholics), and being one of the best fortify'd Citties in Italy, it remains in peace. This whole country abounds in excellent olives etc.' (Evelyn p 150).

Thomas Hill wrote to Abraham in October 1 1657 'I am here at the home of one of the senators Signior Baldinotti; it is pleasantly situated, almost a mile from the city, amongst the mountains, which makes it very agreeable; and as most of the gentry have left the city and come into these parts, it is still more so, by the friendly visits they are continually making to one another.' (*Familiar Letters* 1767. p 16 – in the library of the Royal Society):

2. Giles Lytcott was in partnership with Walwyn Gascoigne at Livorno. This firm acted as factors for John Banks see Centre for Kentish Studies U234.

   Walwyn Gascoigne see Boyd 42683 and the will of his brother Stephen 1688 (TNA: PRO PROB 11/391). A sister. Martha, was the wife of Sir John Frederick.

3. Thomas Hill frequently asks his friends in Italy to send him both music and scientific books. The music would seem principally to be for himself as he had a great interest in Italian music. In his letter to his brother quoted above he wrote: 'Since my arrival in Italy I have missed few opportunities of hearing what music has been publicly performed, especially in the churches'. Lorenzo Penna mentioned here was a musician and composer of arias.

28. (in Italian) **Gioseppe Baldinotti** D[it]to

From my arrival in London I believe you have been aware of my letters already written to Signor Jacopo of the occurrences in this country which are so strange and variable that it will be too tedious to give you them in minute details. In brief, after diverse changes of government there is stability with an assembling of the new parliament on the 25th of next month and there is great hope for the King who is already in Flanders. But God knows that everything is subject to his divine will. It has pleased the same Lord God to take from this miserable world into glory the souls of my dear father and mother who died within a short time one after the other. We are much affected. God grant us his blessed consolation.

I pray that you will accept a present that I make you of a parcel of Indian cloth for you to make use of in shirts. I hope you will forgive the small value of the gift & will accept – it does not do justice to the great affection that I owe you. I send also a piece of Holland cloth which I would like you to have the kindness to have made up for me by the lady nuns into a 'half' shirt similar to those you had in Lucca. The same fashion would please me, the size of the neck and the arms I give you inclosed. You can get the expense from Signor Jacopo who I believe is purse holder in such matters. Through my account with the nuns of Saint Augustine I recall well the name of the convent where are the daughters of Signor Cavre [I should like them to be satisfied with the workmanship?]. When they are made if you would send them to Signors Lytcott & Gascoigne at Livorno, all will be well. Pardon me for this inconvenience and command me for ever with 1000 kisses of the hand to Signor Cavre and his wife the Signor Faneville, the Signors Resina and all my friends generally I remember from my heart.

29. Mrs Pearde[1] D[itt]o

Since the death of my father about three moneths since I have not byn wanting to use all diligence for the handing up that bond in w[hi]ch himselfe & Mr Peard stood bound to the State & now at Length have brought the busines so Farr to an issue, that the bond is in my Custody. Some Charges we have been att, especially to the p[er]son that obtained the bond to whom yesterday I paid five pounds for Charges, and his owne paines, as by his receipt besides there is 12s.6d paid by another in this busenes and about 20s by our selves, though that's not certainly all hath bin disbursed. However, if you please in answer to this to order some freind to pay mee (as my father's executor) these Sumes, in all £6.12.6, upon Receipt whereof I shall deliver up the bond wherein yo[u]r husband stands engaged, that soe a ['quit' x out] quiet end may bee put to this trouble some businesse. I desire yo[u]r speedy Answer.

If you thinck good wee shall showe the p[ar]ticulars of this Charge to any freind you shall appoint.
London 20 March 1659[/60]

1. The Peards were merchants in Barnstaple although Justinian, the brother of Charles, moved to Plymouth and had long been a prominent merchant there and a correspondent of Richard Hill. Charles Peard died

c. 1658 and money was owing to the Hills which Thomas was asking his
widow, Alice, to pay.

30. Mr John Woodroffe

Yo[u]rs of the 12th Currant I have received by the hands of Mr
Thomas King who seconds what you desire that I would Receive
£236 for the present in part of £336 upon that bond due on the
Five & twentieth Currant and that for the other hundred pounds I
would expect yett a moneth longer w[hi]ch, to doe you a favour, I
am Content shall bee, provided I may then have itt w[i]th out Faile
and this £236 before the 25th of this moneth soe that I pray, upon
the answering to this, you give order to Mr Tho[mas] King for
this first paym[en]t and the other £100 in a moneth. I insist upon
yo[u]r punctualitie because our [because our repeated] occasions
depende upon what we are to have from you.
London March 20th 1659[/60]

31. Mr Andrew Hill[1]

I Received yo[u]r letter of the 2[n]d of Febr[uar]y w[hi]ch coming in
a time of much Greif in our famylye could not then bee answered,
especially our Losse being encreased by that of my good mother
also, who departed this [moneth x out] life the 4th of this moneth,
wee must all patiently submitt to the good providence of God. To
my Father's estate I am admitted administrator and am therefore
to Settle w[i]th you the small accompt depending. The Rent from
Rowland and Skerdon w[hi]ch you understan[d] to belong to my
Father only from the time of my Grandfather's death, wee finde
by the writings to bee due to him from the time of the graunt
in Octob[e]r 1639 and no mencon of Reserving any thing to my
Grandfather during his life so that now there comes due for 20
years ¼ £20.5 (besides the highe Rent paid out of w[hi]ch we
haveing Received but six pounds there rests somewhere £14.5.)
[How much of it x o] How much of it as is due from Mr Glasse I
perceive is Ready, soe pray as soone as you cann make it up to mee
by a bill of exchange. I have acquainted my brother w[i]th yo[u]r
opinion & Uncle Sawdy's that hee may have £120 for two lives to
bee added to Rowland's but I think hee will rather stay till itt bee
let at a yearely rent or (iff you would buy itt) hee would sell his

interest out Right but in the meane time pray let mee know w[i]th what both p[ar]cells togeather may yeild if the[y] were to bee sett att yearely rent or what the present title to both may bee worth, to bee sold forever. W[i]th yo[u]rs I write to my uncle Hillary about the £26 due from him. I finde not that my father intended to release itt him, only to doe him the Curticie to lend It him w[i]thout Interest for soe many yeares and soe to have itt againe, w[hi]ch I hope hee will take care to doe. We all present our Respects to yo[u]rself our Aunt, Uncle and Aunt Sawdy And all friends.
London March 20th

The 12th Octob[er] 1639
Your selfe delivered possession and the Tennants attorned to him.

1. Andrew Hill was a brother of Richard. This letter refers to property left by Richard in Devon which had belonged to Thomas Hill, Richard's father.

32. Mr Hillary Hill [1]

Of the late greate Losses in our famalye – I suppose you may have heard from my uncle Andrew Hill. To my Father's Estate I am admitted administrator and thereby [word x out] engaged to looke after all bu[s]nisses and discharge all debts, Lagacies etc. & likewise to recover whats[oe]ver is abroad upon a bond of yo[u]rs in my possession. I find you are indebted £26 – w[hi]ch you have had the benifitt of some yeares. Our occasions now requireing Large somes of money I am put upon demanding this from you w[hi]ch pray take care to satisfy as soone as possible. My uncle Andrew Hill will shortly Remitt mee up some money so you may have a convenience to doe the like w[i]th yo[u]rs in the same bill and save yo[u]r selfe some trouble. Pray favour mee to dispatch this businesse as soone as you can. W[i]th my Respects & my brother & sister.
London March 20 1659[/60]

1. Hillary Hill was another brother of Richard. Richard had lent money to his brothers and Thomas Hill had to try and obtain it although the family had expected that these sums of money would have been forgiven them in Richard's will and they were very reluctant to pay.

33. (in Italian) **Sig[nor]e Vincenzo Piccini**[1] Lucca

I having a little hope that you have not entirely forgotten me, I come with these four lines (badly composed) to admit the obligations received from you. But I would mention in particular [this small gift which is very generous of you ?] and therefore I cast down my eyes to confess that from you I do not deserve to enjoy so much.

O God the delight of that angelic voice of my dear master that I am already longing for Lucca, to have the wings to fly very willingly to San Martino to hear a little of that music truly celestial & to enjoy that choir where my Signor Vincenzo is present but I must not turn to those vain thoughts ever more I must be patient. But I can have some consolation in receiving music from your hand, although not hearing it from your lips, I will be satisfied and assured of your customary kindness. Truly tell me if it were you who granted me this kindness. Signor Jacopo Baldinotti will be the recipient of this letter with a present that I make with the greatest affection (although the gift be small) of two pairs of gloves made to wear as is our custom [with slits below ?] Please accept this feeble demonstration of my love and my commands are for ever, and to all the Gentlemen Musicians I kiss their hands with great affection.

On March 24 1659/60 London

1. Vincenzo Piccini was a friend who had helped Thomas when he stayed in Lucca. It is interesting that Vincenzo Piccini not only had a beautiful singing voice but was also closely connected with the cathedral of San Martino. The composer, Puccini, was born in Lucca two hundred years later. Members of his family had been for many years associated with the cathedral and were noted for their singing. I wondered if there were any connection between the two families but it would appear that the Puccini family did not come to live in Lucca until the eighteenth century.

34. **Mr John Byam**[1] 24 March

S[i]r,

By a letter of yo[u]rs lately rec[eive]d I perceive you would supply father James w[i]th what he might have occasion of to provide the perticulars I desired of him for w[hi]ch I thanck you. I have taken care for yo[u]r Imbursement by Mr Dethick[2] & Compa[ny] of Legorne when you please. Mr Hallet told mee hee would diliver mee a box of strings [ie lute strings] of yo[u]rs desireing that I would dispose them for you w[hi]ch I told him I would endeaver to doe, but as yett I have not received them, but when I doe I shall use all care & diligence to sell them to yo[u]r most advantage. In yo[u]r next pray advice mee (to satesfie a freind) the prizes the[y] may bee bought at w[i]th you att the season, and according to what sortments. S[i]r, Herewith I present you my Respects and thancks for all favours together w[i]th a payre of our Country gloves w[hi]ch pray accept of not as a requitall but a demonstration of my Respects to you. To prevent a mistake that itt's possible [you x out] you may incline to, I must informe you that you are not to take these for weding Gloves.[3] I am soe farr from that we are all in teares for the double losse both of father and mother in lesse then two moneths time. We submitt to Providence. S[i]r I am much yo[u]r servant and would gladly be comanded most freely by you as yo[u]r occasions may require w[hi]ch certainly may [may repeated] be assisted by a diligent freind as I hope you will find mee alwayes. My Respects to Dr Bacon[4] & the freinds w[i]th you.

1. Letters exist from John Byam to the Hills in BL.Add MS 5488. His name occurs in a Chancery case (TNA: PRO C 9/30/142) which concerned John Hallett (believed to be the merchant mentioned here) and the very difficult John Trelawny who had been sent, during his apprenticeship, to work with John Byam who was then it would seem in Rome. He later moved to Naples. For Hallett see Woodhead p 82. For details of the Hallett family see James Derriman, *Killigarth*. (Morden 1994)
2. Thomas stayed with Thomas Dethick in Livorno. His company was one of the largest there and was also closely associated with the Banks family.
3. It would seem from these comments that Thomas's friends in Italy had assumed that Thomas would find a wife on his return to England. His father's death altered his prospects of marriage.
4. Evelyn met Dr Bacon when he was in Rome in 1644. He and a Dr Gibbs were physicians there. (Evelyn p 87).

35. Mrs Groves[1]

It is some moneths since that I writt you by one Mr Elliot that went to Legorne, other Letter of mine has delivered and I hope yo[u]rs did not miscarry. I only wish it least I should undergoe the

danger of being Judged too remisse in paying my thancks where soe much is due especially to yo[u]r selfe to whom I am much obliged for many favours w[hi]ch I'll willingly requite if you please to make use of my service. From Mr Richard Middleton² I suppose you have noe letters by this Conveyance he being lately gon downe to Wales w[i]th his Lady now w[i]th Child. The old S[i]r Thomas is likewise returned after his Long absence and is gon to his Country to stand for Parlam[en]t man now the next Sessions w[hi]ch will bee 25 Aprill. Of Mr Jolife³ I can give you little accompt other then that I see him dayly upon the Exchange but since his Obligations to his Lady hee is altred and quite another man. I hope yourselfe and the Children are all in good health w[hi]ch I should bee glad of. With my Respects to yo[u]r good selfe, Mr Groves, Mr Richard Browne and all freinds.
London 24 March 1659[/60]

1. Mrs Groves was a friend in Livorno to whom Thomas was sending news from England.
2. Richard Middleton was consul at Morea in 1655
3. William Joliffe was in Livorno in 1657 (see letter to Thomas of June 1657 CRO F3/786).

36. Mr William Latham London 23th March 1659[/60]

S[i]r,
By reason of your sicknes and absence you have not byn put in minde of two assurances by you made to Mr William Jenens each for £25 – one upon the body of the shipp *William*, the other upon the goods in her, both w[hi]ch proved to bee dead losses though he hath bestowed much in vaine to recover something in France where the shipp was cast away. So that now take some speedy course for his satisfaction and what your Resolution is pray let me Receive.

37. Mr John Hill¹ London March 24th 1659[/60]

S[i]r,
Itt hath pleased Almighty God of late visit our family w[i]th very much sickness w[hi]ch proved mortall to both our father and mother in lesse then two moneths, one of the other, by w[hi]ch

double losse our greife was Largely increased. We desire the helpe of yo[u]r prayers to beare such afflictions [affair x out] w[hi]ch are the greatest our condicons are Lyable unto. To both the estates of the freinds deceased their desires and conveniences have engaged me administrator to the father and executor to the Latter so that Remaines w[i]th me to look after all things haveing Relation to either. Upon perusal of our books I finde £20 lent to yo[u]r selfe in two summs at severall times and £1.10s to a relation of yo[u]rs, Mr Elliston, both w[hi]ch I suppose you will Reimburse. I therefore desire It w[i]th your convenience the quicke Repaym[en]t of those summs, because our occasions require it.

1. John Hill was another brother of Richard Hill.

38. **Mr James Thierry** London 29th March 1660

S[i]r,

Yours of the 16th/[6th] Currant I have Received. The arbitrators about the *Dolphin's* businesse and the Insurers w[hi]ch my selfe mett two dayes since, where att large the whole businesse was discussed, and at Length when wee had made use of all proofs, it was left to them to determine and the time limited to give up the award is till the first Aprill so that p[e]r next shall send you Coppy of the sentence w[hi]ch I hope will be to your content.

I perceive the *Sevea[n] Starrs* is now returning home, so you would have the pollicys in force. That upon the goods I am advised will be soe, but the other on the shippe not, for the shipp proceeding another voyage it will prove a deviacon and the premio must be paid [word x out] th[e]m and a new pollicye shall shall [sic] be made, though I feare not att the former rate of 6 p[er] C[en]t. I shall doe itt the best I cann: S[i]r to avoide all mistakes, that may hereafter arise, please to take notice that the former pollicye made upon the *Seaven Stars* that is upon the Shipp, the assurers say that the premio is due, because they bore the adventure dureing her stay at Barbad[os], and soe would have donne to Amster[dam] had the shipp not altered her voyage. What they says will prove soe, soe that if you will have any other assurance made, upon the body of the Shipp, pray give your positive order: and It shall be observed. The other pollicye w[i]thout paying for underwritting money will be in force from the landing of the goods.

S[i]r I have rec[eive]d upon the bond due from those of Yarmouth £150, the rest, to make up £236, I am promised in 4 or 5 dayes and the other £100 in a moneth. This latter I am sensible is beyond the time, but could not avoyd itt, the[y] declareing plainly, itt could not bee done sooner. I have hopes they will then be punctuall, w[ha]t passes shall advise.

39. Mr John Woodroffe London 31th March 1660

S[i]r ,

Yours by covert of Mr Thomas King I have Received who hath likewise paid mee in parte upon the bond due the 25 currant – £100 in one paym[en]t before he went out of towne, and £98.12s more he paid mee yesterday the Remainder to make up to £236 (which att yo[u]r request I for the pr[e]sent am contented w[i]th) hee promiseth to pay mee in 3 or 4 dayes w[hi]ch will be well. The other £100 I hope you will take kindly care to imburse me, espetially because this first paim[en]t was not soe punctuall as I in reason expected. S[i]r I Recommend this businesse to yo[u]r care.

40. Mr William Jennens London 3[r]d Aprill 1660

S[i]r,

I have not any of yo[u]rs to answer, which will cause breavetye this serveing cheifly to give covert to the inclosed Received from Mr Gerrards. I hope this will find you in safety returned home, w[hi]ch I should be glad to heare of; and that att yo[u]r leisure you please to make up the *Swann's* tonnage that soe accompte may be adjusted w[i]th Mr Thierry.

41. Mr James Thierry London 6th Aprill 1660

S[i]r,

Yours of the 2[n]d and 9th Currant I have received, in the former the acc[omp]t of the *Swan's* freight w[hi]ch shall bee communicated to Mr William Jennens, and finding it right shall noate accordingly for what concerns our proportion. The arbitrators upon the *Dolphin* have now given up the award, a breviate whereof is Inclosed and I hope will bee to your good Likeing. I writt you fully, and expect yo[u]r order, in causing a new pollicy to be made upon the body of the ship *Seaven Starrs*, the former being voyde on her first departure from Barbados to Guinny so that what fresh order you please to give shalbe observed.

From those of Yarmouth I have received £236 the other £100 in full of their bond I am promised on the 25th Currant when received shall advise you. S[i]r Their are two merchants of this Cittie, Mr John Walthen and Mr Christopher Yardly departed hence 14 dayes since intending for your Amster[dam] to dispatche some affaires. If upon their addresse to you [please x out] you please to afford them yo[u]r Councell and assistance, they will thanckfully accept it and I shall esteeme it a favour donne my selfe.

S[i]r the scrivener haveing failed to give a breveate of the award, pray for the present take this accompt, w[hi]ch is the whole substance, that is, That Mr Fowke & Mr Ellis doe pay mee, for yo[u]r use on the 2nd June next, each of them one hundred & thirty pounds, in full of the £200 by them to you assured in the *Dolphin* and t[ha]t the hopes of Recovery be ['recovered' x out] continued in [you?].

42. Mr Tho[ma]s Dethick Mr Rich[ard] Browne & Comp[any] London 6th Aprill 1660

S[i]rs,

Yo[u]rs of the 29th February I have received, w[i]th an the inclosed accompt Currant to w[hi]ch for the pr[e]sent I must answear that the Summe you say of $271.14. 11 oweing by Bartolimo Scarti for tyn needed some thing of explanacon, for as it is now I cannot understand itt. However [I have x out] itt may be: I hope you use all meanes to prevent a bad debt besides I suppose you have omitted to give mee Cr[edit] for about 100 p[iece]s Hounscotts[1] Sold during my aboade w[i]th you w[hi]ch pray rectifie and endeavour quick sale of what is w[i]th you that all accompt may bee adjusted. S[i]r herewith I send you Invoice & bill of lading for 50 piggs of lead, aboard the *Swallow* bound for yo[u]r port. My desire is that you dispose of them for our most advantage w[hi]ch, whether to sell to Consigne or to expect the markett att arrivall you cann best judge so itt's wholly left to your dispose. The small quantity that goes to yo[u]r port I hope may keep up if not advance the price, a speedy dispatch is our desire, w[hi]ch this Comoditye cannot misse of.

Pray doe us what favour you cann to dispose of this soe that itt may bee an encouragem[en]t to later proceedings.

I perceive how extreame low the exchange rules w[i]th you, and no bills to be had, but I hope w[i]th the first you will comply w[i]th my former desire. I once prayed you to Cr[edit] Mr John Byam to $50 a 60 for my acc[omp]t w[hi]ch I confirme.

1. hounscotts – Possibly Suffolk 'says' for these 'imitated the earlier textiles from Hondeschoote, which Florentine merchants had distributed throughout Italy in medieval times.' Gigliola Pagano de Divitiis *English Merchants in seventeenth-century Italy* (Cambridge 1997) p 173

43. Mr Alex[ander] Travell[1] London 11th Aprill 1660

S[i]r,

I am indebted answer unto your severalls of the 23th July & 17th January. The former received by Mr Birch, togeather w[i]th yo[u]r Gunn made up in Canvas. As you desire I have made enquiry for the old man that made itt, and am Informed hee is yett liveing but as yet I cannott finde where, I shall use all diligence to get it fixt by him or Barnes, in time for the first Conveniance to you. I give you my harty thanks for yo[u]r courteous invitation in to yo[u]r parts, no doubt the Caracter you give of them is exact, but my fate, I feare, will oblige to this Ile for some yeares, especially because of late itt hath pleased the Divine Providence to deprive us of both father and mother in a very little space, of the former on the 15th January, the latter on the 4th March. So that I am Involved in a world of businesses by being administrator to the estate of my Father and Executor to my mother's. So you must Imagine I have not a little to doe w[hi]ch would bee much more had I not my Brother's Assistance. Our businesses goe on well and I hope will find a good Conclusion. I perceive Mr Hunt[2] is Returning home once againe and resolves By way of Germanye, which will certainely give him Content as it did to mee, but it wilbe Chargeable. The Lowe Countrys and the industry of those people is pretty, but I like the airy disposition of the French. I take notice how yo[u]r businesse stands in Relation to Mr Newman. I hope itts to yo[u]r satisfaction and may prove yo[u]r benifit to your undertakeing. I wish all good successe.

I strange Mr Dethicke stayed soe long abroad rather then that's hee is now coming home. Mr Lytcott is likewise leaving Livorno. Mr Jonathan Parker was my Fellow traveller and I thincke intends not to leave England any more; Mr John Trelawny is here alsoe haveing left Legorne not w[i]thout some disgrace. Hee was some time here in the Counter[3] but if hee has adjusted his busenesse w[i]th all I know not, my Respects to the freinds w[i]th you.

1. Alexander Travell was a merchant in Aleppo later in St John d'Acre. In the introduction to *Familiar Letters* (1767) Abraham Hill is mentioned as contracting 'an intimacy with two amiable young gentlemen, Mr Alexander Travel, and Mr John Newman, who, pursuing their travels, became known to each other in Turkey. Their expressions of esteem and affection for him, and indeed of all his correspondents, throughout these letters, shew how valuable he was to all his friends.'
2. Mr Hunt is George Hunt
3. The Counter. A name given to three prisons owned by the city corporation & used for the punishment of civil offences, one being in the Poultry (see Letter no 6). (Pepys X p 76)

44. Mr Henry Mellish, Mr Henry Browne London 11th Aprill 1660

Much Respected friends,
Your courteous Letter of the 8th past I have Rec[eive]d w[i]th an inclosed receipt for a small box, directed to mee and by you Laden on the *Mary Bon[aventu]re* for yo[u]r Extraord[ina]ry care therein I give you my hearty thancks, and that to this favour you will add yett another, in takeing care of those 3 Jarrs of Lucca Olives rec[eive]d from my Patrono Sig[nor]e Baldinotti. What charge soever may arise upon this Businesses I shall most thanckfully repay, as you please to order wishing for some occasion to balance this accompt of Courtesie. *Dear Signor Harry Browne I kiss your hand with very great affection.*

45. Mr William Jennens London 12th Aprill 1960

S[i]r,
Yo[u]rs of the 6th currant I have received, with the inclosed for My Hugh Squier[1], which I delivered to him. I thank you for the advice of Tonnage upon the *Swann* which shall bee observed in making up the accompt of freight w[i]th Mr Thierry. I am very mindfull of what was heare promised the the [sic] perfecting your accompt,

which shall bee donne therein, you may be confident yours shall bee the First. In the meantime I hope itt's not to yo[u]r least prejudice. The news now talkt of is the Lord Lambert's[2] escape out of the Tower on Tuesday night, some feare disturbances may thence arise.

1. Hugh Squier was a special friend of the Hill family.
2. Lord Lambert was the most feared of the Republican generals. He escaped from the Tower on 10th April. '. . . it seems that he had persuaded the maid who tended his chamber in the Tower to don his nightcap, sleep in his bed' and then he slid down a rope into a boat waiting in the Thames. The escape was not discovered until the morning. The government were frantic to recapture him. Lambert intended to gather together the rebellious forces at Edgehill but, as this became known, Lambert was recaptured and re-imprisoned in the Tower. (Hutton p 113)

46. Mr Francis Selwyn London 13th Aprill 1660

Yo[u]rs of the 25th past I have received. The things I have bought for you are aboard the *Hanniball*, destined for yo[u]r port, bill of Lading is inclosed. My deligence putt them aboard before I knew any other bound thither, besides Capt. Haddock[1] and cheifly a freind of mine, the purser, will take speciall care of them, and because it will soe happen that Mr Gayre will bee departed before any Conveyance could bring the Dictionary to him, I hope itt will not bee much amisse, the other things stay some time by the way if the[y] come safe at Last which I wish, and to yo[u]r Content, the cost etc. you have underneath, w[hi]ch I passe to yo[u]r D[ebit] in accompt.

I thank you for yo[u]r Loretto's Musick, which I may expect by the First. This weeke dyed Mr Toby Crisp, a person I thinck knowne to you, his disease was a feaver of but few dayes durance. I much pitty that Lady to whome hee was Last a servant, and the[y] say soe much in earnest thatt all things were [– ?-hole in text] even agreed upon. There was Lately (by the malice of some) a book printed (and soone became very publique) wherein this Mr Crisp[2] but Cheifly his brother Mr Sam[uel] Crisp, were grossly abused, the Author bringing them upon the stage like Knight Errant, under the title of the Knights of fond Love. The booke I have perused, the stile and Caracter itts printed in, is purely

Romance, the worst sort Like the Seven Champions[3] dividing the History into severall Chapters with the Contents perfixt. In fine itt's what might almost bee said of any one, supposing '[to be hired' x out] a person that was hired to abuse those he knew nott but 'twas those Gentlemen's misfortune to bee the subject of that pamphlett. I hope itt hath not prejudiced Mr Crisp in his last sicknesse, though some say hee did much resent itt. Heaven defend my freinds from such abuses. Mr Sam[uel] Crisp is lately gone into Flanders and France, where I suppose may spend some time. Excuse this story I relate it's because I thinck you know the persons. The L[or]d Lambert who has for some weekes prisoner in the Tower did on tuesday night Last, make an escape thence. Since which [since which x out] is no news of him. Pray my Respects to Sig[nor]e Hales and if you are soe familiar with Him, pray tell him to be mindfull of a wager betwixt himselfe & mee, what would happen to mee in six moneths after my arrivall in England, which time is now past,[4] and I am still in *status quo prius*. My service to Mr Breyden, Mr Hobson and all freinds.[5]

For 4 doz paire of white gloves	£ 4.8.0
A beaver hatt, band & case	£ 4.7.6
An Italian Dictionary	£ 1.4.6
The box, lock & portage	£ 0.2.0
	£10.2.0

1. Captain Haddock in this case is thought to be William, not his son Richard.
2. Sir Nicholas Crispe was a noted merchant before and after the Civil War, he was a pioneer of the West Africa trade and a commissioner for the customs. Whether Samuel and Tobias were his sons is not known.
3. Seven Champions. This is a reference to a book by Richard Johnson *The Seven Champions of Christendom* which appeared in print in the 1590s, the seven champions being the patron saints of seven countries. The book had a great deal of influence on subsequent writers such as John Bunyan. See *The Seven Champions of Christendom* edited Jennifer Fellows, Ashgate 2003
4. There had been a wager between Thomas and his friends that he would be married within 6 months of his return.
5. Mr Breydon, Mr Hobson and Mr Hales would seem to have been English merchants in Venice.

47. Mr James Thierry London 13th Aprill 1660

S[i]r,

Yo[u]rs of the 16/6[th] Currant I have rec[eive]d w[i]th the inclosed for Mr Rogers which shall be forwarded to him. Herewith you have an abstract of the award about the *Dolphin*. It's under the scrivener's hand that drew them up As to the *Seaven Starr's* businesse ['under' x out] I cann say no more then formerly: that the policy on the boddy of the ship runns that the [Assurers x out] Assurers are to beare the adventure att and from Barbados to Amst[er]d[am], soe that after her departure from Barbados [to Guinny is a certaine breach of the Pollicye x out] if she keep not her direct Course to Amsterd[am] and should miscarry, the Asurers are nott concerned and shee sayling from Barbados to Guinny is a certaine breach of the pollicye, and the Assurers will expect the premio as much as if shee had sailed to Amsterd[am] which the[y] are obliged to have borne if so it had pleased you.

This is the opinion of Court Registry. The other policy on the good[s] will be in force, so that if you please to have an ensurance made on the body of the shipp pray give mee yo[u]r order w[hi]ch shall bee observed, they demand 10 p[er] C[en]t I have payd Capt Will[iam] Bray £40 st[erling] upon yo[u]r bill of Excha[nge] w[hi]ch I past to you D[ebto]r.

48. Mr Bernard Sparke London 14th Aprill 1660

S[i]r,

Yours of the 11th Currant I have Rec[eive]d, the inclosed was last night forwarded to Mr Thierry. I perceive you have disposed the rest of the *Swann's* Oile att £39 p[er] ton, which I thinck is very well. Att yo[u]r conveniency the ac[comp]t of all would be welcome. Those from Mr Thierry I see you have perused, and have satisfaction from him in the Error you found. Yo[u]r thoughts upon the whole pray give us att yo[u]r Leisure for better *governo*.

49. Mrs Peard

[repeats letter 29]
The above is coppy of what I writt you some time since to which not haveing received answear, I send this to acquaint you what I then desired, intreating you answer by the first.
London 14th Aprill 1660

50. Mrs Eliza[beth] Mourton London 14th Aprill 1660

I have Received your letter of the 29th March under Mr Roger's covert to whose care I recommend this. What you therein desired I shall do accordingly, haveing to send downe by sea to Penrin so I intend the gowne which my mother left you, shall bee sent with them to a freind there who will take care of 'them' x out] itt. I shall then write you more perticulars. With my Respects to your self & freinds.

51. Mr Bryan Rogers[1] London 14th Aprill 1660

S[i]r,
The present is cheifly to give covert to the inclosed Received yesterday from Mr James Thierry. S[i]r I thanck you for the letter you put covert to from our Mrs Mourton. Please to afford the like favour to the inclosed w[hi]ch is in answear to the former. W[i]th my Respects to Mr Jennens, yo[u]r selfe and freinds w[i]th.

Pray S[i]r If yo[u]r brother[2] and Mr John Bawdon[3] are still att Barbados, or to w[hi]ch of them I may write to entreat their assistance to recover a debt there. Yo[u]rs T.H.

1. Bryan Rogers had married the daughter of Ambrose Jennens and was possibly by this time living with his father-in-law and handling much of his business.
2. The brother mentioned is possibly Bryan Rogers' brother-in-law George Thomson for I do not know that Bryan Rogers had any living brothers.
3. John Bawden was a merchant in Barbados, possibly born in Bridgewater in 1635 and with an estate in Barbados. (see Woodhead p 27)

52. Mr Bernard Sparke London 17th Aprill 1660

S[i]r,

Yours of the 14th Currant I have received w[i]th the accompts of the *Swanns* Oiles w[hi]ch I suppose may be right, upon further perusal finding otherwise shall advice you: In the intrim pray endeavour to imburse yo[u]rselfe to what is standing out and as itt comes in. Please what is for ¼ [a quarter x out] belonging to my father deceased to my selfe being the only person to act in businesse relating to his estate, I haveing obtained Letters of Administration from the Court of probate of Wills. Yo[u]r inclosed for Rouen was forwarded yesterday pray God send us good newes of the *Swann* which coming first to you pray advise.

53. Mr John Woodruffe London 17th Aprill 1660

S[i]r,

The time now drawing neere which you desired for the sattisfying the Remaineing £100 upon your bond I thought itt convenient to give you timely notice to provide accordingly which I hope you will take Care may be punctually performed, the rather because the former were not imbursed att the time expressed. S[i]r I leave itt to [you x o] yo[u]r Care intreating yo[u]r farther directions for delivering up your said bond, which as you shall order, shall be donne accordingly.

54. Mr James Thierry London 20th Aprill 1660

S[i]r,

Yours of the 23/[13] currant I have received, giving you thancks that you will afford my freinds your assistance when they arrive with you. I shall be ready to serve in the like occasion when you please. S[i]r as I remember itt hath byn more then once advised you, that Mr Gifford Bale, who assured £200 to you on the *Dolphin*, is long since retired to the King's Bench prison, or itts priviledges where he remaines without giving satisfaction to his creditors. Whenever hee comes to an agreement with them, I shall bee very carefull to looke affter what belongs to you. I hope the *Dolphin's* businesse will not prove soe dead a losse as att p[re]sent itt seemes to bee but that when the new K[ing] of Sweden[1] is better setled we may by yo[u]r meanes have Justice done us, w[hi]ch I hope you will fully endeavour.

S[i]r I would willingly bestowe my paines to the utmost in serving in [the] *N[orth] Lyon's* ['*7 Stars*' x out] businesse so that if you have or cann procure proofs sufficient to manifest the losse, I shall really endeavour what might bee to doe your self and freinds service, not in this onely butt in what else may occurr. The news is great expectation from the party att Breda,[2] who is here expected suddenly some say against the parliam[en]ts sitting, w[hi]ch is to bee on the 25th Currant. 'Tis said the Marquisse of Ordman[3] and Newcastle[4] are both arrived in England, the L[or]d Goreing[5] hath been here some time. On the 24th Currant will bee a General Muster of the Citty forces (where Major Crusor[6] is now Collonell) Consisting of the Trained Bands, the Volonteers and Auxiliarys whose number, by Compute, may amount to Thirty thousand, the Rendevous is to bee in Hide Park.

1. Charles X, the King of Sweden, died in 1660, he was succeeded by Charles XI.
2. Charles II was by this time at Breda,
3. James Butler 12th Earl of Ormond. Made a Duke at the Restoration. (Pepys X p 50)
4. William Cavendish, 1st Duke of Newcastle, a Royalist commander.
5. Lord Goring in this case was George Goring 1585–1663 a diplomat. His son George, the Royalist commander had died in 1657. 'This day [April 10] my Lord Goring returned from France and landed at Dover.' Note says 'Probably George (Goring), Earl of Norwich. Royalist leader in the Second Civil War; abroad since 1650; still often called by the title of his barony, since his earldom was a civil war creation.' (Pepys I p 106)
6. Crusor ? Is this John Cressnor, grocer A Customs Officer in 1640 and c. 1661-1666. (Woodhead p 54).

55. Mr William Jennens London 21th Aprill 1668

S[i]r,

Yours of the 17th Currant I have received, to which I hope this will be a satisfactory Answear. S[i]r It's true Mr Elliott's servant, Mr Hodge, was here with us and intreated £5 to w[hi]ch hee had deniall and reasons for so doing which very well satisfyed him w[hi]ch If hee did us the right to acquaint Mr Elliott[1] with fully,

I doubt not, but that he will see [that x out] we beare him as much respect as ever, knowing well his quality and the esteeme my father had alwayes for him. Had he given a Letter directly to us, itt should have byn honoured w[i]th punctual performance for a farr greater summe, but not doing so and a late losse by money paid a relation to a freind neere you, makes us very scrupilous of these things but upon the least word in writing, any freind's request shall finde due honour. We give you hearty thancks for your freindly excusing us in this thing to Mr Elliott. Pay our Respects to him att yo[u]r convenience assuring him fully that wee doe much esteeme him and shall be ready upon least command to serve him.

S[i]r, yo[u]r advice that I should honour my Father's ould freinds is a principall I hope is well fixed within mee which I doubt not [inserted] any freinds shall find to the contrary in any action and that you seeme to understand otherwise. By the want of your accompt wee shall endeavour to rectify that, by the perfecting itt with the first itt's easy to suppose, the many businessesse [sic] we are now engaged in, that hinders the punctuallity wee would use in affairs of this nature. S[i]r you may expect itt suddenly and be fully sattisfied. Wee have and shall ever continue to you a very extraordinary respect and shall be ready to serve you on any occasion. Wee suppose Mr Sparke hath forward to you Mr Thierry's acc[om]ts of the *Dolphin* with his thoughts thereon. Upon our short view wee found parcell that ought to bee rectifyed att your *Comodo*. Pray a word of this perticular.

1. Mr Elliott. Is this one of the Elliotts of St Germans?

56. **Mr William Jennens** London 28th Aprill 1660

S[i]r,
Since my last I have not received any of yours. Herewith is Coppy of what we found in Mr Thierry's accompts to be queryed w[hi]ch may bee of some use to you. ['accompt' x out] Your accompt is now making up and as soone as possible you shall have itt. In the intrim pray advise the perticulars of what you Charge my father's last accompt w[i]th in £22.10s for ½ of goods sent per *Dolphin* w[hi]ch I thinck you were formerly desired to send us. The Parliament have adjourned till tuesday morning, when 'tis supposed they will enter on that which is termed the great worke.[1]

1. 'the great worke' The Declaration of Breda was presented to the Council on 29 April and to the House of Commons on May 1. The Lords and Commons agreed that the English Government was by the King, Lords and Commons. The Restoration of the King was, in other words, formally agreed upon. (Hutton p 118)

57. Mrs Alice Pearde London p[ri]mo May 1660

I have written you twice to the same effect, to acquaint you that the bond wherein your husband stood bound to they Excise Com[missione]rs is now taken up and in my possession the Charges as I have said is £6.12s.6d which I pray take Care to satisfie mee speedylye that so you may have up the bond. This is but very reasonable what I demand. I question not but you know that your Husband gave Counter bond to save my father Harmlesse and defray w[ha]t charge might arise in this businesse, that is still in force and I assure you shall be made use of except there be some care to imburs mee. Itt's a badd requitall for a Courtesie of that nature, to bee putt to trouble meerly upon another's businesse. If this be yo[u]r Concernment or more properly yo[u]r Sonn's I know not, butt whomsoever itt concerns, I hope their Civilitye will give some answear, w[hi]ch you have not hitherto done. I expect a letter by the first.

58. Mr John Woodruffe London 3rd of May 1660

S[i]r,

I formerly received yo[u]rs of the 20th & 27th past and yesterday yours of th 30th with an Inclosed bill of exchange upon Mr John Hill which hee hath satisfied. I say £40. The letter to Mr Thomas Barnes hath hath byn carried severall times to his lodging, but the messenger could not yet meet with him, If ought happens before the post's departure shall noat herewith. I am sorry you have byn disappointed and Consequently my selfe, but 2 or 3 dayes import is not much in which time being satisfied the remaineing £60 I shall cancell your bond, and send itt you a[s] desired.

S[i]r, The answear I have from Mr Barnes is that the £60 you mention hee hath already rec[eive]d and disposed as hee gave you notice per last post, so I must pray you to take some speedy care for mee elsewhere.

59. Mr James Thierry London 4th May 1660

S[i]r,

This post brings mee none of yo[u]rs, which will cause breavitye – of the £100 resting on Yarmouth men's bond, I have received £40 – the rest am promised speedily. The news is the Parliam[en]ts receiving his Maj[e]sties Letter & Declaracon to which the[y] unanimously resovle [sic] to give a suitable answearr and to make a present freely of £10,000 st[erling] from the Cittye, and £50,000 st[erling] for the supply of the present occasions. The house of Lords have chose some of their members to waite on the King, their names are the Lord of Oxford, Warwick, Hereford, Brook, Barkley, Middlesex.[1] The Comons have not yet resolved on their members.

From the Cittie goe as Com[missione]rs the Recorder Wilde, Ald[ermen] Adam, Robinson, Bateman, Renoldson, Langham, Bunce, Mr Bludworth, Chamberlain, Vincent, Ford, Biddulph, Bromfield,[2] their departure hence is intended tuesday next; the present affaires give a generall satisfaction to the nation, God send us a good issue to all

1.
Aubrey de Vere 20th Earl of Oxford. Imprisoned during the Commonwealth. (Pepys X p 462)
3rd Earl of Warrick. 'patron of the Essex presbyterians' (Hutton p 152)
Hereford = William Seymour, 1st Marquis of, 2nd Duke of Somerset ?
Robert Greville Brooke. 2nd Baron Brooke. (Pepys X1 p 119)
George Berkeley, 9th Baron (1st Earl in 1679). one of the original fellows of the Royal Society. (Pepys X p 27)
Lord Middlesex. Lionel Cranfield, Earl of Middlesex (Pepys XI p 73)

2.
Sir William Wilde. Recorder of London 1659–1668. (Pepys X1 p 311)
Ald. Adam = Sir Thomas Adams ? Sheriff 1639–40, Lord Mayor 1645–6 described as 'Darling of the City' knighted May 1660 (Woodhead p 15)
Sir John Robinson 1625-1680. Lieutenant of the Tower 1660–1679, Sheriff 1657-8, Lord Mayor 1662-3 knighted and later granted a baronetcy. He was said to have played a large part in bringing about the Restoration. N.B. he married the daughter of Sir George Whitmore Lord Mayor 1631–2. She was the niece of Alexander Daniell of Penzance. Her mother was the half sister of Alexander and George Whitmore was formerly the partner of Richard Daniell of Truro, the father of Alexander. The Daniells had important relatives.

Sir Anthony Bateman. knighted 1660, Sheriff 1658, Lord Mayor in 1663. He
was ruined by losses in the Great Fire. (Woodhead p 25)
Renoldson = Ald Abraham Reynardson ? born Plymouth 1590. knighted
July 1660. Lord Mayor 1648–9 but removed as a leading City Royalist.
(Woodhead p 137)
Ald. Col. John Langham MP knighted May 1660 a Presbyterian
Sir James Bunce. Sheriff 1643, knighted May 1660, created baronet 1660
(Woodhead p 41) Presbyterian and firm Royalist.
Sir Thomas Bludworth. Turkey merchant knighted May 1660, Sheriff 1662–
3, Lord Mayor 1665. (Woodhead p 33)
Sir Thomas Chamberlain. knighted May 1660 Governor of the East India
Co 1662–3. (Woodhead p 44 and Pepys X p 56 – some discrepancies in
these two accounts)
Sir William Vincent. knighted May 1660. MP London 1660. d. 1661.
(Woodhead p 168)
Sir Richard Ford. His father was Thomas Ford merchant of Exeter. Richard
was knighted May 1660, Sheriff 1663, Lord Mayor 1670. FRS 1673. He
was active in promoting the Restoration and was well-known to William
Jennens and Bernard Sparke. (Woodhead p 71, Pepys X p 149)
Ald Sir Theophilus Biddulph. Master of the Drapers' Company. MP for
London in 1656 and 1659. (Woodhead p 38).
Sir Lawrence Bromfield. knighted May 1660. He had been committed for
high treason in February 1660 (Woodhead p.38)

60. **Mr Roger Street** London 5th May 1660

S[i]r,

Yesterday's post brought mee a letter to my Father from your
self which caused [mee x out] us something to wonder, that you
should not have understood the great losses wee have received in
our familye by the death of both our deare Parents. The former
departed this life, the 15th January last, the latter the 4the of
March following, to our unspeakable greife. This advice will bee
answear to what you desire. If in anything I cann serve you: I shall
be ready.

61. **Mr William Jennens** London 5the May 1660

S[i]r,

Herewith is your accompt as itt stands in our books the ballance
we forbeare to adjust, till wee have made an end w[i]th Mr Joyner
both for the Cottons and the losse, which hope may bee in 2 or

3 dayes In the mean time pray peruse this, w[hi]ch hope you will finde right. You are not charged w[i]th port of l[e]tters, because you ordered itt to be placed to Mr Thierry, soe hee allowing it hereafter will be well. The Citty Coun[cil]l[or]s are prepareing to wait on the King at Breda and may depart on tuesday, Captain Stookes[1] goes Com[man]d[e]r of the Squadron that attends them.

1. Captain Stookes = Ald. Stokes (see letter 62)? Is this Humphrey Stokes goldsmith at the Black Horse Lombard Street ? (Pepys X p 404)

62. Mr Giles Lytcott London 7th May 1660[1]

It's some time since I writt you, being still an expectation of some letter from you w[hi]ch I feare are miscarried for I have answear to that w[hi]ch did accompany your two borders of haire nor any advice whither Capt[ain] Paine delivered you a doz[en] bottles of sack and a small packett of letters I sent by him. I doubt something in these perticulars because I am well acquainted with your punctuallity to advice the needfull. I am now with yours of the 10th Aprill informing mee your sudden intentions to leave Rome; t[ha]t you have minded mee with *carissima* I kindly thanck you. Mr Byam I hope was well, and all other our acquaintances but of these, and thousand other perticular, *we will speak soon*. July is drawing and if your thoughts are to passe Germanye and to the lowe Countrys you may possibly arrive there in the Criticall minute to waite on his Maj[es]tie our King who is now at Breda prepareing for England. The houses of Lords and Comons have chosen Com[missione]rs to waite of him there and present him their allegiance. The Citty does the like, by their Com[missione]rs who present him £10000 st[erling] in pure guifts and £50000 st[erling] lent to supply his occasions. These persons may depart in 2 or 3 dayes. The squadron of Ships that attend the Com[missione]rs are commanded by our Ald[erman] Stockes who is much your servant, as himself tould mee lately. The King is not yet proclaimed but itts suddenly expected so that now their no doubt butt thing will runn in their antient Channell. I am solicitous to sell the barb[2] butt cannot yet meet a Chapman, every one Comends him, as in reality hee deserves, but the objection onely is that hee is to little, butt I hope may Growe. You may be Confident I doe what I cann.

Deare hart, lett mee hear how you dispose of yourself in your Journey that I may still meet you with a letter and with myself upon the first English ground you tread. I thanck your Care about the barber I hinted in my former's, but now it matters not much. I hope you have the much esteemed society of Dr Finch[3] and Dr Baines[4] to whom my due respects. The former's brother (as I take itt) Mr Hennage is a Parl[iame]nt man. With huge applause things goe on mighty satisfactory to the generality of the Nations – no partye discontented but such as are distinguished by the name of Phanatique[5] that is a medlye of the sextaryans. Two statutes are in hand of the late and the present King, to whom wee are growne so charitable to pray for him publiquely giving him his due and antient titles.

1. The King was proclaimed the following day i.e. May 8th.
2. a barb = Arab (i.e.Barbary) horse (Pepys X p 569)
3. Dr Finch, the brother of Heneage Finch. There were two cousins called. Heneage Finch. This one would appear to be the 1st Earl of Nottingham, later Lord Chancellor and the second son of Sir Heneage Finch.
4. In a letter dated November 24 1663 (*Familiar Letters* p 84) Walter Pope FRS mentions Sir John Finch and Dr Baynes 'whose reputations are very great here'. They had recently returned from Naples 'and viewing its natural curiosities, they killed dogs, cats etc. with those steams, and afterwards dissected them'.
5. There was a great fear of 'fanatics' a term which included the Quakers.

63. Mr John Hill London 10th May 1660

S[i]r,

Yours [I have received x out] of the 13th Aprill I have rec[eive]d and perceive your are willing in some short time to pay £10.-. of w[ha]t is demanded of you w[hi]ch I desire may be done as soone as your one Conveniency will permitt to Mr Tho[mas] Dennys of Barnstaple [1] upon notice whereof Mr Hugh Squier will imburse us here. The letter w[hi]ch you have by you & intend to send mee I shall expect for the cleering the other £10.

1. Mr Thomas Dennys was a merchant of Barnstaple.

64.Mr John Woodruffe London the 10th May 1660

S[i]r,

Yours ['I have received' x out] of the 7th Currant I have received with an Inclosed bill of sixty pounds att 4 dayes sight upon Mr James Johnson[1] w[hi]ch he hath accepted and promiseth punctuall payment att the day which I doubt not off, when itt's rec[eive]d I shall cancell your bond, and inclose itt p[er] first post.

1. James Johnson – a goldsmith ? (Woodhead p 99)

65. (in Italian) [to Signore Jacopo Baldinotti but no name is given]

My Master etc.

It has been my misfortune that your letters (always very dear to me) have not been safely received since after those which I got in Venice I have not received even a word. Those for my friends in Lucca, as I mentioned to you in my last, I sent by a friend of mine who left a month ago by sea for Livorno. On his arrival you will receive them with other things that I send you.

I have already received your welcome one of the 31st March by way of Venice and by sea from Mr Harry Browne. The casket that I ordered from you is there within are the books of Signor Sbarra[1] with the music which without doubt is rare being chosen by you but the letter that ought to accompany it I do not find, therefore I cannot know what I have to do with an old shoe that was inside. With your next, two words please with your orders concerning this shoe which instantly will be acted upon. I believe it is for a pattern but not having an order I can do nothing. I see how great is my new obligation to you Signor with a gift truly royal of two casks of olives and oil besides which I should receive with the next ship from Mr Browne. This has reproached me but rest assured that I will do my best in everything that I can and will have much pleasure that you command me freely and tell me what things would please you to have from our country that I will try to serve you immediately. At the proper season of the year you will receive flowers that will please you, I taking pleasure in finding some for you that are beautiful. I will not fail to serve you with all my power and therefore tell me freely. I am pleased Signor Gioseppe is married and so much to his liking. [You use him as an example?] To him and to his wife I humbly kiss their hands and indirectly

to all my friends in my dear Lucca. Mr Samuel[2], not rejoicing in perfect health, has not yet thought of leaving soon but if he ever comes into Italy he will come to revere the Signors Loroda. Here, in recent days, it has been declared that our King Charles, with general applause of all the people, will shortly be here to rejoice in his inheritance and the government of his people, as Mr Giles favours. As before I salute you very dearly.
11 May 1660

1. Francesco Sbarra was a writer of librettos and operas. The first public opera theatre opened in Venice in 1637. http://www.fathom.com/ feature/121321. Seen 24.02.05
2. Mr Samuel i.e. Thomas's younger brother Samuel.

66. Mr James Thierry London 11th May 1660

S[i]r,
Being without any of yours the two last posts shall bee the breifer, the present serveing for covert to the inclosed from Mr Ber[nar]d Sparke. On tuesday last the King was proclaimed with the usuall ceremonyes and to the generall satisfaction of all the people.[1] Wee are every day expecting his arrivall with us which god grant. S[i]r If in any thing I can serve you pray freely Comand.

1. 'My letters today tell me how it was entended that the King should be proclaimed today in London with a great deal of pomp.' (Pepys I p 21)

67. Mrs Alice Pearde London 12th May 1660

I have att length received [your x o] answear to [you x o] my severalls, but not what I expected; how you are provided w[i]th money I cannot tell, but itt not reasonable that w[ha]t have disburst to save you harmlesse (besides much time and paines) should prove to my one damage. I beleive six months agoe you would have given ten times w[ha]t I now demand, the businesse had byn donne but now you thinck your selfe out of danger, you make little of itt, but you mistake for I have your Husband's bond, w[hi]ch I assure you shall be made use off except you some speedy course [bee x out] be taken to satisfy mee. I am as civill as any man, but yet cannot endure to bee a sufferer, by doing another a Courtesy when itt's in their power to prevent itt. I desire by the return of this post yo[u]r answear.

68. Mr Bernard Sparke Exeter London 12th May 1660

S[i]r,

Yours of the 9th Currant I have received w[i]th the Inclosed accompts which I am glad you find right. Yours to Mr Thierry was forwarded the last night. I perceive the good newes of the *Swan,* god return her in safety. The proceed of her oyles being received you will remitt for our part w[hi]ch will bee well. Wee are all bigg w[i]th expectation for his Maj[es]ties safe arrivall w[hi]ch may bee very suddenly. The Citty Commiss[ione]rs are this day departed to attend him..

69. Mr Thomas Trewoolla[1] London 12th May 1660

Yours of the 26th past I have received, the inclosed was safely delivered. The side saddle of my Cousen Betty is put aboard W[illia]m Rogers[2] , who was the first conveyance and I hope will arrive in safety hee going with Convoy, att present is in the downes expecting a faire winde. I thank you for the advice of tyn If I cann serve you here pray Comand mee. My Respects to my uncle, your selfe and Cosens.

1. This is Thomas Trewolla junior.
2. William Rogers was a noted Falmouth captain of one of the 'tin' ships i.e. the ships which carried the Cornish tin to London.

70. Tho[mas] Dethick [etc]. London 19th May 1660

What my bro[ther] hath above desired you concerning his Coxall bays[1] I request the Same for our peece goods resting in yo[u]r hands for our joynt acc[omp]t that soe an end may bee to yo[u]r acc[omp]t pending. I hope our Lead, 50 piggs, will finde a good markett w[i]th yo[u]r care, w[hi]ch wee desire.

1. coxall bays. Are these the same as Colchester bays?

71. Mrs Pearde London 19th May 1660

I have received your letter but cannot from thence understand your meaneing, what I have said in my former letters I am still [I x o] to insist upon for your spedy satisfying mee what I have disburst to save mee [sic] harmlesse which I pray take care that it may speedilye bee donne, the somme is not of much concernment that you say you are not able to satisfy itt's too much for mee too loosse and upon noe other score then for doeing a courtesie to another; I am unwilling to trouble you or my selfe with many Letters. Pray therefore by returne of the post take some course to pay mee, and soe avoyd any further troble.

72. Mr John Woodruffe London the 22th May 1660

S[i]r,
I forbore to write till I had received the £60 upon the bill of Exchange you sent mee, w[hi]ch is now donne so I herewith send your bond Cancelled as you desired. I pray advise mee when you have rec[eive]d itt. S[i]r if in anything I cann here [inserted] bee servicable to you [here x out] pray Command mee freely.

73. Mr William Jennens London 22th May 1660

S[i]r,
Since my last have not rec[eive]d any of yours. Inclosed you have the accompt of the Cotton 4 baggs sould Mr Joyner w[hi]ch you may please to noate without our prejudice till received, wee not being yet able to adjuste [itt x o] with Him. Att the request of our ould acquaintance Mr Geo[rge] Putt[1] I am to entreat you to pay to his sister (I suppose well knowne to you) Ten shillings hee haveing paid mee soe much here. Pray excuse the trouble & Comand.

1. George Putt? There was a 'Putt' family who lived at Combe House, Gittisham in Devon

74. Mr James Thierry London p[ri]mo June 1660

S[i]r,
Yours of the 28th past I have received perceiveing you [would x out] endeaver to get some farther proofes about the *N[orth] Lyon*[1]

which will doe very well. I have at length received the full of that bond from the Yarmouth men which is delivered up to them. The time draws on for the paim[en]t of the losse on the *Golden Dolphin* which shall be demanded of them to procure paim[en]t as soone as may bee, and what passeth shall advise. Wee Heare how nobly our King was treated at the Hagh, he since safely arived and made his entry into the Cittie w[i]th great solemnity on the 29th past being his birthday. Here is so universal Joy that theirs yet noe news or any thing donne then giveing and receiveing visits.

S[i]r, there is a gentleman, Mr Giles Lytcot, who some yeares hath lived abroad as a merchant, in severall places, the last at Legorne, where his name runs in a cheife house [place x out] there. This Gentleman is now returning home and will passe your Cittie, he is my most intimate and esteemed friend, and therefore I desire him to waite on you & that besides p[re]senting you my service hee may give you some accompt of the trade of those places he hath been att w[hi]ch I am Confident he cann doe as well as any p[e]rson whater. S[i]r, pray ecuse the liberty I take & Comand mee.

1. *North Lyon* There is no indication how this ship was lost.

75. **Mr Lytcott** Amst[erdam] London 1 June 1660

I have before mee yours of the 21th past from Venice, Perceiving you are now in earnest in your thoughts homewards, Heaven crown yo[u]r journey with succese, and give us a good meeting. You could never chuse a tim[e] to finde soe universall *allegrezza* as now possesseth us for the safe returne of his Maj[es]tie and the two Dukes[1], who made their entry into the Cittye[2] on tuesday, the 29th past being his Maj[es]ties birthday. Little newes there is these few days being spent in giving and receiving visitts. Severall Noble men went nare Dover to attend his Maj[es Landing (w[hi]ch was on the day senight being fryday), w[i]th troops of gentlemen hugely rich in apparrell. One troop went out of the Citty under the Command of their Collonel, now S[i]r John Robinson, under the title of the batchelours troops of w[hi]ch yo[u]r servant was one, our habitt was all alike which gave us the title of the most gallant though others were farr richer but theirs being various appeared not so well as ours w[hi]ch in breife was Horse and armes well fixed, a Buffe Coate w[i]th the sleeves all laced, a white hatt w[i]th a black Feather and a greene Scarfe w[hi]ch was oure colours and our motto was 'alwayes Loyall'.

1. The two Dukes i.e. the Duke of York (later James II) and the Duke of Gloucester
2. Evelyn describes the King's entry into the City on the 29 May.
   'This was also his birth-day, and with a triumph of above 20,000 horse and foote, brandishing their sword and shouting with inexpressible joy; the wayes strew'd with flowers, the bells ringing, the streets hung with tapistry, fountaines running with wine; the Maior, Aldermen, and all the Companies in their liveries, chaines of gold, and banners; Lords and Nobles clad in cloth of silver, gold, and velvet; the windowes and balconies well set with ladies; trumpets, music, and myriads of people flocking, even so far as from Rochester, so as they were seven houres in passing the Citty, even from 2 in the afternoone till 9 at night. I stood in the Strand and beheld it, and bless'd God . . .' (Evelyn p 265)

76. Mrs Alice Pearde London 2[n]d June 1660

I have yours of the 22nd past wherein you desire time for the payment of what ['which' x out] is due unto mee. You well know itts some moneths since I first demanded itt and many when the money was paid by us so that itts strange to mee you require a longer time, nor doe you say how long you would be forborne. However I am content that you take a months time for the paym[en]t of the somme of £6.12s.6d that so I finding your punctuall performance I may noe farther troble you or my selfe.

77. Mr Bernard Sparke London 2nd June 1660

S[i]r,

Yours of the 30th past I have received with the inclosed from Mr Butson[1] and the good newes of the *Swann*'s arrivall for which I thanck you. I perceive you were offered £38.10s p[er] t[on] for 50 Pipes you know best what's to be done, itt's a wasting Com[modi] tye espetially the heats coming in with us, the very high of the markett is £39 p[er] t[on] seller cleering the excise which is 35s p[er] t[on]. Att Bristoll they say itt sells att £40 so that if your markett corresponds with that you may possibly obtaine your demand. For my Concerne I leave itt to your dispose being Confident you will doe for the best. If you are in Cash upon the last Sales pray remitt up att your Conveniencye. If you can dispose this parsell of Oile for money itt would doe very [will x o] well and much for our occations.

1. John Butson was a partner of Bernard Sparke and his brother-in-law.

78. Mr John Pascoe London 2nd June 1660

I am to give you answear to yours of the 6th february wherein you desired forbearance for your rent w[hi]ch you may perceive was granted. My present request is that you would cleare the whole accompt of Rent due to Mich[ael]mas last, deducting what taxes was to be allowed, for from that time the land will belong to my brother Mr Abraham Hill, who will in time write you and no doubt but will forbear yo[u]r rent till September next. If my Cousen John Trewoolla should have any demands upon the land for a herriott or such like Pray referr him to mee, so may him Satisfaction.[1]

1. This refers to the dispute about the ownership of Trelevan.

79 Mr Ben[jamin] Childe London 4th June 1660

Much respected friend

I am to give answear to your letters of the 23rd past fro[m] Florance *I am obliged to remember it for all its pleasures and what a paradise* you see the effect of thinking on delicate florence. I pitty you really that trobles & disturbances disquiet you and have prevented yo[u]r executing the thoughts you entertained of a speedy returne but itt may possyble be more for your benifitt, though to yo[u]r lessor satisfactions, to remaine still abroad. If you were now with us you would perceive that by sence w[hi]ch att the distance you are, cannot enter yo[u]r imagination, so universall a Joy att the safe retrune [sic] and settlement of his sacred Maj[es]tie that himselfe could not expect nor his subjects expresse more. Himself with the two Dukes made theire enter into the City on tuesday the 29th past (his Maj[es]ties birthday). Att Dover where he landed he was rec[eive]d and attended by the L[or]d Monck and 4 miles on this side by diver troops of gentlemen, under the Command of Ald[erman,] now S[i]r John, Robinson, consisting

about 100 horse, besides servants, of this troops was yo[u]r
servant. Our habitt, w[hi]ch in disigne was alike, made his Maj[es]
tie take perticular notice of us when with the rest of the Volenteers
we were martialled to receive him upon Barham Downes¹ 4 miles
from Dover: to be perticular we wore Buff Coats the sleeves all
laced, white hatts w[i]th Black feather and large greene Scarfe,
suitable to our colours the motto of w[hi]ch was alwayes loyall. I
may seem partiall in this [last?] as being a pertie but in the opinion
of the ladyes the Batchelours troops (w[hi]ch was our title) boare
the vante of all. We attended him hither and found the Cittie fitted
for his reception, the streets all rayled and lined with souldiers
and furr gownes; the Conduits blushing att his joyfull arriveing,
turned their water into wine & shouts raysed many notes beyond
the Scale of Musique. In the Churchs the Common Pray[e]r is
generally used. Yesterday being Sunday Bishop Ween, and another
Bishop preache before his maj[es]tie in their usuall antient habitts
and on the 29 past 7 bishopp sung Te Deum at Westminster, so
wee have hope things will move in the right sphear.[words x o]
His Maj[es]tie hath made a proclamation against Debauched
persons for their diseiante naming and bringing to punishment
w[hi]ch highly satisfieth the sober and ingenuous partie. Hee has
byn with the parlam[en]t and gives them counsell to be moderate
in their proceedings and a noble expression was used that they
should provide that the plaistering may be wide enough for the
Soare. Deligent search is made for the late king judges of which
Greg[ory] Clement² is taken and secured in the towerr. Others
no doubt will quickly accompany him because everyone is their
enimy. The L[or]d Lisle is escaped into France³. Things move on
highly satisfatory God continued itt. Mr Lytcott is on his jurrney
and I hope wilbe quickly here. Prithee love Mr Angier for mee and
salute him kindly.

1. The reception at Barham Downs was organised by the Heneage Finch
   who was 3rd Earl of Winchelsea. He was appointed by Monck to be
   the Governor of the castle and town of Dover and on the 25th May he
   marshalled the nobility and gentry of Kent to welcome Charles II on
   Barham Downs. (*DNB* Vol. 19 p 566) From Thomas Hill's account there
   were many others besides the people of Kent who went to welcome
   the King.
2. Gregory Clements (1594?–1660 was a Devon man, the son of John
   Clements of Plymouth (who was Mayor in 1614). He must have been

well-known to the Hill family as he did business with Richard. He was said to have been captured because a blind man recognised his unusual voice. (*DNB* Vol.12 p.28)
3. Lord John Lisle regicide – he escaped to Switzerland but was assassinated by a Royalist agent.

80. Mr Will[iam] Hill[1] London 5th June 1660

S[i]r,
I hope this finds your selfe and freinds in good health. The Hopps and Iron by Rogers I suppose may 'ere this bee safely arrived and Landed for itts dispose I leave itt wholly to your Care being confident you will endeavor for the best. [word x o] With us hopps are riseing but I am willing you take the best markett price for mine and the Iron too [the x o] that full returnes may come by the first and alsoe the money I furnished you with Here may be Invested to the best tinn att the best & cheapest rates you cann procure itt. Speedy returnes are that will encourage mee to continue this trade which is wholly in your diligence & Care to effect. I have not elce but my Respects to your selfe, my aunt, & the freinds with you.

1. Mr William Hill, younger brother of Richard and therefore uncle of Thomas. He went to Truro after the Civil War and then moved to Falmouth.

81. Mr John Byam ['Byme' x out] London 8th June 1660

Yours of the 22th past I have received giveing you [word x o] many thancks for your kind proffer to provide [for us x o] for us what was desired of father James, who I thought would have done mee that or a greater Courtesy but since he failes I must pray your excuse. If I troble you, with [sic] assure me that if I cann serve you here, you will make use of mee with all freedome. What I desired of him you will perceive by the Inclosed note, of which the thing you cann doe conveniently pray forward to us as best you cann. What's to bee had of F. Kirker[1]. F. James is the fittest person, because he was with mee when I bought His books. The $50 or 60 I desired Mr Dethick to imburse you withall was to have satisfied for what you might have disburst to F. James for the things I desired or itt the same thing still if you take the trouble on your selfe. Mr Hallett once mentioned your box of strings and prayed my assistance for their dispose, which readily assured him of but since have not heard of them, though doe often see him on the exchange. Our freind Mr Lytcot is on his way through Germany and hope may bee here by all the next month. Of our King's safe arrivall and reception I suppose you have advise. The parliam[en]t are upon the act of generall pardon, which may bee quickly publique. The other maine businesse is of the 7 excepted persons that were of the King's Judges. As the Report goes their names are Harrison, Jones, Scott, Saye, Lisle, Holland, Baxter, of which the two former are onely Incustable.[2]

1. There are several references to Father Athanasius Kircher (the spelling varies) in Evelyn's *Diary*. Evelyn met him when in Rome in 1644. Kircher was professor of mathematics and oriental studies at the Jesuit College there. He took Evelyn into his study 'where, with Dutch patience, he shew'd us his perpetual motions, catoptrics, magnetical experiments, models, and a thousand other crotchets and devices, most of them since published by himselfe or his industrious scholar Schotti'. (Evelyn p 91). Evelyn himself later sent to Kircher drawings of some hieroglyphics which were on a stone given to Evelyn. These hieroglyphics were later mentioned in one of Kircher's many publications. In 1655 (p 244) James Usher, the Archbishop of Armagh, described Kircher as a 'mountebank' to Evelyn and, in a letter dated from Rome, November 24 1663 (*Familiar Letters* p 84) Walter Pope FRS informed Abraham Hill that 'Since I came to Rome I have more than once visited Kircher's and seen his tradescant's shop; but he is so continually accompanied with his admiring countrymen, that I have not yet had any competent time of discourse with him. He has lately printed here a book, which, if we may believe him, is very curious . . . it pretends to teach one of an indifferent capacity, in a small time, to understand all languages, and to make himself understood to all'.
2. The King's Judges. For a discussion on the 'Regicides' see *DNB* Vol. 46 pp 365-368
The fate of the so called Regicides varied, many escaped the death penalty but 'For others it was a different story. Men like Thomas Harrison, John Carew [from Antony] and Thomas Scott, who were entirely unrepentant, could expect no mercy . . . Three others who sat in judgement on Charles I, John Jones, Adrian Scrope and Gregory Clements were only slightly less defiant . . . They too were convicted and executed.' (*DNB* Vol. 46 p 367) Ten men were executed as a result of the 1660 trials, six of the sixty-nine commissioners who sentenced Charles I to death or signed his warrant of execution, plus four others.

Three more were executed in 1662.
Major General Thomas Harrison (*DNB* Vol. 25. p 529). Pepys describes his execution on 13 October. (Pepys I p 265)
Col. John Jones executed 1660
Thomas Scott (Pepys I p 263 & note)
William Saye escaped to the continent.
Lord Lisle (see letter 79)
Richard Baxter. (*DNB* Vol. 4) was not described as a regicide 1615–1691 Puritan minister. 22 June 1660 he, with others, was appointed chaplain to Charles II and on the 22 July preached before Charles II. One of Baxter's best known publications was *A Holy Commonwealth* (1659) which contained an appendix with an explanation and justification of his actions and allegiance at the time of the Civil War. This was used by some at the Restoration to show that he was seditious. In 1670 Baxter withdrew the book but it was burnt in 1683 as seditious by a decree of the University of Oxford.

82. Mr Giles Lytcot London 8th June 1660

I writt you on this day senight but then forgot to advise you that your freind Mr Elizabeth Harvey[1], who ridd right Hand man in our troope received the Honour of Knighthood from his Maj[es]tie att Canterbury. The Parliam[en]t are earnest upon excepting from pardon 7 out of the late Kings Judges some give their names which as the Report goes you have in the margent. I lately spoke with your Couzin Overbury[2] (who lived once w[i]th S[i]r John Robinson) and he promised upon timely advice to attend your land which pray as certain accertaine as you best cann Conveniently that so wee may not faile to waite on you. Mr Byam kindly salutes soe doe all the freinds from Venice. You may probably att your arrivall finde with us Mr Alex[ander] Travell from Aleppo who taking the Conveniance of a long vacation will visitt His friends here, & hitherto wee understand no other businesse. Hee was att Leg[orn]e the 21th past and intended within a day or two to beginn his Journey. Pray my Respects to the doctors and George Hunt if with you. Pray favour mee to visitt Mr James Thierry, giving him my Respects as I desired in my last. Wee have from Amst[erdam] the badd newes of the losse of the *Reformation & Freetrade*[3] I have not elce but my most affectionate embraces.
[at side] Harrison etc.

1. i.e. Eliab Harvey who had traded as a merchant in Italy. Knighted at the Restoration and later an MP He was the brother of William Harvey who discovered the circulation of the blood. He had business connections with the Noy family of Penwith see CRO GB/15/20.
2. Cousin Overbury. Giles Lytcott's mother was Margaret Overbury the daughter of Sir Nicholas Overbury.
3. The loss of the *Reformation* and *Freetrade* was a great blow as it came just as peace with Spain was about to be signed. The ships contained valuable cargoes from the Near East and were taken into Gibraltar.

83. Mr James Thierry London 8th June 1660

S[i]r, Yours of the 11/[1] Currant I have received, perceiving the safe arrivall of the *Phenix* from Barbados, w[i]th 26 Butts sugar and 10 Baggs Cottons. Upon returne of the *Dolphin's* Cargo pray endeavour the dispose of all and att your Convenience the accompts of what you received by the *Gustavus Adolphus*. I shall consult with Mr Jennens, who is now In towne, about the fittest meanes to procure letters from our King in our behalf concerning the *Dolphin's* busines, & advise you. I have made demand of your award upon the *Dolphin*, which the assurers promise me satisfaction of in a short time.

Our Publique affaires goe on very smoothly: the Parliam[en]t are upon an act of general pardon w[hi]ch in few dayes may bee published. The 7 excepted persons of the late King Judges are as itt's reported Harrison, Jones, Scott, Saye, Lisle, Holland, Baxter, of which the first two are onely in Custody. Wee expect confirmation of your advice concerning *the Tweed* & *Deane*.

84. Mr Francis Selwyn London 8th June 1660

S[i]r,
I have received yours of the 28th past with an inclosed bill of Echange on Mr George Robinson for £7.0.6½, w[hi]ch I shall demand of him and doubt not satisfaction. The Song booke you sent by Mr Saunderson, I have received and give you thancks for your care therein. You have heard of his Maj[es]ties safe arrivall and noble reception by the Cittie. The Parliam[en]t are earnest upon excepting from pardon 7 out of the late Kings Judges some give their names which as the report goes you have them in the

Margent.[Harrison etc.] Your brothers and sisters came from
Friston to see the King's *entrata*, the same did most of the Gentry
w[hi]ch made the solemnity huge splended. Dobly returne my
Respects to the freinds you mention. The fish designe we consider
of and possibly may doe some thing in itt.

Mr Robinson hath promised *to remember* to satisfie your bill.

85. Wor[shi]ppff[ull] Justinian Pearde London 12th June 1660

I suppose before this you have other wayes heard of the decease
of my good father to whose estate I am administrator with the
will annexed for the adjusting thereof with everyone. My present
request is that you please with your first conveniency to send mee
coppy of what in acc[omp]t hath lately past between your selfe and
my said father. The present offers not elce but my respects and in
what I can serve you freely comand.

86. Mr Giles Lytcott London 15th June 1660

The two foregoing posts, I writt you since w[hi]ch I have not any
from you, and though your last was from Venice not accertaineing
your departure thence, yet I hope this may meet you in safety at
Amst[erdam] w[hi]ch I should gladly heare and that you resolve to
see us w[i]th the first good oppertunity. Of news here's little other
then the Confirmation of the losse of the *Reformation* & *Freetrade*
carried into [Giblato x o] Giblater, the 16 or 17th past our stile.
His Maj[es]tie writs to the K[ing] of Spaine att the request and on
the behalfe of the Turkey Company here concerning these two
ships, and the Company have hopes to get a restoration. The letter
is intended to bee sent by Mr Paige[1] a very worthy gentleman- and
one that stood to bee Consul att Smirna. He departs in a day or two
to prevent Imbezzlement of goods, w[hi]ch may bee, Heaven bless
his Indeavour to the benefitt of the Intressed. The Parliam[en]t are
still upon the act of pardon and besides the seaven excepted for life
and estate (as in my last) t[ha]t were the King's Judges for estate all
they said judges will bee excepted and 20 principall men besides
those the[y] have already past of 20 as p[er] margent.

[In margin] Speaker Lenthall, St John, Vane, Sidenham, Ireton,
Haselrigg[2]

1. Mr Paige – which Mr Paige? See Steckley for discussion of the family. (G.F. Steckley ed. *The Letter Book of John Paige, London Merchant 1648* London 1984) John Paige, the cousin of the John Paige in London, would appear to have left Plymouth about this time.

2. William Lenthall d 1662. Speaker of the House of Commons 1640–1653, of Parliament 1654–5, 1659–60. d. 1662. (Pepys X p 231)
Oliver St John d 1673. (Pepys X p 373) He was related by marriage to Oliver Cromwell. Chief Justice of Common Pleas in 1648 but refused to sit on tribunal which tried the king. He was declared incapable of office in 1661 and went into exile in Germany in 1662.
Sir Henry Vane was imprisoned in the Scillies. Tried and executed 1662
Col. William Sydenham was expelled from Parliament. (Pepys I p 21 & note 2)
Ald. Sir John Ireton (brother of Henry) in the Tower until death in 1689.
Sir Arthur Heselrig died in the Tower 1661.

87. Mr James Thierry London 15th June 1660

S[i]r,

Yours of the 18/[8] Currant I have received with the inclosed for Mr John Sparke w[hi]ch shall bee forwarded. Herewith you have one from Mr Bernard Sparke. I am Considering with him and Mr William Jennens about procuring letters from our King to the King of Sweden about the *Dolphin* to effect which Mr Sparke will use his interest with Sir Richard Ford, so I hope some good may come of itt. I shall endeavour to farther itt the most I cann. The summe I rec[eive]d from they Yarmouth men, was £336 st[erling] of w[hi]ch you shall have a perticular account p[er] next, how much is the principell and what for interest.

I am glad to heare of the safe arrivall of the *Halfe Moone* with returnes upon the *Dolphin*'s Cargo. Pray use all diligence to dispose of this and the former parcells as soone as you cann, to adjust all accompts upon your award about the *Dolphin*. I have not yet received any thing but am promised paym[en]t sudenly which I shall endeavour and advise you. I thanck you for your courteous offer concerning my freind Mr Lytcott I shall be very ready to serve you upon the Like occasion.

88. **Mrs Pearde** London 16th June 1660

I have received your letter and considered the Contents to which I am willing to consent provided you will then be punctuall which is but very reasonable you should after soe long time, the time you desire is till the 12th of August w[hi]ch I am satisfied with upon yo[u]r promise t[ha]t then you will order mee punctuall payment here, which you may easilie doe by a bill of Exchange. I leave it to your Care for the performance.

89. **Mr Bernard Sparke** London 16th June 1660

S[i]r,

Yours of the 13th Currant I have received with the inclosed to Mr Thierry which was forwarded, inclosed is one from him to you. I perceive you have sould 10 Pipes of the *Swan's* Oile att £40 p[er] t[on] I wish it were all disposed att that price. Att yo[u] r convenience pray bee remitting mony as you are in Cash. If you please to advise to what ¼ of the *Swan's* freight may arise to, I shall make it good to Mr Thierry in accompt. Our Court is not soe much setled yett that wee know what person about the King are fitt to assist us in our *Dolphin* businesse, but in the Intrim if you thinck fitt to write to S[i]r Richard Ford, I shall deliver him the letter, and use all diligence to the forwarding the businesse as hee shall direct.

90. **Mr Will[iam] Hill** London 16th June 1660

S[i]r,

I writt you on the 5th Currant since which nor since your departure have I had any of yours which I something strange att but I hope you will lett slipp no good oppertunity to dispose my hopps and Iron to my most advantage, that so full returne may bee made in the best Tynn by the first good conveyance. The successe of this first good adventure, will engage for the future, w[hi]ch I hope will bee an argument, to use your utmost care. Inclosed you have a rec[eip]t for a small bundle directed to your selfe aboard the *Willing Minde*,[1] Contayneing a blacke Cloth Gown, for my Aunt Moreton; w[hi]ch pray receive, and forward p[er] first, the charge she will thanckfully repay you.

1. The *Willing Mind* was a 'tin' ship It is mentioned in the 1661 port book for Falmouth with William Bewes as captain.

91. Mrs Eliza[beth] Moreton London 16th June 1660

This I send under covert to my Uncle Mr W[illia]m Hill entreating his care to receive and send forward to you togeather w[i]th the gowne I formerly writt you my good mother had given order should bee presented you. I am sorry itt hath laine to long from you, but of late here hath not byn any other convenyance then that itt goes by. I hope itt will arrive safe, and fitt to doe you service.

92. Mr Giles Lytcott London 22nd June 1660

I am now bigg with expectation of some good newes of your safe arrivall in Holland, but the last post [brought x out] brings none. I hope the next may. However I very willingly write you though there's little more then you have in my formers. George Hunt is here arrived and tells mee you intended to depart Venice in few dayes after him, w[h]ich makes mee beginn to looke out sharpe. Yet I allow time for your visiting the Emperour's Court etc. in Germany. Holland I suppose Cannot entertaine you long having seene the varities of Italy, but lett mee mind you (though to my Longer want of you) not to loose the sight of Antwerpe which will recompense the time you spend. The Chappell in the Jesuitts Church[1] I esteem [word x o] a rare peece of workmanshipp soe are the paintings of Father Leigers of that society. Yesterday Mr Richard Middleton Christned his sonne and heir *cosi va crescendo il mondo.* Jo[hn] Kent is expected here every day, soe is Dr Bacon who [word x o] takes his passage on the *Maidenhead.*
His Maj[es]tie hastens the Parliam[ent] to dispatch the act of Pardon the Judges of the late King doe many of them render themselves to the speaker, who committs them to the serjeant at Armes, 'tis reported that Scott, one of the judges fled into flanders but was taken att Gant and is brought back againe. My wonted respects to yo[u]r deare selfe and the worthy gentl[emen] your Companions.

1. The Chapel in the Jesuits' church in Antwerp In 1615 architects of the Jesuit Society started to build a new monastery and Baroque Church which was at first dedicated to the Virgin Mary but later to St Ignatius

Loyola. (It is now called St Charles Borromeus.) Rubens was asked to
paint two large altarpieces. The interior was destroyed by fire in 1718
and the paintings by Rubens and presumably those of Father Leigers
were lost http://www.geocities.com/Paris/9974/Jesuits.htm seen
24/02/05
Evelyn visited the Jesuit Church in 1641 'The Church of the Jesuits
is most sumptuous and magnificent, a glorious fabriq without, and
within wholly incrusted with marble, inlay'd and polish'd into divers
representations of histories, landskips, flowers etc. . . . There are rare
pictures by Rubens, now lately deceased, and divers votive tables and
reliques.' (Evelyn p 34)

93. Mr Roger Street London 23 June 1660

Yours of the 19th Currant I have received. I suppose you have
understood that the present Com[missione]rs for the Customs are
to be continued for yett a month longer and Consequently officers
under them, after w[hi]ch new ones will be chosen, of which
number itts supposed Sir Richard Ford will be one. Considering
his relations to Exon 'tis probable you may engage him by some
freind their, when not, I shall bee very ready to speake with Mr
Foxcraft or some one else to doe you all the Courtesie and service
I cann.
However pray endeavour what you cann by meanes to Sir Rich[ard]
Ford w[hi]ch I esteeme the surest way.

94. Mr Bernard Spark London 23 June 1660

S[i]r,
Yours of the 20th Currant I have rec[eive]d w[i]th the inclo[sed]
for which thank you. I perceive you goe on selling the *Swan's* Oile
and endeavour to gett the parcell arrived att Dartmouth in your
hands to prevent the falling [word x out] of the price, w[hi]ch
will doe very well. The *Swan's* freight I perceive for ¼ amonts
to £55 w[hi]ch must be made good to Mr Thierry but I suppose
somew[ha]t will be coming due [inserted] on what goods shee took
at freight. The parcells of sugar & Cotton arrived at Amsterdam.
Mr Thierry hath advised mee. Likewise 6/mo[nths][1] of some
sugars hee was to received out of the *Gustavus Adolphus* upon
acc[omp]t of the *Dolphin*, but of late hath said nothing of them
though I have often hinted itt to him. I returne you my thancks

for your kind offer – that I might intrest my selfe in some designes w[i]th you. My answear must bee that for the present itt will not suit with my occasions, although another yeare I should willingly embrace some such like voyage as you mention, w[hi]ch appears very pro[fit]able.

'Tis reported that the Ostenders Comissions are called In, and wee have hopes a cessation may quickly follow, because letters to that effect have past between us & the Spaniard, and no doubt but a peace would readily be entertained [betweene x out] by both partyes. Sir Rich[ard] Ford is likely to bee a Comiss[ione]r for the Customes, possibly hee may do us some favours about the *Dolphin* espetially to S[i]r William Morrish who being moved likewise, from Mr Will[iam] Jennens possibly some good may come of itt. If I cann bee servicable to present yo[u]r letters or w[ha]t else may bee neccessary I shall be ready.

1. Payment was to be made in 6 months.

95. Mr Will[iam] Hill London 23 June 1660

Yours of the 18 Currant, I have rec[eive]d [From] the incloseds [today?] I perceive Will Rogers was arrived and t[ha]t of my parsell of Iron you had then sould 4 cwt of 4 tons and hoped to dispose of the remainder & the hopps in 2 or 3 dayes. I leave it all to your care, not doubting but the tryall of this first adventure will encourage for the future. Tynn it seemes is risen w[i]th you – however you will not faile to make mee full returnes in the best of that comodity p[er] the first. If you cann give mee advice of some small things that might find quick sale w[i]th you I am willing to provide and send you itt's your notice that must bee my direction, which being punctuall I shall observe itt. All the freinds you Visited I am glad were in good health. Wee have considered of w[ha]t you writte concerning our Uncle and Aunt Vincent. Pray our respects to them, and att your Leisure acquaint them that, other then the freinds at London, there not any rings presented, had itt byn otherways the[y] would have byn Remembered among the Cheifest. If it so happens that there presents with you a conveyance for Smirna before one for London pray Loade what Tynn you may have bought for my acc[omp]t. As itt is in blocks agreeing for freight, as best you can, consigneing itt to Mr Samuel Taylor, for my accompt. This mention because the shipp *Prosperous*,[1] now on departure, is intended for that port. With my Respects presented I Remaine

1. There are references to the *Prosperous* in the 1660 port book for Penryn in June 1660, Charles Hatsell being the Captain. It had come from St Kitts. Another *Prosperous* occurs in the 1661 port book for Falmouth but on a coastal voyage with a different captain and presumably a different ship

96. Mr James Thierry London 29th June 1660

S[i]r,

Yours of the 2 July [/22 June] have ['have' x out] received for answer the some I received of the Yarmouth men was £336 as appeares by Coppy of there bond which I sent you of w[hi]ch as I am informed by the accomptant of the prize office £300 was the principall and £36 for Interest two yeares and upon making up the accompt when this bond was received for you, there was Cr[edit] given to the office for one yeares interest £18 by agreem[en]t, upon the Restoration made. This I suppose is w[ha]t you desire of Mr Thomas Fowke & Rob[er]t Ellis. I have received £260 by vertue of the award [word x o] concerneing the *Golden Dolphin's* assureance w[hi]ch I give you Cr[ed]it for in acco[mp]t. I have perused what you say about the intended designe for Barbados and Guinny itt's a probable buisnesse [sic], and I thanck you for offering mee a part but my present occasions will not conveniently permitt mee to intrest my selfe in itt, however I shall bee very ready to assist Mr Whiting the best I cann, itt will requisitte hee bee very understanding and resolute man, that undertakes this businesse, and that hee goe well mann'd for itt has byn knowne to offten that they blacks (if that bee his designe) have endeavoured the [l x o] mastry of all, and how fatall that would prove, is easye to suppose. If you are satisfyed that hee is a fytting person [inserted] hee may deserve what he demands because the good successe of the voyage will depend on his care and diligence. I wish a good issue to your owne satisfaction. I perceive you endeavour the dispose of the Cottons & sugars arrived w[i]th you from Barbados upon the *Dolphin's* acc[omp]t the sooner disposed the better. With us here's little newes other then t[ha]t advice from Turkey sayes that Galata (a part of Constantinople) is burnt downe to the grownd. The Letter was from Mr Jonathan Dawes,[1] an Englishman resideing there. Yesterday, being Thursday, was a Publique thancks-giveing for His Maj[es]ties safe returne and settlem[ent] and the next thursday himselfe and the Dukes and both houses of Parliam[en]t dine att Guild Hall being thither invited by the Citty.

1. Jonathan Dawes, an East Indian and Levant merchant. (Woodhead p 58)

97. (in Italian) [**Signore Jacopo Baldinotti** ? no name given]

My master etc.

I hope that you have received mine of the 10[th] May sent by way of Venice in which I let you know that the parcels of books and other things sent by Mr Harry Browne are safely received as you would understand from my previous letter.

With my friend on the *Hannibal* for Livorno I sent you a letter etc. that I believe is arrived, if it is it will have had much care. The casks of oil and wine that you sent me have not yet arrived but we are expecting every hour with the ship *Virgin*. I am obliged to you greatly for presents so large. At the proper season of the year I will serve you with some seeds of flowers which you desire. My respectful salutations to all gentlemen and patrons of Lucca with every great affection. With very great affection I kiss their hands. London 5 July 1660

98. **Mr William Jennens** London 7th July 1660

S[i]r,

Yours of the 3[r]d Currant I have rec[eive]d and for answear please to noate that to foot of the acc[omp]t sent you there ought to be added in your Cr[edit] £31.10s for the losse from Mr Joyner of £50 and £21.19.3d for the nett of your Cotten wooll, 4 baggs and then the ballance to you will bee £23.15.3 ½ which if you find accordingly, I shall desire Mr Sparke to pay you w[i]th the 10s yo[u]r serv[an]t paid att my request. Our hearty respects presented.

Foot of former acc[omp]t	£1427.05.02½
By Cotten wooll	£ 21.19.03
Mr Joyners losse	£ 31.10.00
by Cash paid	£ 00.10.00
	£1481.04.05½
former accompt	£1456.19.02
	£ 24.05.03½

99. Mr Roger Street London 7th July 1660

S[i]r,

I have yours of the 30th past. For answear, I have spoken w[i]th a freind belonging to the Customhouse here, who tells mee that very many make addresses to they Com[missione]rs in the same manner as I intend to w[hi]ch they have this generall answear that they know not of any altera[t]ion or new Com[missione]rs but if t[ha]t should happen and they of the number, they will doe any Courtesie, thus the[y] give the same dispatch to all that solicite them. I shall be carefull in case of alteration, timely to move Mr Foxcraft[1] in yo[u]r behalfe. I am told itt's a sure way to make the Collector yo[u]r freind, for those he [ls x o]presents are oftenest confirmed. I shall bee mindfull to doe what I cann for you.

1. Mr Foxcraft was a Customs official.

100. Mr Thomas Dethick, Mr Richard Browne London 9th July 1660

S[i]rs,

Yours of the 18th and 25th past are come to hand and w[i]th the former first bill of exchange on the Wor[shi]pp[fu]ll Will[iam] Williams for $800 att 3 m[onths] ex[ch]a[nge] at 54d in £180 sterl[ing] w[hi]ch said bill is accepted, and good paim[en]t I hope will followe. By the latter I have accompt of the 50 Piggs lead you received p[er] the *Swallowe* the price is lower then was expected, but wee hope itt was to the height of the markett, but as wee have here calculated itt, there is a difference in the weight of about 500 lb w[hi]ch pray examine least some mistake hath byn att itts delivery. The Charges too, are something high, being sold I suppose to consigne, itt's left to yo[u]rselves to rectify. With thancks for your advices I Remaine

Post Script I pe[r]ceive y[o]u have rec[eived] $50 upon Scarti's debt. I hope y[o]u wilbe carefull to p[re]vent any other losse besides time, and will follow Sig[no]re Viale the securitye. Our says w[i]th y[o]u I could gladly heare were sold for our conveniencye. My Resp[ect]s to Mr Angiers.

101. Mr William Jennens London 12th July 1660

S[i]r,

Since my last of 7th Currant I have not rec[eived] any from you w[hi]ch will cause Breavitye. The present is for Covert to the Incloseds and for advice that from Mr Tho[mas] White of Oporto I have bill of lading for Ninetye seaven Mill and five hundred Reis by him putt aboard the *Kingfisher,* consigned to mee, for accompt of yo[u]r Lady, Mrs Jenne[n]s, being a Leagacye left her by Mr Rob[ert] Trelawny[1] deceased, by the Inclosed you will perceive the needfull. The ship is arrived and when comes higher up I shall [waite x out] take Care of the perticulars and attend yo[u]r order for their dispose. Mr James Thierry mentions the endeavouring to get the King's Letters on our behalfe about the *Dolphin*, if you have any acquaintance att Court, that could procure them in our favour itt might do well. I suppose hee writs the same to you.

1. William Jennens wife, Elizabeth, was a Trelawny. Robert, her brother, would appear to have died in Oporto and this was a legacy left to her.

102. Mr Bernard Sparke London 12th July 1660

S[i]r,

I have not any of yours, which causeth breavity. Herew[i]th you have an inclosed. You advised mee a while since, that I might except some mony on accompt of the *Swann's* Cargo att the end of last moneth. That time being past I hope for bills w[i]th yo[u]r next and a larger [word x out] summe.

103. **Mr James Thierry** London 13th July 1660

S[i]r,

Yo[u]rs of the 16/[6] Currant I have rec[eived] w[i]th the inclosed for Mr William Jennens, w[hi]ch was forwarded and I have desired his advice about procureing Letters for us about the *Dolphin*, for as I am told, hee has acquaintance with S[i]r William Morris, Secretary[1] of State. I am expecting [yo x out] his answear and w[ha]t passeth shall advice you. I perceive you have sold all the sugars at 8d & Cottons att 15d 3 /mo[nths]. The accompt of all pray, att your conveniency.

The news with us is the committing to the Tower, the Marquesse of Argile[2], the Lord of Antrim[3], S[i]r Arthur Haselrigg and S[i]r Henry Vane divers others are under the Black rodd a few dayes will produce more. The Parliam[en]t have voted that his Maj[es]tie doe Imedeately take possession of all lands belonging to the late King; though purchased by private persons. Here you have incloseds from Exon and Plymouth. With my respects to yo[u]r selfe and Lady.

1. Sir William Morice was born in Exeter in 1602. He purchased Werrington (then in Devon) from Sir Francis Drake in 1651. MP for Plymouth 1660. He was related, through his wfe, to General Monck and acted as a go-between with Monck and the King. He was knighted in May 1660 a baronet in 1661 and became Secretary of State. He died at Werrington in 1676 and was buried there.
2. Archibald Campbell, Marquess of Argyle, was beheaded in 1661. (For details see *DNB* Vol. 9 pp 705-716.)
3. Lord of Antrim. Randall Macdonell was 1st Marquis of Antrim 1609–1683 (Pepys X p 162) Originally a royalist but joined with the Cromwellians in 1650. At the Restoration he was imprisoned in the Tower but later released and granted a full pardon.

104. **Mr Bernard Sparke** 14th July 1660

S[i]r,

Yo[u]rs of the 11th Currant, I have received With an inclosed bill for £100 att 6 dayes sight upon Mr Laurence Blancart[1], itt's with him for acceptance and shall be noted underneath. I perceive the price of Oile is advanced. I wish you may attaine your demands for itt, the whole managem[ent] I leave for my concern to your care. It's Mr Jennens' opinion that we petition his Maj[es]tie about the *Dolphin*. I should bee ready to use my utmost here, and Mr Jennens hath so much intrest with they secretary, S[i]r Will[iam] Morrice, itt's a probable meanes to doe us much good. What you two shall direct I shall endeavour to accomplish.

1. Laurence Blanchard was a London merchant. Mico & Blanchart are mentioned in the Exeter port book of 1661 (TNA: PRO E 190/953/6)

105. Mr Bryan Rogers London 14th July 1660

S[i]r,
This serves cheifly for advice that in the absence of my brother, Mr Abraham Hill, I have satisfied your draught on him for £5 payable to Mr James Haton w[hi]ch pray noate accordingly. My Respects and ready service to your good father Mr Amb[rose] Jennens, yo[u]r lady & self.

106. Mr Will[iam] Hill London 19th July 1660

I have long expected to receive some letter from you, with advice of the sale of my hopps & Iron, but have had none but that of you beginning to sell which though you say not is not quite, yet I hope ere this is fully ended and the whole proceed invested in they best Tyn to come p[er] first. You once promised a quick dispatch and confessed that that onely encouragem[en]t in the trade hitherto. I perceive but little for this first tryall, I leave it wholly at yo[u]r dispose praying to heare what's donne.

107. Mr William Jennens London 19th July 1660

S[i]r,
Yours of the 10th Currant I have rec[eive]d, the Inclosed for Holland [have x out] forwarded and that to Mr Squier's delivered. I perceive your objecting to the £20 charged for provision of monys paid and rec[eive]d by yo[u]r order. That such things betwixt my Father and your self were used to bee donne gratis, itt's likely for small paym[en]ts or had there byn any equality of business but your occations requiring more by farr with us then what wee had to trouble you with I suppose itts very reasonable what is demanded and upon perusall, you will finde itt's within

the ordinary Comission. [Ietter x out] However if you look upon itt as to much, I shall not for a small matter insist of itt with you, but leave itt to yo[u]r one dispose, to doe as you please, on answear whereof I 'll take care to Imburs you. The two assurers on the *William,* are under a Cloud and small satisfaction to be expected from them. I shall be carefull if they pay their Creditors to putt in for you. Your mony p[er] the *Kingfisher* is not yett rec[eive]d. I looke after itt with some of my owne in the same shipp

108. Mr Will[iam] Hill London 26 July 1660

[Loving U? x out]

I have yours of the 16th Currant, adviseing the sale of my parcell of Iron, att severall prices. I strange the bagg of Hopps should prove damaged, here there was not the least appeareance and to my Remembrance the[y] are alwayes kept upon boards in the Cellars, 'tis Likely it was donne att sea which should have byn Lookt too at takeing ashoare. £3.10s per cwt for hopps is soe low a price [words x o] that after that rate there will be noe encouragem[en]t for a Continuance, espetially Tyn being at soe High a price, and should you give so much as the Curr[en]t demand is, I feare mony would be Lost by itt. The whole managem[en]t I leave to you and In the Conclusions wee shall if businesse of this nature is worth the continuing. By Will Rogers I expect full returns and the investm[en]t of what I furnished you w[i]th here w[i]th the 20s. to my Coz. William. I have not lately seene Mr Delaplace when I doe I shall give him yo[u]r Resp[ec]ts. I thank you for forwarding the small bundle to my Aunt Moreton.

109. Mr Bernard Sparke London 26 July 1660

Yours of the 18th Currant, I have received, your draught on Mr Lawrence Blancart for £100 [I have x out] hee hath paid mee, w[hi]ch I passe to yo[u]r Cr[edit], as more money comes In I desire you please to be remitting itt.[of x out] The proofes taken in our adm[iral]ty Court about the *Dolphin* were all sent to Mr Thierry when he dispatch an expresse to Gottenburgh but they may be had againe if you thinck itt worth they Charge of Coppying them Here. I hope ['suppose' x out] Mr Jennens hath Consulted w[i]th you and resolved upon something. I shall use my uttmost to prosecute the businesse here as you two shall direct. I perceive you goe on selling the Oiles w[hi]ch is well that those acc[omp]t may bee ended. The Antient Com[missione]rs for the Customes do now sitt again. S[i]r Job Harby S[i]r Nich[olas] Crispe

110. Mr Thomas Dethick, Mr Richard Browne & Compa[ny] London 27th July 1660

S[i]rs,

Yours of the 2/[22 June] Currant I have received, w[i]th the needfull advice concerning yo[u]r *raggion* which I have acquainted my brother withall to which both hee and my selfe wish all prosperity. Itt's both his desire and mine, that with the very first oppertunity you please to dispose of our peece goods, if not for money, then for silke or, w[hi]ch I suppose may alwayes bee donne, bartered against Flo[rence] silkes, Our occasions require the adjusting of all accompts, therefore I urge it the more. In the receiving what Com[modity] soever pray have a great care they be answearable to [you x out] the agreements you make w[hi]ch too often fall out otherwise. (I suppose you minde remitting home the proceed of our Lead 50 piggs.)

111. Mr James Thierry London 27th July 1660

S[i]r,

Being without any of yours unanswered, cau[s]eth breavity, this serving for Cover to the inclosed for Mr Will[iam] Jennens. Mr Sparke is att Plymouth, consulting about the *Dolphin's* businesse of meanes to petition his Maj[es]tie on our behalfe. I shall use my utmost Businesse to solicite the businesse t[ha]t some good may follow. This day were erected on the Excha[nge] the statutes of the late and present King. Wee have not yet any news of the Indian shipps.[1] God send them In safety.

1. i.e. the ships of the East India Company

112. **Mr Will[iam] Jennens** London 28th July 1660

S[i]r,

Yours of the 15th [Curr x out]and 24th Curr[en]t rec[eive]d. The incloseds were forwarded. I have minded Mr Hugh Squier of your businesse att Barnstaple. Your Portugall money 97½ M[il] R[ei]s I have rec[eive]d and haveing paid the freight one p[er] Cent the Rest I delivered to Ald[erma]n Backwell's¹ servant as p[er] th'inclosed receipt. S[i]r to cleere up to you farther the Clause of provisions which you scruple, please to take notice, that that I do not Looke back into ould accompts and charge itt on them but I find the last acc[omp]t sent you by my father was 30th Sept[ember] 1656, since w[hi]ch the severall summes being Considerable were received and paid by your order. I see no reason for not charging provision as is Customary & I know itt's the same what my father intended to doe and I finde you charge 2 p[er] Cent in the Newfo[undland] bill, on acc[omp]t of the *Swann*, I would willingly that you had full satisfaction in this perticular. If I have occasions in yo[u]r parts I shall give you troble and I desire you free disposall of mee here as oppertunity presents. If your selfe, with Mr Sparke have resolved how to proceed about the *Dolphin's* businesse I shall follow. All the examinations are in the Am[ira]ltys Court to be made use of [word x out]
as need requiers. I hope some good issue to itt, if the businesse come once to heareing.

1. Alderman Edward Backwell 'The most important goldsmith of his day'. (Pepys X p 16) (See *DNB* Vol. 3 p 113)

113. **Mr Ambrose Jennens** London 2[n]d August 1660

S[i]r,

Yours of the 28th past I have rec[eive]d by the hands of Mr Joseph Allen, according to yo[u]r order therein I have paid said Mr Allen Ten pounds, he telling mee his occasions requireing such a sume. I passe itt to yo[u]r accompt. I have offered him my service and assistance. if his affaires require itt w[hi]ch I shall most willingly doe and not to him only but any other recomended from your selfe. S[i]r Wee all present you our due Respects.

114 (in Italian) [Signor Gioseppe] Baldinotti

My master etc.

Your very welcome letter of the 24th July I have received with the orders to us to make a dozen shoes, half for the summer and the rest for the winter with two soles [to withstand] water, the size intended should be the height of the old shoe sent by Signor Jacopo. In conformity with which you will be served with the greatest punctuality and I hope much to your taste. In addition you asked me to have made three pairs of boots, two for the winter and one for the summer conforming to the inclosed measure; but I find it a little difficult and do not know how we can take the measure of the foot, there is not much height to the instep [?] but the size of the calf for the other pair is strange to us in every way. I will do what can be done with great diligence and speed so that they will be dispatched with the shoes ordered for Signor Jacopo. I give infinite thanks to you, my patron, for your kindness in offering to provide and serve us with the cloth of your city but the worry is that our business, little as it is, goes another way from here straight to Turkey and we do not find much satisfaction in trading with Livorno particularly when it means exchanging our bays (imperial measure) against the drapery of Florence or Lucca because at the moment the cloth is lower in quality and is not as good as that which can be bought for the same amount and for the same reasons we favour it very little and I bring to your attention that I have had in hand from my friends in Livorno for longer than two years a quantity of the aforesaid stuff, no return from which has yet been seen.

I hope that my dear Signor Piccini will have such virtuous curiosity to come and find us, being as near as Paris to this our London not more than five days' journey. All is now stable with our King and all is at peace and not a little of joy. If Signor Vincenzo had thoughts of staying with us for a little he would find satisfaction to be near the King who is a great virtuoso and loves greatly music. He would earn enough money which is not to be sneezed at. Signor Ciccolini of Florence is on a voyage and desires to come here to serve the King and it seems to me that Signor Vincenzo and he would be able to stay readily and I would serve with pleasure my dear master and welcome him with great warmth into my home.

I would give you thanks for the oil and olives that you send with Mr Browne, but the ship on which they are loaded is not yet arrived but I cannot miss the opportunity in this our country to thank you for your kindness. Kiss the hand of your Lady wife and all my patrons etc.

In London on the 4th August 1660

115 (in Italian) **Sig[no]re Jacopo Baldinotti** ['Bla' x out]

My master etc.

My last was of the 5th past since which I have gratefully received yours. The shoes, which you ordered, are being made with every diligence and I hope successfully to your taste. The seeds of the flowers that you desired are very rare and I intend to do nothing until a friend will give me what are best which you will have together with the shoes.

This my friend (who at this moment is on a voyage for Livorno) has taken a letter which, after he has arrived safely in that city, will take his departure for Lucca where he will deliver a letter to you by kissing your hand on my part.

When our King is crowned you will have a medal but for now there is not much urgency for a coronation since it has already been declared throughout England.[1] I would dearly have loved to hear the composition produced for the reinstalment of our King, it does not appear to be dear, the subject being good. I have told Sir Eliab Harvey what you ordered me to. That gentleman has had a great honour from the King with the title of Knight of England, an honour which is much esteemed we have to call him 'your most illustrious'. To you as to all my dear patrons, I kiss your hand with great affection.

On the 4th August 1660 London

1. Medals of famous events were frequently made and collected at this time. Abraham Hill was a noted collector.

116. **Mr James Thierry** London 3th August 1660

S[i]r,

Nott haveing any of yours p[er] this week's ordinary shalbe the breifer, this serving to give Covert to the Inclosed from Mr

W[illiam] Jennens, from him I am to present a letter to the Cheife secretary of State on our behalfe concerning the *Dolphin* I hope some good may come of itt. I shall doe my utmost in the businesse. S[i]r if I cann bee serviceable to yo[u]r selfe or freinds, pray comand mee freely.

117. Mr William Jennens London 4th August 1660

S[i]r,
Yo[u]rs of the 31th past, I have received. The inclosed for Mr Thierry forwarded. That for S[i]r Will[iam] Morris[1] I was with this morning to have presented him, but could not have an opertunitye, his multiplycitye of business makes itt difficult to speake with him. Hee is removing his Lodgings into Whitehall where I shall waite on him some morning earley and give you acc[oun]t. The Papers concerning yo[u]r father shall be made up in a box, and sent.

1. William Morice had been made Secretary of State.

118. Mr Justinian Pearde London 7th August 1660

On the 12 of June I writt you which I suppose you have received. What my request was then I now confirme the rather because because [sic] the Com[missione]rs of the prize Office are disatsified in a summe [?] which an accompt from you may possibley suffitiently Cleere. Att you convenience pray doe mee this favour and Command

119. Mrs Pearde London 7th August 1660

The time is now drawing on, which your selfe desired for the payment of the £6.12.6 you are indebted to mee. I therefore desire that upon receipt hereof to take speedy care for my satisfaction, that any further trouble may bee prevented both to you and my selfe. Pray let mee heare from you by the returne of this post.

120. Mr Will[iam] Jennens London 11th August 1660

S[i]r,

I have not any of yours unanswered. This is cheifly to advise [you x out] that I was severall times to wait on S[i]r Will[iam] Morrice w[i]th your Letter in vaine but have lately had an oppertunitye. The Letter appeareing something Long he did not p[e]ruse itt but was soe much satisfied with my staying [sic] the Case, that himselfe writ a letter to the Swedish Embassador on our behalfe (coppie is inclosed) which I shall take care to deliver him, and endeavour what's possible, of all w[hi]ch you shall have advice. I was acquainted by a freind of the *Olive branch's* arrivall by your letter which was wellcome news, our concerns in her being 1/8 p[ar]te.

121. Mr Bernard Sparke Londo[n] 11th Aug[u]st 1660

S[i]r,

Yours of the 8th C[urr[ent]I have received with an inclosed accepted bill for £100, on Mr Fr[ancis] Tyssen, att day I shall demand itt, and being satisfied noate itt accordingly. I have obtained a letter on our behalfe to the Swedish Embass[ado]r which I shall deliver him, and use all meanes that some good may followe.[1] S[i]r I thanck you for yo[u]r kind offer in yo[u]r intending designe to w[hi]ch I pray good successe but my present occasions will not suite with a concernm[en]t therein, though att some other time itt's what I should willingly Imbrace. I perceive you goe on in selling the remaineing Oile. Pray continue yo[u]r care in their dispose that they acc[omp]ts may be ended. My Respects presented I Rest.

1. Thierry, Sparke, Jennens and Hill are still trying to get compensation for the *Dolphin* which it would appear was attacked by a ship under a Swedish commission. In spite of all their efforts they do not seem to have succeeded.

122. Mr William Blunden[1] London 13th August 1660

S[i]r,

This is cheifly to give Covert to the inclosed from Mr Tho[mas] Hollis – of itts receipt pray a word, and your opinion to what port of Italye hee will bee induced to goe too which will bee a Conveniency for Us to knowe.

1. William Blunden, the son of William Blunden of Basingstoke, was originally apprenticed to Richard Hill. Thomas Hollis was a partner of Richard Hill who it would seem still owed money to Richard Hill's estate.

123. Mr Will[iam] Jennens London 14th August 1660

S[i]r

Yesterday I was with the Swedish Embassador and presented him (by his secratary) the Letter from S[i]r Will[iam] Morrice on our behalfe, to whom hee professeth great respect and hath promised because I come with His recomendation that he will give mee a Letter in few dayes to the Cheif att Gottenbergh that will cause a revision of the whole businesse. If the partye that mannages for us there can showe some Just reason which I thinck may bee very easie to doe. By the next I shall advise Mr Thierye that he give timely advice to the freind at Gottenbergh to have all proofes ready.

124. Mr Hillary Hill London 14th August 1660

I have received your letter and perused the Contents, in answear to which pray take notice that my father hath not in his will released you the £26 hee Long since Lent you, but left that and many other debts to my care for the speedy recovery w[hi]ch I must by all meanes endeavour to doe for the satisfying of Legacy[es? -blots] and other debts for his estate in short time to be paid which forced mee to call upon you. However I should bee very ready to doe you all the courtisie I can, which is onely to the time, and if you take six moneths to pay the whole I shall be content to expect soe Long. My advice is that you take care to be paying in some mony as you find conveniencye rather then by delay to put mee upon inconvenience of other proceedings which I shall unavoydeably [due x o] bee ingaged to doe because of an Inventory I give in to the court. Here, whereby this some you owe, will appeare to be due upon bond, and thereby I shall be forced to take such remedyes, as would be very contrary to my present Intention, or desire. With my Respects to your selfe and the freinds with you.

125. Mr W[illiam] Hill London 14th August 1660

The want of any from you so Long time makes mee wonder, were I not well assured of your care in the managem[en]t of my small concernm[en]ts. I should not tell how to understand yo[u]r silence, but my hopes are that good accompts, and full returns will make full satisfaction, in confidence of which, I enlarge not, but leaveing all to yo[u]r dispose.

126. Mr James Thierry London 17th August 1660

S[i]r,

I am still without any of yo[u]rs unansweared, since my Last I have been endeavouring about the *Golden Dolphin's*[1] businesse. I first waited upon S[i]r Will[liam] Morrice, Secr[eta]ry of state to our king, and acquainted him of the whole businesse, and soe urged the Justnesse and reasonablenesse of our case, that hee writt a letter on our behalfe to the Swedish embassador, Frisendo, residing here, which I delivered to his secratary and hee to the Embassador, whose answear was, [word x o] That hee doubted not but those of Gottenburgh would doe us right, but I tould him, wee had found the Contrary, in conclusion, he hath promised mee a letter to the Judes att Gottenburg, which will bee efectual to have a revision of our cause, if good reason bee shewed that It ought to bee soe, which I suppose is easie to doe. The letter I am promised the next weeke, if soe you shall have itt. I give you this timely advice that you may have time to write to the freind that followed the business, to have all proofes in readyness now in case those people make us noe satisfaction, then the whole proceedings are to bee ['authorised' x out] authenticated and removed into our admiralty Court where upon peruseall, and the equaty of our demand considered, wee may peticon the King and obtaine Letters of M[a]jaet[ie] but till wee are denied iustice att Gottenburgh nothing farther is to be done here.

1. The two ships which suffered disasters were the *Golden Dolphin* and the *Dolphin.* Here there would seem to be some confusion for it was the *Dolphin* which was captured by a Captain under a Swedish commission.

127. Mr Philip De Pape[1] London 17th August 1660

Middleburrow

S[i]r,

I have since the death of my good mother, Mrs Agnes Hill, rec[eive]d yours of the 9 & 14 Currant, the former by Mr John Lane who is a p[er]son wholly unknowne to mee but I cannot doubt him to be otherwise then the person he pretends by the papers and many publique writings he hath[word x out] with him. The businese of the Shipp *Eagle* which he speakes of I am very much unacquainted w[i]th, itt being transacted so Long before my time, but perusing [words x out] some papers, I find a bond (Coppie enclosed) of Mrs Ellen Lane, the Grandmother, & Mr Ric[hard] Lane, the Uncle to this Mr John Lane obleigeing themselves to save my father harmelesse for whatever either him Selfe or any by his order, should act for them in this businesse. The Coppie I send you, in case Mr Lane should Joyne with Mr Colwell in prosecuting the suite, it might doe you service, for if this Mr Lane should desire his right[inserted] title from either his Grandmother or Uncle Ric[hard] Lane (as certainely he does [NB bracket missed out] then this bond obleiging them to save harmelesse my father or any acting by his order, will most certainely cleere you, and will bee by far the easier way, then if any damage should arrise and you forst to pay, should endeavour to recover it of us, and wee returne again of him, w[hi]ch must Consequently follow, but this a great time and expence whereas you have now a better meanes in yo[u]r owne hand espetially if you insist upon this -That Mr Richard Lane was yo[u]r principall & Correspond[en]t through the whole businesse, w[hi]ch I suppose you may easily make appeare by his letters to you & yo[u]rs to him, besides as I understand this Mr John Lane desires not his title from Mr Richard Lane, so you may the easier defend yo[ur]selfe for his Joyning w[i]th Colwell is for noe other way then to recover of you what you have so long defended.

1. Philip de Pape was a merchant in Middleburg who had been a correspondent of Richard Hill many years previously. The whole episode shows the necessity for merchants to keep their accounts and copies of letters for a long period of time in case there should be any queries many years later.

128. Mr Tho[mas] Trewolla sen. London 21th August 1660

By yours to my brother, I take notice w[ha]t you say co[n]cerning
Mr Cotten[1] to w[hi]ch I answeare That by my memory I doe not
remember any thing of the businesse, but itt's Likely that my father
did receive £10 of you which was allowed by Mr Cotten, upon my
father's note to the sub Com[missione]rs of the Prizes office at
Plymouth, and they, if itt bee paid him, will charge us with itt in
our accompts, if not and produceing the note (which is the only
proofe that itt's unsatisfied) I shall take care that right bee done to
all partys. Our Respects to your selfe, our Couzens and the freinds
w[i]th you.

1. This episode again shows the difficulties Thomas Hill was having with
   transactions which had happened many years before. It would seem
   that some were trying to take advantage of his lack of information in the
   hope that he would not be able to trace the papers concerned.

129. Cosen Tho[mas] Trewolla London 21th August 1660

I should bee very willing to imploy a stock to your Towne & selfe
if you could give mee advice of some goods with us that would
find a quick dispatch, as Iron, Hopps, Cloath, Hatts or what else
your shopps might vent upon a little encouragem[en]t. Some thing
might be done for a tryall and as that succeeds, soe wee might
proceed. Pray att Leisure Lett mee have yo[u]r advice fully. My
Respects to all friends.

130. Mr Will[iam] Jennens London 21th August 1660

S[i]r,
For answear to yo[u]rs of the 14th and 17th Curr[en]t The Inclosed
to Mr Pate was delivered. The *Dolphin's* I am mindfull of and doe
make use of my Lord Whitelock's[1] Intrest with the [letter x out]
Embassador which I hope may doe us much good service. The Letter
which The Embassador hath promised, will bee delivered mee to
forward and I have advised [word x o] Mr Thierry the needfull,
that there may be a timely provision made att Gottenburgh to have
all proofes in readinesse.
    The £20 in dispute upon yo[u]r acc[omp]t I remaine much
unsatisfied of, knowing itt was my fathers Intention to charge itt

and that Itt should not bee soe, I perceive noe reason besides yo[u]r pleasure but because I am very uwilling to differ with an intimate freind upon cleering accompts, if you please to send mee [words x out] a generall discharge, I shall order you the balance. I formerly desired a perticular of £22.10s for goods sent per the *Dolphin* w[hi]ch att yo[u]r Leisure pray lett be drawen out. Mr Robert Swale (of whom you desire an accompt) is by profession a Cheese monger, hee keeps a shopp att Billingsgate, and esteemed a man of a faire estate, and the person that gave mee this Information used this expression that hee was an Alderman fellowe.

1. Bulstrode Whitelocke, the father-in-law of Abraham Hill, had been the ambassador to Sweden at the time of Cromwell. (*DNB* Vol. 58 p 694)

131. Mr William Jennens London 28th August 1660

S[i]r,

Yours of the 21th & 24th Currant rec[eive]d with the inclosed w[hi]ch were from Mr Tho[mas] White who laded yo[u]r 100 m[il]reals[1] upon the *Kingfisher* his request is that your please to give him a discharge for said Legacye and send itt mee for hee hath entreated a Brother of his to call for itt. I have beene twice to waite on the Sweedish Embassador for the Letter hee promised on our behalfe, but cannot yet obtaine itt. As you desire I shall send you an acc[omp]t firmed, & request the same from you. I have acquainted Mr Squier what you desired. The papers you desire shall bee Looked out and sent you. The perticular of the £22.10s when the[y] come before you, pray Lett us have a Coppy. Herewith you have an Inclosed from Mr James Thierry, which is what the present offers.

1. This refers to the legacy to Elizabeth Jennens mentioned in an earlier letter.

132. Mr Barnard Sparke London 28th August 1660

S[i]r,

Yo[u]rs of the 22th Currant I have rec[eive]d the Inclosed forwarded. The letter of the Swedish Embass[ador] I am to have it from him and forward itt which I suppose may doe us some service, espetially our

freind att Gottenburgh p[re]senting itt, besides our businesse will
in a perticular manner be recommended to the L[or]d Fleetwood[1]
now on departure, soe that there appeares some hopes of a good
Issue, when not, and that wee cann there procure noe Justice, wee
may have redresse in our King's Court by Letters of Maj[es]t[ie]
as my Procter of the Adm[ir]alty adviseth, what passeth shall be
advised.

1. Lord Fleetwood. There is a problem of identity here. According to the
DNB there were two Lord Fleetwoods, both Parliamentarians. George
(*DNB* Vol.20 p.25) was a regicide and was imprisoned. Charles escaped
punishment in 1660 but was disabled for life from holding office. Neither
of these therefore would seem to fit the description. Therefore was it
another 'George Fleetwood' who was a soldier in the Swedish army
and a diplomat and a friend of Bulstrode Whitelocke? (Ruth Spalding,
Contemporaries of Bulstrode Whitelocke Oxford 1990 p 93)

133. Mr Roger Street London 28th August 1660

S[i]r,
Yo[u]rs of the 20th Curr[en]t I have received. Mr Gregory Alford[1]
to whom you desire mee to speake on yo[u]r behalfe, is a person
wholly unknown unto mee but I have [tould x out] acquainted
Mr Sowden what you desire, his answear is that the party is very
Little of his acquaintance, however wee have joyntly resovled [sic]
to find him out, and to endeavour a promise from him of what
you desire. I wish itt may succeed to your minde. I shall In this
and any thing else bee most ready [serve you x out] to afford my
utmost assistance.

1. Gregory Alford. The Alfords were a Dorset family. One Gregory Alford
was Mayor of Lyme.

134. Mr Will[iam] Hill London 28th August 1660

I have yours of the 16th Currant perceiveing how you have
disposed of my Iron, and one bagg of Hopps, the paym[en]t to
bee att Mich[ael]mas which I suppose you know is not for my
greatest conveniency because quicke returns is Like to be the
onely encouragem[en]t of this trade, since itt's done, 'tis well, but
pray take the buyers note payable to my selfe or order, for some

reasons. That you are proffered £4 per c[w]t for the remaineing bagg of Hopps I take notice you know what's to be done for my most advantage, soe pray act accordingly.

I mett Will[iam] Rogers upon the Excha[nge] [1] but find you have not made mee any returns upon him, which expected and you offten promised. Most men would have advanced mony haveing goods in their hands, and y[ou]r selfe espetially some mony That I lent you, being long since due, I shall say noe more but desire an end of this small acc[omp]t by w[hi]ch may bee guessed what encouragem[en]t there will be to continue the trade.

1. The Exchange. A description was given by Schellinks when he went to the Royal Exchange in August 1661. (Maurice Exwood & H.L. Lehmann eds.*The journal of William Schellincks' travels in England 1661–1663* London 1993 p 51) 'This building is very similar in style to the Bourse at Amsterdam, but somewhat more square; it has a tower in Cornhill, on whose top, as well as on the four corners of its roof and above every arch, stands a gilt grasshopper. In niches all round stand the statues of 26 Kings and queens . . .'

135. Mrs Alice Pearde London 30th August 1660

I writt you a few dayes since to which I have not any answear although itt might well have returned before this. You knowe what my desire is, to w[hi]ch I pray a speedy answear and Complyance in paym[en]t of the small some you owe mee, to avoyd the trouble and charge of more Letters and other inconveniencys to you if you longer dely mee. Pray a word per the first.
[words x out]

136. Mr John Byam London 31th August 1660 [words crossed out]

S[i]r,
Yours of the 7th Currant I have received with the inclosed folio from Kirker, for which I thanck you. The Pope's medalls formerly desired, since they wilbe deare, itt matters not to buy them so wee shall save you that troble.[1] The gloves I hope will come safe to hand. Pray make use of mee here with the same freedome you see I make w[i]th you. A friend of mine is willing to have a trade of strings[2] from Rome to entertaine such a Corrispondency. Let him writ mee and what Method must be used for his Imbursement

of the cost and Charges and How the[y] can be dispatched and what else is necessary. I wish this may find you [inserted] with content resetled at Naples. Our freind, Mr Lytcott is in safety with us. Yesterday came out the Long expected act of Oblivion.[3] The act for the Pole money[4], for Intrest [expected x out] 6 p[er] C[en]t and for Juditiall proceedings. Of your Couzen Hatsell I cann give you no acc[omp]t onely that I spoke with him here about 4 mo[nth]s since and suppose him still att Plymouth. If I heare any thing otherwise shall advise you. I am sure your occasion sometimes require a freinds assistance here. Pray make use of mee in what ever I may be serviseable to you & Comand mee with all freedome. Yesterday were Chosen foure Com[missione]rs out of whome the King Chuseth two, to Consult with them for the most advantageous manageing the Italian trade. The names as p[er] margent. all traders to Spaine, Portugall, Turky etc. have donne the Like. [names at side] Mr John Mico, Mr W[illia]m Will[iam]s, Mr Giles Lytcott, Mr John Lewis.[5]

1. The Pope in 1660 was Alexander VII (1655-1667)
2. strings i.e. strings for musical instruments such as lutes.
3. The act of Indemnity and Oblivion for all offences committed in the Civil War and during the Commonwealth. The regicides and a few others were exempted. Bulstrode Whitelocke escaped partly by paying a man heavily for an introduction to the King. (Hutton p 133) His loyalty to Cromwell had been rewarded in 1652 when, as Evelyn says the Queen's House in Greenwich was 'given by the rebels to Bulstrode Whitlocke, one of their unhappy counsellors, and keepers of pretended liberties'. (Evelyn p 220)
4. Pole money i.e. the Poll Tax. In order to raise the huge sum to pay off the army the Commons had decided on June 12 to impose a poll tax, by which each individual paid a fixed sum according to his rank in society. (Hutton p 138)
5. Re the commissioners for Italy Thomas later says Samuel rather than John Mico. Samuel Mico was a merchant in Italy.
   William Williams (see Woodhead p 177).
   John Lewis = Sir John Lewis? East India merchant. Member of Council of Trade 1660 (Pepys X p 232)

137. (in (Italian) **Gioseppe Baldinotti** Lucca

My Master etc.
Your welcome [letters] of the 24th July and the 4th August I have received with an inclosed for Sir Eliab Harvey which he has safely received. The boots and shoes which you ordered are all ready for dispatch at the first opportunity, which will be the ship *Providence* which starts her voyage for Livorno with another ship, with hope that she will go in safety. The boots have been made with great diligence and I do not doubt that you will find they conform to your order and please you. I would like you at times to have a little grease put on the boots to make the leather more flexible and more resistant to water which is a good practice but not to the foot nor to the oil cloth within the two soles which water will not pass. The shoes also are strong, those for the country, and the others for the city are fine. The spurs are three pairs all different with six pairs of spur points which I have sent because they cost little and these I believe are not found everywhere which possibly will be useful.[words x out] The account of all I will send.

If I had had occasion for cloth from your city rest assured that I would give you the inconvenience but the cloth is not for us. I have given you the reasons in my other letters. When the shirts are finally made I would be grateful if they could be sent to Messrs Lytcott & Co at Livorno as I mentioned in another letter. To all my friends I send greetings to each one and particularly to your wife. I kiss her hand with very great affection etc.

31st August 1660

138. (in Italian) **Sig[no]re Jacopo Baldinotti** Lucca

My master etc.
Together I have received yours of the 28th July and 4th August with the enclosed which are received. Mr Richard Middleton will reply to you shortly. I see how you are so obliging to me with new favours and my happiness is so great that I cannot repay you with deeds nor with words for our language is unknown to you and yours is foreign to me and what little I know is not enough to express those true words only ungratefully, as I would if it were my natural language.

Come now we are friends and therefore we have no need of compliments. The shoes that you ordered are ready for dispatch as I have written to Signor Gioseppe. The spectacles for distant sight you will receive together with the shoes and flower seeds of the country if I receive them in time. The music which you will send will be gratefully received. I would dearly love Signor Piccini to favour us and come to us [with such wonderful music?]. He would find the stay enjoyable and much to his liking. We are not strange people as perhaps some believe. Sir, we have much bread, wine and good meat and he would not die of hunger even if all Lucca came.

See how I speak to you but to end for a time, grant my due reverence to all patrons and to you particularly.

Last August 1660 London

(On the other side) – I know nothing of Mr Riccaut[1], the debtor of Sig[nor]i [?] Burlamacchi.

1. Riccaut. Is this Paul Rycaut who later accompanied Heneage Finch, the Earl of Winchelsea, to Turkey?

139. Mr Tho[mas] Dethick Mr Richard Brown & Compa[ny] London 31 August 1660

S[i]rs,

Yours of the 13th Currant I have received with an inclosed bill of exchange for $320 att 52d per dollar 3/ mo[nths] on Mr Samuel Barnardiston,[1] which said bill he hath accepted att day I question not punctuall payment which shall bee noted to yo[u]r Cr[edit] upon accompt of lead.

I hope you have before this found to dispose our Hounscott Sayes which have layne by too long, I feare to their prejudice. Pray favour me to dispose them as soon as may bee according to former requests, that all accompts may be ended for our greater conveniencye. Yesterday being appointed to choose four of the most understanding merchants trading to Italie (out of w[hi]ch his Maj[es]tie choose two) to bee Com[missione]rs to bee by the Counsell consulted with for the advantageous managem[en]t of that trade, the choise was made accordingly which were Mr Samuel Mico, Mr W[illiam] Williams, Mr Giles Litcott and Mr

John Lewis. The long expected act of Oblivion is now published with them for pole money, for interest of mony att 6 per cent and judiciall proceedings.

1. Samuel Barnardiston. Knighted. Deputy governor of the E. India Company 1668. (Woodhead p 137)

140. Mr James Thierry London 31st August 1660

S[i]r,

Yours of the 17/[7] Currant I have received the Inclosed forwarded at your conveniency shall expect the acc[omp]ts of the returnes from the Barbados on the *Dolphin's* accompt. Herewith you have an inclosed from Mr Bernard Spark. I have byn severall times with the Swedish Embassador for the Letter he promised on our behalfe [to] the Cheife of Gottenburghe about the *Dolphin's* businesse. I am now goeing again for itt and if I cann obtaine it shall goe Herewith Inclosed. I am often demanded for Barrillia[1] if you could with conveniency order some Hither I doubt not but itt would turne well to accompt, as you have encouragem[en]t please to proceed, and in all things shall bee servisable to you to the uttermost.

1. barillas were soda plants see Roseveare *Markets and Merchants* p 190

141. Mrs Alice Peard London 15th Sept[ember] 1660

I have received [your Letter x out] and perused yo[u]r Lett[e]r that when I forbore you the payment of what was my due for three months [word x o] at your earnest request and promise that I should then bee fully satisfied, I expected your punctuall performance, and not the Least thought of y[ou]r desireing Longer time, which I resolute not to grant for I perceive my former civility but [I x out] ill requited, your answear, to my full satisfaction I expect by the first, if not when you heare from mee next it shall be in another manner which is for yo[u]r interest to prevent. I am in earnest & will not bee any Longer delayed.

142. Mr Will[iam] Jennens London 15th Sept[ember] 1660

S[i]r

Yours of the 11th Curr[en]t I have received that to Mr Thierry forwarded. Mr Squier shall have his att his returne from Gravesend, which may bee in a day or two. When I meet Mr White I shall acquaint him what you write. I have att last procured the Sweed[ish] Embassador's Letter on our behalfe to the cheife att Gottenburgh, itt sealed soe I have not the Coppy, but If it be needfull I suppose with gratuity to the secratary its may be procured, by the next I intend to send it to Mr Thierry together with a Letter of a freind who is intimate with the Lord Fleetwood gonne now to reside theire recommending our businesse to him, and to intreat his assistance. What passeth shall advise you. On Thursday night dyed the most hopefull Duke of Gloucester[1] to the unspeakeable greife of his Maj[es]tie and the whole Cort.

1. The Duke of Gloucester, the younger brother of Charles II, died on the 13th September 'either from complications resulting from smallpox or from the attentions of his doctors'. (Hutton p 149) This was to prove a major disaster for the later succession and brought great grief to the King.

143. Mr Bernard Sparke London 15th Sept[ember] 1660

S[i]r,

I have not any of yo[u]rs unansweared. This serves for advice that I have received £100 St[erling] by the bill you sent mee on Mr Francis Tyssen which I pass to yo[u]r Cr[edit]. I have at Last etc. as is above written.

144. Mr Roger Street London 15th Sept[ember] 1660

S[i]r,

Yours of the 11th Curr[en]t I have received & enquired concerning Mr Corbin who you mention. Mr Sowden I have spoken with who saith he knowes him nott and Ald[erman] Stock is continually out of towne and how to have a Letter to him on your behalfe I know nott, nor from whome to desire itt. I am sorry that what you request is not in my owne power to performe [where x out] were it I assure you [should x o] I would doe you any Courtsie, but itt falling otherwayes, you are not to blame mee.

145. Mr Ambrosse Jennens [illegible scribble] London 18th Sept[ember] 1660

S[i]r,

I having understood by Mr Bryan Roger's Letter to my Brother that Mr Joseph May had paid him £10 which I lent him here Inclosed send you the note hee gave mee desireing that summe may be paid you, and that itt be past to the Cr[edit] of my father in accompts betwixt you – and upon the same accompt I have ordered Mr Pascoe to pay you some money which I suppose hee will shortly doe and entreat you to receive itt for cleering the whole accompt betwixt your selfe & my father, very many occasions have deffered itt longer then I expected but now itt may be donne upon advice from you what summe you will please to allow upon accompt of Provision for the Prize office[1] for my uncle Will[iam] Hill's part. I formerly paid £10 to Mr Joseph Allen upon yo[u]r Letter which I noate to accompt.

1. Ambrose Jennens himself had been the Prize Officer for Falmouth.

146. Mr John Pascoe London 18th Sept[ember] 1660

About three moneths [agoe x out] since I writt you intreating that you would pay the rent due from you till ['Chrmas' x out] Mich[ae]lmas last to Mr Ambrosse Jennens, who I have advised may expect it from you, so therefore I desire you not to faile of a steady paym[en]t and for what will bee since due is belonging to my Brother, Mr Abraham Hill, who will write you him selfe. Pray cleere this businesse as soone as may bee.

147. Mr Andrew Hill London 18th Sept[ember] 1660

I am to entreat you at your owne conveniency & the sooner the Better that you would favour mee to even all accompts betwixt the old Rowland & Skerdon of S[outh] Bovey that is for what is due from them to the Last Chr[ist]mas for that belongs to mee to looke after butt from t[ha]t time itt is my Brother's who will agree with Mr Tho[mas] Glasse to whome hee hath sould the House and land for £255 w[hi]ch wee suppose is to the full value.

148. Mr James Thierry London 21th Sept[ember] 1660

S[i]r,

Yo[u]rs of the 14/[4] Currant I have received. The Inclosed from Mr Hans Hanssen.[1] I have Likewise understood the Contents which gives small hopes about the *Dolphin's* businesse – however wee must use all meanes. I have att last prevailed with the Sweedish Embassador for his letter on our behalfe to the Cheife att Gottenburgh which you have inclosed & I wish itt may doe us service. If wee perceive itt helps us not some other Course must bee thought upon. I take notice what Mr Sellis Marcelles writes you that hee intends to give his Letter of Atturney to S[i]r Richard Ford to recover his losse from the Assurers on the *North Lyon*. I wish he may recover what's his due but other proofes must be produced and more Authentique then what wee have had- and if such could be sent us wee have often desired no doubt but wee might bee as serviceable to you as another, however hee may dispose of his owne businesse as hee pleaseth, but any other that manages this businesse must unavoydably bee att an expence by renewing the whole which continued in our hands will be saved.

1. Hans Hanssen was a correspdondent of Thierry in Sweden

149. Mr Tho[mas] Dethicke, Mr Richard Browne & Compa[ny] London 21th Sept[ember] 1660

Sirs,

Yours of the 3rd Currant ['I have' x out] is come to hand with an inclosed bill of Exchange for $270 att 53 7/8 [d] 3/mo[nths] in £60.12s.2¼d[1] by Mr William Gardiner[2] which hee hath accepted, and att day I question not punctuall complyance which shall bee noted accordingly. What I formerly entreated of you about the probability of an errour in the waight of our Lead 50 piggs by the *Swallowe,* I hope you have examined and finding itt accordingly will passe it to our cr[edit] in accompt. I perceive the fall of the discompt upon silcke, if I mistake not you had in time our desires to dispose the Peece goods in your hands as best you could which probably would [have x out] have byn to our advantage but now I feare the Contrary. Pray therefore to end all accompts dispose of them all as best you cann to our most advantage.

1. The bill for $270 was at an exchange rate of 53 7/8d per $ to be paid in three months.
2. William Gardner (Woodhead p 75)

150. Mrs Alice Peard London 22th Sept[ember]

I have received your Letter and desire that, if on receipt hereof, you want convenience to remitt what you owe by exchange that then you please to pay itt to Mr Thomas Dennys of Barnstaple for the use of Mr Hugh Squier who upon notice will repay mee here.

151. Mr Bernard Sparke London 22th Sept[ember] 1660

S[i]r,
Yours of the 19th Curr[en]t I have received. The inclosed forwarded. Herewith you have coppie of Mr Hans Hanssen's Letter as I had itt from Mr Thierry, by the Contents there's but little hopes of the *Dolphin's* businesse. When you have perused itt pray send itt to Mr Jennens, in the intrim I have sent Mr Thierry the Letter I obtained from the Sweedish Embassador and what Good success follows wee must expect and accordingly proceed, as you dispose of more Oiles I shall desire advice.

152. Mr Will[iam] Jennens London 22th Sept[ember] 1660 a letter forwarded to Mr Wil[iam] Browne of Plymouth

S[i]r,
This serves cheifly to give covert to the inclosed from Holland and for advice that the Letter I obtained from the Sweedish Embassador on our behalfe I have forwarded to Mr Thierry from whom I attend notice of the successe.

153. Mr Philip De Pape London p[ri]mo October 1660

S[i]r,

Yours of the 11th past I have received. Mr John Lane (the party formerly with you) hath showed mee the Letters of administration to him selfe for the estate of his uncle Mr Richard Lane whose wife now living did refuse itt, as appears by the Letters soe that I suppose hee is the partie in Law that is capeable of recovering and discharging debts due to the estate of his deceased Uncle. If a freindly conclusion of this businesse could be made I suppose itt would be most agreeable to both partyes for your security hereafter. I question not but this Mr John Lane will give you what reasonably may bee desired to defend you & yours against the Claimes of all persons whatsoever. Pray S[i]r if [he x o] you come to a Conclusion with him, and he gives you a generall discharge, procure one for me giving mee a word of advice. If I may in the least be serviceable to you here freely Command.

154. Mr Benja[min] Childe London 28th Sept[ember] 1660

I am indebted answear to yours of the 20th past and perceive the new obligation you have upon mee in the huge Civility you were pleased to afford my friend Mr Angier for which I give you my hearty thanks and should gladly requite itt. Your excellent Company was much wanted, and as much desired att Mr Thomas Stone's[1] wedding w[hi]ch was yesterday celebrated his Lady young and handsome with £1,500 they say. Mr Lytcott and your Servant were in a strict relation Obliged to attend the Lady Bride in the Capacity of Bridesmen, a honour Mr Mellish was designed to but why he did not performe I must not Judge, his companye wee had with divers more who wee two entertaine this night *according to the English custom. If you had been here, dear one, you would have enjoyed it greatly, we have always longed for the consolation of so much happiness.* Secretary Thurlo[2] is retired from any publique imploym[en]t but is not in his Maj[es]tie's displeasure that I heare of. I have bin favoured with the relation of your *allegrezze* upon his Maj[es]tie's safe returne which was very noble & splended and could not be otherwise when you were soe cheife an Instrum[en]t.[3] This goes by our freind Mr Jonathan Parker whom god send in safety and good successe to his designes w[hi]ch I should gladly see. Pray my hearty Salutes to your *Sig[no]ra Comadre* when you writ her, the lik[e] to all the freinds with you. If I can be any way of Serviceable to you here freely Comand mee.

1. Thomas Stone. I have several references to 'Thomas Stone' but it is not clear which one this is – possibly the Thomas Stone of Bristol who was apprenticed to a grocer in 1643, the son of Edward Stone? There would seem to be several weddings celebrated as the various merchants returned back to England.
2. Secretary Thurlow. John Thurlow had been Secretary of State during the Interregnum. He was described as 'one of the best administrators England has known, his speciality being the gathering of intelligence'. (Hutton p 13)
3. This remark 'you were so cheife an Instrument' is puzzling.

155. Mr Selwyn London 30th Sept[ember] 1660

The good opertunity of Mr Parker intending for your Citty is the occasion of my Letter. I am to thank you for many Civilities but more espetially for the huge favour you shewed to my friend Mr Lytcott as hee pased your parts. I am uncapeable of requiteing of the least of the many I stand Obleiged for but in whatsoever I may seeme serviceable to you pray comand mee. Mr Parker (whom God send in safety to you) will be able to give you a full relation of the late transactions in England perticulars there are too many for the narrow Compase of this paper, to which I referr you to your good selfe Mr Dreydon, Mr Hobson etc. my kindest salutates & wishes for all hapinesse.

156. Mr Groves

I am to give you my hearty thanks for a most Courteous Letter of yo[u]rs which was delivered mee by Mr Rich[ard] Middleton for your expression of respects therein I am hugely obleiged. Such favours being far beyond my small deserts. The Civilities you showed to Mr Angier I esteeme them as donne to my Selfe, and noate itt ann aditionable obligation to your former. This goes by our friend Mr Jonathan Parke[r] whom I intreat to kisse your hands on my behalfe. My Respects to Mr Groves, Sig[no]re Riccardo and the frends w[i]th you. London Sept[ember] 30th 1660

157 (in Italian) **Sig[nor]e Jacopo Baldinotti**

My master etc..

This will be presented to you by Mr Jonathan Parker together with the six pairs of glasses which your ordered, the one pair of which is bound with gold as also two razors. They are the best found here and I hope they will be to your liking. The seeds of flowers promised from my friend have not yet been received but shortly they will be despatched to you. I believe in your parts there are better flowers and seeds than we have in these cold countries. Your letter to Sir [Eliab] Harvy is received safely and when I receive a reply I will send it to you but I believe that he has in fact forgotten the Italian language.

158. **Mr Will[iam] Jennens** London 2th October 1660

S[i]r,

Yours of the 25th past I have rec[eive]d. The inclosed forwarded. Herewith you have your acc[omp]t, the ballance whereof being £44.5.3½. I doe by this post intreat Mr Barnard Sparke to Imburse you. Only please to take notice that for some yeares wee have disburst a Considerable Summe for port of Letters which by your order will be placet to Mr Thierry's accompt but in Case hee doth not wholly allow itt itt itt [sic] must afterwards be charged notwithstanding what now paseth between Us. Inclosed you have a Letter from Mr Thierry.

All your papers with us shall in a few dayes be Lookt out & sent as you order. I shall give your respects to Mr Squier. I have not heard that hee intends into the Country.

159. **Mr Bernard Sparke** London 2[n]d October 1660

S[i]r,

This serves cheifely to give covert to the incloseds and to entreat you att your conveniencye to pay unto Mr Will[iam] Jennens £44.5.3½ out of what may be due to our part out of the *Swann's* Oiles. I pray the favour of you itt being to ballance accompt betwixt us, soe accordingly pray take an acquittance.

160. Mr James Thierry London 5th October 1660

S[i]r,

This serves cheifly to advise the receipt of yours of the p[ri]mo currant. The incloseds forwarded. By the Contents of Mr Hans Hanssen's Letter I perceive Little hopes of the *Dolphin*'s businesse, wee must have patience and expect the effects of the Embassador's Letter to those att Gottenburgh when not, and that wee cann have noe Satisfaction this way, some other course is to be endeavoured. I shall attend Mr ['Sparks' x out] Jennens' and Mr Sparke's opinion, and act accordinglye from the former you have an inclosed.

161. Alice Pearde Barnstaple 6th Detto 1660

That I had rec[eive]d £6.12.6 of Mr John Clerk & dil[ivered] to him her husband's bond & the security given to R.H. That she should ord[e]r J[oh]n Clerk to make mee some pr[e]sent for the paines in the businesse.

162. Henry Mellish & Browne 8th d[et]to

To understand the disposal of 3 Jarrs Olives they rec[eive]d from Baldinotti of Lucca w[hi]ch they promised to send p[er] the *Maidenhead*.

163. Samuel Taylor[1] Smirna 16th Octob[er] 1660

S[i]r,

I am indebted answear to severall of yo[u]rs. The latter having inc[uded] Invoice & bill of lading for Three bales Ardasse[2] silk by the *Greyhound* w[hi]ch I have rec[eive]d & noate upon acc[omp]t betwixt yo[u]rselfe & my father. The ballan[ce] whereof being $5.09 I pray make good to the Acc[omp]t of my bro[the]r Mr Ab[raham] Hill w[hi]ch shalbe well etc.

1. Samuel Taylor was a merchant in Smyrna see TNA: HMC Finch 1 p 300 1663
2. Ardass silk. 'The least desirable export grade [of silk] was *shirvani* silk, called *ardas* by the Europeans . . . but . . . was not necessarily unpopular in Europe.' Rudolph P.Matthee *The Politics of Trade in Safarid Iran: Silk for Silver, 1600–1730* (Cambridge 1999) p 37

164. (in Italian) **Sig[nor]e Gioseppe Baldinotti**

My Master etc..

This serves solely to dispatch the bill of lading enclosed for the shoes and boots with the ship *Providence* which goes consigned to Messrs Lytcott & Gascoigne for your account as you will see by the aforesaid letter which should arrive in safety. Oblige me by paying the charges for all to the aforesaid Lytcott if you find the enclosed account to your liking. Your letters to Sir Theophilus Biddulph in your last letter of 25th ult I have received as also the other for Sir Eliab Harvey. The latter is in the country for the most part and I believe has almost forgotten the Italian language and more he has not much liking for writing but any way he recommends himself to you with much kindness and has given order for making mention of his friendship for you and your wife and all the friends and patrons. London 12th October 1660

Sig[no]r Gioseppe Baldinotti owes for the cost of the
articles described below

Shoes 24 pairs at 5s per pair	£ 6.00.00
Boots 3 pair	£ 4.10.00
Spurs 3 pairs, 6 pairs of spur points & the case	£ 0.11.00
Spectacles 6 pairs two of which bound with gold, ordered by S[igno]r Jacopo	£ 0.12.00
Two razors sent with the spectacles consigned to Mr Jonathan Parker	£ 0.06.00
	£11.19.00

@ 51½d per $ = $56.05.00

165. **Mr James Thierry** London 12 October 1660

S[i]r,

Two dayes since Mr De Peister delivered mee yours of the 15th Curr[en]t with three certificats concerning the Three shipps you have Loaden and intend for the barbados. Withall I perceive your doubt, because of the Late act published of Navigation, which prohibitts all Strangers to trade to the English plantations in forraign Ships. Now Shipps belonging to English men thought Dutch built will have the Privilidge of English Ships upon ordinary Certificate that they really belong to English men that is, till the first Aprill next, after which time the Act orders what shall be a proofe t[ha]t a Ship is English, which is, that the Owner or Owners shall personally appeare before the cheife Custome-house officer of the nearest port to his aboade and there depose upon oath to whome the Shipp and loading Really belongs, So that your Shipps are not att all concerned in the act espetially if you order their dispatches from the Barbados to be before the first Aprill next w[hi]ch I suppose you may doe & order them for England as you intend. That I might have all the necessary advice for your Satisfaction I have byn with the Secretary of the Com[missioners] of the Custome and with him perused the act for Navigation upon which he gave mee his opinion w[hi]ch you have inclosed. I desired some publique writeing to send with the Shipps but his answear was hee could not give any such thing and besides though[t] itt uselesse espetially if you send by the Captaines the Authentique Papers you sent mee which I herewith returne you I question not the least of Danger if you cann dispatch them att Barbados before p[ri]mo Aprill as above for Engl[and] att their arrivall, if you cann or in the intrim may be serviceable to you or freinds pray Comand mee.

I doe not conceive that their is anythinge in the Act for Encourageing and Encreaseing of Shipping and Navigation that doth P[ro]hibit a Ship dutch built belonging to English men as proprietors and right Owners thereof to trade to the plantations or other parts beyond the seas and from thence to bring backe goods & Merchandize into England, Sam[uel] Whittell 12th Oct[ober] 1660

166. Mr Giles Lytcott, Mr Walwin Gascoigne 14th Octob[er] 1660

Sirs,

This serves cheifely for advice that I have past my bill of Exc[hange] on you for $600 paya[ble] [at x out] three monthes after date to Mr Hugh Squier or order to which pray ['pay' x out] give acceptance, and att day, punctuall payment Reimbursing your selves out of my 1/6th p[ar]te of 420 barells of Salmon consigned you p[er] the *Providence* which God send in Safety, the next proceed of which I suppose will advance this $600 besides what is to be sent by the Shipp in her future proceedings in w[hi]ch my concernm[en]t will be 1/12th as in the Joint Letter, when not you will suddenly have other effects in your hands, as 1/3rd of 1000 barrells of herrings, p[er] the *Griffen* and 100 Piggs Lead which I Lade in p[ar]ticular I thank you Mr Gascoigne for your care about my small things to Lucca & Rome of their [word x o] receipt I have had advice. Pray comand me freely.

167. 14th **October** 1660 London 1600

Three months after date of this first bill of Exch[ange] second or third not being paid pray pay unto Mr Hugh Squier or order Dollers six hundred effective Civill [Seville] & Mexico[1] for the value of him self placeing itt to acc[omp]t as p[er] advice Thomas Hill [$600 at side]

1. Civill & Mexico i.e. Seville & Mexico These dollars were the ones trusted to be of full weight.

168. **Mr Will[iam] Hill**[1] London 18th October 1660

By yo[u]rs of the 16th August I perceive the Sales of the Iron that remained in yo[u]r hands at £18 pts to be paid at the 29th past w[hi]ch time being e[x]pired I doubt not but you are fully Imbursed the proceed and have sould the remaineing bagg of hopps soe that now I expect acc[ompt]s and the full proceed returned mee in the Best Tyn and by the first Conveniancy. I cannot but wonder so many Good opertunityes presenting, I have not received something from you all this while espetially because of your often promiseing soe to doe. You have not taken care [word x out] to Supply my Coz[e]n Will[iam], your Sonne, with any apparrell and other necessarys since he hath byn with [us], and you cannot but know he wants to provide what is needfull for the p[re]sent I have p[ai]d him 20s more on yo[u]r acc[omp]t w[hi]ch pray give mee your approvall of. I should offer on his behalfe that you give him the £40 you weare to pay Mr Newball that hee may Imploy itt and so find him selfe Apparrell if you approve itt pray give mee your order by some means to make him good so much for he wants very many things which must necessarily be ['had' x out] provided. I pray Consider it and give me answear.

1. William Hill, Thomas's uncle, had two, if not three, sons, Peter the second remained in Falmouth where he became a well-known and

respected merchant. The eldest son, William, was sent to stay with the Hills in London but the uncle seemed not to be interested in this son and Thomas had difficulty in obtaining supplies for him. He later left the Hills' house but what became of him later is not known.

169. Mr Bernard Sparke London 23rd Octob[er] 1660

S[i]r ,

Yours of the 17th Curr[en]t I have received and give you thanks for makeing good to Mr Will[iam] Jennens £44.5.3½ w[hi]ch you have cr[edit] for in acc[omp]t. S[i]r Mr Thierry, itt seems, hath written you fully about his Shipps and goods now on departure for the Barbados etc. – all the Service I could doe him was to go to the Sec[retary] of the Custome-house and stating the Case to him procure his opinion in writing and firmed by him, which I forwarded to Mr Thierry itt being short, you have Coppy herewith. But to gett some publique act as hee called to send p[er] the Shipps, that the Customs would not doe, except the Shipps had byn cleered here. Now the clause you mention for the proprietors' personall appeareing to make oath for the Cleering Shipps is not in force till p[ri]mo Aprill next before which time I suppose the Shipps may be dispatcht and on their way home.

170. Mr James Thierry London 26th Octob[er] 1660

S[i]r,

With yours of the 19th Curr[en]t I have received the former Despositions, about the three Shipps and Loading of yours bound for the Barbados. I addressed my selfe to the Com[missione]rs of the Customes, intreating their directions for the secureing yo[u]r Shipps & goods, when the[y] should hereafter arrive, to which their answear was That they cannot give the Sence or interpretation of the act for Navigation, espetially to a clause that's not yet in force and if you will Dispatch yo[u]r shipps they will take noe notice of itt nor make any question except shee arrives after the first of Aprill next, w[hi]ch unavoydably must bee and then the[y] referr to the expresse word of the Act, as in the 10th page of the act (w[hi]ch I suppose you have w[it]h you) is to be observed whereby all shipps of a forrayne built and the whole Ladeing are forfeited, except the proprietor a native of England, (& that is easy enough to prove you S[i]r), doe personally appeare before the cheife custome house or officer in England nearest to his aboade, That the ship or ships w[i]th their lading doe truly & *bona fide* belong to him selfe or if there bee other proprietors they are all obleiged to doe the same for the more certaine and safe proceeding herein I have had the advice of some very able Councill who have strictly perused the Act and agree in their opinon that their is noe way possible to avoyde your personall appearance in some port of Engl[and] to make oathe, as the act directs & requires. I produced then your Letter of attorney impowring mee to make oath on your behalfe, or give Security or what else was necessary that these Shipps & Lading should returne (the Dangers of the Sea excepted) into Some port of England. They answeared, that according to the former Act, Such oath on your behalfe might have byn accepted, but this p[re]sent Act positively requireing & directing to take the p[er]sonal oath of the proprietor, their was noe way possible to avoyde itt. I am very sensible of the inconvenience of such a voyage would bee to yo[u]r selfe and affaires, w[hi]ch made mee use all meanes posible to have prevented itt but itt cannot by any way be prevented without the certain Seizure of both ships and goods when it please God they shall arrive. Another clause their is in the act most espetially to be taken notice of, w[hi]ch is that three fourth of the Seamen must bee English and so must continue all the voyage w[hi]ch is to be proved upon oath & was inserted to p[re]vent [s]trangers, and being nere home, to discharge them & take aboard English, soe that nothwithstanding the oath as above, any Shipp sailing with less then 3/4 Engl[ish] will Loose the privilidge and be forfeit as a Forriegner which clause you must carefully observe. I noate this more perticular because I finde the masters of yo[u]r Shipps to be English but no mention what the Companie are. [words x out] Now S[i]r if you should resolve to come into some port of England and make oath as is required (w[hi]ch by all is esteemed the best, safest, and only way to prevent an unavoydeable danger, they will without such certifycats fall into) you will have great conveniencyes by itt as the provideing her w[i]th Engl[ish] Marriners which is a principall thing to be regarded, next the haveing the Custome certificates [w]ith them, which besides makeing them cleere Shipps att the Barbados, itt cleers them from any of the King's men of War who, without finding such proofes, will make t[he]m prize. Besides your Shipps will make a huge Voyadge being free, for most have ordered returnes from the Barbados to Engl[and] by which means freight is advanced to six pounds st[erling] per tunne, & will continually go riseing notwithstanding the Directions of the Act. I have procured the regristring of the three Ships in our Admiralty court, to serve as occation may require. The most convenient port for your makeing oath and Dispatching the shipps I suppose to be Dover espetially because their Marriners are alwayes to bee had. Now whether you resolve upon the port of Dover or any other place I desire your timely advice, that I may wait on you, and do you what Service yo[u]r occasions require. If you think itt best, itt will bee well you come on yo[u]r owne Shipps to p[re]vent Losse of time. I should be hugely glad to see you and returne my thancks for the Civilitys Received. If in any thing I cann be serviceable to you pray freely command mee My Respects to yo[u]r good selfe and Lady.

171. Mr Bernard Sparke Lond[on] 6 November 6th 1660

S[i]r,
Since my last of the 23th past I have not any of yo[u]rs. Mr Thierry not being satisfied with w[ha]t I sent him from the Custome-house concerning the three Shipps bound for the Barbados, desired the[y] might bee registered in our Admiralty Court, which is done accordingly but I feare that will doe little good if hereafter any dispute should arise. I tooke advice of very learned Councell upon the Act for Navigation, and the result of all is that itt's the only way for making these Shipps to passe as English, and have free and Secure traffique at the Barbados and when the[y] returne here that Mr Thierry make a voyadge into England and cleere them him selfe without which the[y] lye subject to seizure, bothe [here x out] att the Barbados, to any of the Kings men of war that meet them or when the[y] arrive in any port of England, thus much I have advised him and attend his answear. S[i]r I suppose by this you are imbursed the full proceed of the *Swan's* Oiles at your Convenience, Pray a word.

There lately departed from Amsterdam three Ships (Dutch built) with their Lading bound for the Barbados, which said shipps in all probability cannot bee dispatcht from thence on their Voyage homewards (t[ha]t is for England whether they are intended)

till after the first of Aprill next after which time the late act for
Navigation directs, that for the proveing a forraigne built Shipp
to belong to the Subjects of this Kingdome itt's required t[ha]t the
proprietor or part owners shall *viva voce* make oath before the
next Custome house Officer to his aboad, the part or proportion
he or they are concerned in such shipps. Now whereas the above
s[ai]d Shipps and Lading doe wholly belong to Mr James Thierry
a native of the Cittie of London and freeman of the Companie
of Weavers now resideing at Amsterdam being diseased in body
and the season of the yeare hindring his undertakeing such a
voyage, without much prejudice to his health & affaires, so Hee
humbly prays that his Maj[es]tie would bee gratiously pleased to
give order to his Com[missione]rs of the Customes in the port of
London (whether Commission from his Maj[es]tie's high Court
of Admiralty for the proveing said Shipps & Lading to belong
wholly to him selfe or of my testimony) who by Correspondence
with the said James Thierry understand the whole Conduct of the
businesse and t[ha]t the said Shipps, returning as aforesaid to the
said James Thierry or in his absence to my selfe. I humbly conceive
the scope and reason of the Act to be Complyed with without
any Contradiction to the words thereof. London 8 November
Tho[mas] Hill

172. Mr James Thierry London 9th Novemb[er] 1660

S[i]r,
Yours of the 12th Currant I have received from Mr de Peyster
but [but repeated] the shortness of time permitts not to send you
yo[u]r Certificates from the Admiralty Court, which you desire,
however by the next you may expect them. In the meane time I
have engaged a Courtier very neare the King's person, to present
him the whole state of the case as you may perceive by the inclosed,
to which I have hopes to procure answear in few dayes, or in Case
t[ha]t faile you may depend on the writings I shall send you from
the Adm[ira]lty. I shall really doe what possibly may bee to serve
you.

173.Mr James Thierry London 16th Novemb[er] 1660

S[i]r,

Since my Last of the 9th Curr[en]t I have not received any from you. Herewith I send you three Certificats out of the Adm[ira]lty Court, concerning your three Shipps gone for the Barbados and other three I have given order for, to send by the first conveyance to Mr Sparke and Bawdon. I hope they will come safe to your hands, and doe Some Service, t[ha]t may equall the Charge w[hi]ch will be about £20 st[erling]. S[i]r I have not yet my answear from my freind at Court but expect it dailey, what passes shall bee advised. I shall certainely use all care for yo[u]r most advantage. I formerly writt att large t[ha]t your Shipps must be sayled according to the Rules of the late Act for Navigation w[i]th three quarters at least English, if that hath not byn strictly observed pray by all meanes give positive order to the Barbados that the Dutch men bee discharged, and English [men x out] taken in their places, without which the Shipps and goods will unavoydably be Seized when the[y] arrive w[i]th us.

174. Mr Philip De pape London 23th November 1660

S[i]r,

I have received yours of the 8th Currant, being sorry to heare of your late Sicknesse but hope itt's past over. The 2 bills of Exchange you mention to have sent the 3d of October 1639 each for £200 st[erling] I answear that as they faling due the[y] were placed to the cr[edit] of Mr Richard Lane for whose acc[omp]t you say they were sent. This Letter I send by Mr John Lane who itt seemes have byn forced to make another voyadge into England upon a mistake in the Letter of Administrat[ion] hee formerly Obtained, but that being now rictified and hee haveing very Sufficient and Authentic proofe that hee is the Person he pretends to bee, I hope you will even the accompts depending betwixt you, and may hereafter be some way Serviceable to you which pray Command freely.

175. **Mr James Thierry** London 23th November 1660

S[i]r,

My last was on the 16th Curr[en]t cheifly to accompany the three Exemplifications taken out of the Adm[ira]lty Court for your Ships bound for the Barbados which said writings I hope you have received, other three I have by mee to send by the first [word x out] convenyance to Mr Sparke & Bawden as you order. I have not any any [sic] of yo[u]rs p[er] this post so shall be the Breifer only am to advise you that this day I have received from Mr De Peyster your Letter to S[i]r Arnold Breames, with Coppy of what I have delivered to bee presented the King which I was with [sic] to [word x out] deliver S[i]r Arnold, but his relations to the Court engage him often abroad, so that I have not yet met with him, but shall Endeavour itt toMorrow and acquaint him whose assistance I have desired att Court that soe both Joyneing intrests [word x out] may the Speedier be dispatch yo[u]r businesse which I heartily wish were effected to your own satisfaction.

176. **Mr Will[iam] Hill** London 24th Novemb[er] 1660

I question but that you have received a Letter of mine dated a moneth since, but why I have not answear is strange to mee for this beginning of businesse I have byn long silent, expecting the performance of what you so offten and fairly promised – but there is a great distance betweene your word and deed [word x out] Not a little to yo[u]r discredit and my disatisfaction I must be plaine with you and Say that from noe man must I be so delt with. I could Say much more but I forbeare. Mr Hayes, of whom I bought the Hopps, complaines of you much and sayes that of you which I should not heare if I knew itt not to be true, for your owne sake S[i]r, give better satisfaction to those you deale with, and let mee receive Answear to the Perticulars of the last & this Letter.

177. **Mr William Mico** Leg[horn] London 26th November 1660

S[i]r,

I am indebted answear to yours of the 24th past. The *Jeremiah* from your port wee heare is arrived but not yet come about. I take care by a timely Letter to the Master to secure the small box you put aboard him directed to me for acc[omp]t of Mr John Byam. I hope shall Obtain it without trouble notwithstanding crosse accidents hindered your taking a bill of lading. If Mr Harris the Passenger delivered the box to the Master I shall doe well enough, but if he keeps it him selfe (as I shall knowe in answeare of mine to the Capt[ain]) then I must inquire him out according to yo[u]r Directions. I shall use all needful care. S[i]r I give you my hearty thancks for your ['high' x out] huge Civilities to my freind Mr Angier a person well deserveing and able to requite the favours done him, for all yo[u]rs to mee I cann give you noe other returne but certaine assurances of the desire & readiness I have to serve you. By Mr Alex[ander Travell], who begins his journey in a day or two, through france for Leg[horn] you shall receive the small treatise you desire of modern policye. I am glad the little trifle I formerly presented you found so good acceptance, if there be extant any other such piece you shall have itt. S[i]r I wish you all prosperity in yo[u]r intended removeal to Naples, the pleasures of which [letters x out] Paradise I feare will engage you there, and deprive us of yo[u]r most esteemed Society. During which if my utmost abilitys may bee in the Least Serviceable to you Pray S[i]r, use the priviledge of a Patrone upon [me].

178. **Mr John Byam** London 29th November 1660[1]

Yours of the 9th & 13th past I have received with an inclosed to Capt[ain] Hatsell which I have Left for him att his Lodging he being here in London. From Mr Will[iam] Mico of Leghorn I have advice that by Mr Bernard Harris a Passenger on the *Jeremiah,* hee sent the box rec[eive]d from you, but have noe receipt or bill of lading, a noat he gives mee of his Lodging in King Street, where I have byn but cannot heard of him. The Ship is arrived and I hope may in a day or too come up then I shall use all diligence by the master or some else to find him out, and receive the goods but it seems the parcell of strings are not so many as you formerly advised what ever they are. I shall, when rec[eive]d, dispose of them to your best advantage. I have not yet any advice of a greater parsell of strings you say Mr Ephraim Skinner he will send mee togeather with a box of songs. I thank you very kindly for your care of these trifles, their cost I shall readily imburnse you, the large quantity will prevent my giving you any further trouble in that kind. My Respects I pray to Dr Bacon and thancks for his remembring of mee. I have not seene Mr Stefkins[2] since his being in England but when I am able to deliver him his box of strings I question not quickly to find him out. S[i]r, I perceive your removall to Naples was suddenly to bee. I wish all success to your designes, and shall be ever ready to promote them by giveing you your deserved Caracter and what else may be needfull to doe you Service. I shall consult with Capt[ain] Hatsell and be forward to engage with him in a pilchard ship to you, though that Com[modity] is very scarce & I am already concerned in three fish ships to Leg[horn] one of which might probably have gonne to Civita Vecchia if wanted a m[a]rk[e]tt att Liv[orno].

1. November 29th The previous evening Abraham Hill had attended a lecture at Gresham College by Christopher Wren, he and others had then withdrawn and discussed amongst themselves the founding of a society which became the Royal Society. Abraham Hill was therefore one of the original founders of the Royal Society.
2. Theodore Stefkins was a musician, viol player and composer born in Germany but who spent much of his life in England.

179. Mr Walwyn Gasoigne London 29th November 1660

Yours of the 29th past I have rec[eive]d with an Inclosed bill of Lading for a small box rec[eived] from Lucca and by your favour put a board the *Leicester* which God send in safety. I feare my acquaintance of Lucca gives you troble about my small businesse with them, but I must pray you to excuse itt which if you doe will shew you have more charity then I for at this instant in two posts I have noe lesse then Eleaven Letters from them. *God give me patience to reply to all of them.* The 2 jarrs of Olives I perceive arrived to late to enjoy the Conveya[nce] then in port, pray lett them come with the first, herewith you have bill of Ladeing for 100 Piggs of Lead which goes consigned you p[er] [by x out] the *Griffen* which God Send in Safety. I leave itt wholly to your owne dispose only if you could sell att above $30, to Consigne itt might doe well. You are my freind and I being convinced of itt I [word x out] esteeme itt the best way never to oblige you to any strict order. My concernm[en]t in said Shipps lading of Herrings you will understand from the Joint Letter.[1] The Lead deserves not any

Invoice So onely for yo[u]r governm[en]t please to note itts waight
to be 281cwt.1qtr.27lbs.
[H at side]

1. 'joint letter'. This shows that other correspondence re trade was taking
   place (i.e. from Abraham and Thomas jointly) besides those letters
   copied into the letter book.

180. Mr James Thierry London 29th Novemb[er] 1660

S[i]r,
My last on the 23rd Curr[en]t advised the needfull. Since which have
rec[eive]d yo[u]rs of 26/16 detto perceiveing that you will approve
of what I drew up to present the King I am glad I happened on
what was to yo[u]r Likeing. The Coppy you sent & Letter to S[i]r
Arnold Breames I have delivered him, and had much discourse
with him, and he gives mee his promise to endeavour what may
bee that you may have what you desire. I am to attend him in a day
or two according to his owne appointment to understand what hee
hath donne, w[hi]ch shall advise you.

The Certificates to bee sent to the Barbados about your three
Shipps shall be sent the next weeke, by an acquaintance of our
going thither which I rather Chose for their better security and a
safe delivery.

181. (in Italian) Sig[no]re Jacopi Baldinotti

My master etc.
With the two last posts I have received from Signor Giuseppe
and yourself eleven letters. I am so very sorry that to hear you
gentlemen suffered so much trouble in serving [me]. I would gladly
[beat myself?] four times a month if only I could know you were
well. I thank Signor Jacopo for my shirts which are already loaded
on the ship *Leister* I cannot doubt at all but that they have been
well made. I do not doubt. Your account I have received on which
there remains owing £18 shown from Lucca. You must be able
to deduct the expenses of the goods dispatched with the ship
Providence but the present which you have made me of olive oil,
olives, [soap powder?] and a thousand other curiosities which
make one wonder and marvel at I cannot ever respond to such

kindness. I would dearly wish that you would tell me the cost of this gallantry so that I could at least reimburse you and you must do me this favour in the future so that I do not become your poor debtor.

The boxes of wool, and of silk, the ribbons, buttons etc. will be almost at once ready to take advantage of being transported on our ship which is the *Society* which goes to Livorno and the account will follow in due time. Signor Nicolo Santini is with us but he will leave in 4 days time for Paris. I believe that he did not have much pleasure as it was a very bad winter season, The work of the nuns is just beautiful. I will show it to certain ladies, my friends and, if they would buy some like it I will give a share to you. I apologise meanwhile for such brevity in answer to your dear letters and a thousand kisses of the hand to all Gentlemen patrons at Lucca, whom I remember with all my heart.

London 30th Nov[embe]r 1660

182. (in Italian) S[ignore] Gioseppe Baldinotti

My Master etc.

I cannot ever thank you sufficiently for the present sent me of oil and olives which by misfortune arrived at Livorno two days after the departure of the English ship *Patience* perhaps they will come together. [words x out] In the past year you must remember that, when I parted from Lucca we were of agreement not to make these presents without accompanying them with a bill, and your not doing so mortifies me greatly.

The boots and [word x out] shoes I hope are safely arrived I would dearly like to know that you have found them to your liking.

The liquid for the boots is given below:

8 oz of tallow which is used for candles.

4 oz grease

2 oz oil of turpentine

2 oz of yellow wax fresh

2 oz olive oil which together make a liquid for the boots which is put on the boots by the fire by hand whilst on the feet as is usual.

Your letter to Sir Harvey is not yet received, he being in the country, but you must rest assured that I will present it into his

own hands and ask for a reply. To you and your wife I send my sweetest remembrances.
London 30th Novem[ber] 1660

183. M[essr]s Giles Lytcott Mr Walwyn Gascoigne London 4th Decemb[er] 1660

S[i]rs,
Haveing ['occasion' x out] occation to furnish Mr Alex[an]d[er] [ie Travell] with some mony att Leg[horn] I make bold to entreat the favour of you, the Certaine some I know not but Suppose itt may be about $1,500 – which pray Supply him, takeing his receit for what you pay him upon accompt of my brother Mr Abr[aham] Hill. Now for yo[u]r reimbursem[en]t of this mony I hope the ship *Griffen* may oppertunely arrive but in Case that should not bee however I desire hee may be furnished and for yo[u]r being in disburse, I am willing to give allowance. But if itt should so happen that the *Griffen* miscarry (w[hi]ch God forbid) in t[ha]t Case, pray passe yo[u]r bill on my brother, Mr Abr[aham] Hill, w[hi]ch shall find punctuall Complyance.

184. Mr Will[iam] Hill London 4th Decemb [er] 1660

Yo[u]rs of the 25th past I have received, not a little wondering att the contents. I must conclude the goods of mine in yo[u]r hands all sould, and you imbursed the proceed and why I am without accompts I know not, but more strange itt is t[ha]t you imploy my effects to yo[u]r private use and why you should prefer my Couzin Peter to yo[u]r eldest sonne I know not [put at side] who I am confident could advantagously manage w[ha]t you give him but t[ha]t others of my Letter you answear not. Supposeing their were garm[en]ts fitt for my Couzin William's use yet you cannot but know there must bee some charge upon them, w[hi]ch and other charges he cannot posibly live without. You take no care att all to supply him. S[i]r I hate to stuffe a Letter with repetitions of this businesse when you well know hee was entertained att yo[u]r earnest request and now you esteeme us as obliged [word x out] to doe what wee have, and yet more for him. When Mr Peak's bond fall due I shall demand itt. Mr Travers & Captain Horner [Homer?]

complain much of you and Say t[ha]t unlesse they Speedily here from you you shall from them to yo[u]r disadvantage. S[i]r, pray for yo[u]r owne Creditt minde these businesses and say something to Mr Hawes that I hinted in my last [word x out] but you say nothing to itt. [at side in fainter writing] – send mee some oysters and 2 barrels of Sampier.

185. Mr Arnold Breames Dover[1] London 5th December 1660

S[i]r,
By order of Mr James Thierry of Amsterdam I send this to accompany a black box containing [words x out] severall writings out of the Admiralty Court Concerning some Shipps of his bound for the Barbados of which one is the *black horse*, who I suppose may before this be in Dover Roade. If soe or when ever shee arrives there is aboard Mr John Sparke[2], to whome please to forward the above said box, w[i]th all speede and care adviseing the needfull to said Mr Thierry, and my selfe if you please.

1. Arnold Braems was the nephew of Sir Arnold Braems and was a merchant in Dover who acted for James Thierry when shipping arrived at that port.
   Sir Arnold Braems of Bridge in Kent was knighted in 1660. He was of Flemish descent. He claimed to have secured the fleet for the king through his friendship with Sir John Lawson. 1st Chairman of Dover Harbour Board. (Pepys X p 41) Also see article by P.C. Elgar in *Bygone Kent* Vol. 18 No. 9
2. The relationship, if any, of this John Sparke to Bernard is not known.

186. Mr John Sparke London 5th December 1660

S[i]r,
By Mr James Thierry's order I send this to accompany a black box containeing three Exemplifications taken out the Adm[iral]ty Court concerning the *black Horse, Goulden Fox & Seaven Starrs* bound for the Barbados, which said Writing coming Safe to yo[u]r hands, please to followe his ord[er]s for there further Dispose. This wishing you a Safe and Happy Voyage.

187. Mr Bernard Sparke London 6th Decemb[er] 1660

S[i]r,

My last was on the 6th past. Since which I have not any of yo[u]rs. Herewith is a Letter [word x out] from Mr James Thierry directed to Mr John Sparke, att Exson, and in another to mee hee mentions such a person aboard the *Blacke Horse* bound for the Barbados so that probably, itt may be a mistake in the Superscription of which you may consider when re[eive]d. If you have ended accompts about the *Swann's* Oile I shall pray the perusall of them, to see what may be coming to my proportion. Pray S[i]r advise if their bee any exchange betweene yo[u]r Cittie and Falmouth. I have hopes to bring Mr Thierry's businesse, concerning his three Ships gone for the Barbados, to a good issue haveing my petition presented to the King yesterday and a promise that it will be granted.

188. Mr William Jennens London 6th Decemb[er] 1660

S[i]r,

My last was on the 2nd October and since which I have not re[eive]d any ['from you' x out] of yours. The accompt then sent I hope you finde right, the ballance being £44.5.3½ I entreated Mr Bernard Sparke to make good to you which hee advised mee is donne accordingly, of which pray a word in your next. Herewith you have an Inclosed from Mr James Thierry.

189. Mr James Thierry London 7th December 1660

S[i]r,

I have yours of the 6th & 10th Currant and according to yo[u]r order therein, I imediately dispatched the Exemplyfications out of the Adm[ira]lty Court to Mr Arnold Breames the younger in Dover, With order that they should be forwarded into the Downes to Mr John Sparke aboard *the Black-horse* which is there arrived. I sent him Likewise the former Certificates you sent mee, of there receit I expect to heare. Two dayes since I drew up a petition to the King in your behalfe which my friend promised to present itt and when any thing was donne I should have notice soe that before my next I have hopes to received itt backe granted. What further passes shall advise.

190. Mr Arnold Breames Dover London 20th December 1660

S[i]r,

Under covert of Mr De Peyster, I have received yo[u]rs of the 11th Curr[en]t adviseing the receit of mine with the box of writings [word x out] etc. I am glad the Shipp *Black-horse* is dispatcht to content, what that is, pray advise mee, which if I had knowne timely Enough might possibly have prevented much trouble, & charge att Court to procure [word x out] Licence for Mr Thierry's other three Shipps gone for the Barbados but that I have at length procured by perticular favour of his Maj[es]tie and though not yet in my Possession I may have itt timely ['enough' x out]] to give good accompt to Mr Thierry, by tomorrow's post. Although it be altogether impossible for Mr Thierry to continue in this way of trading durring his forreigne Residence As S[i]r Arnold, yo[u]r Uncle, hath well noted upon the late act for Navigation, yet I have hopes of hereafter his occasion should require to procure him the like petition.

191. Mr James Thierry London 21th December 1660

S[i]r,

The inclosed in yo[u]rs to S[i]r Arnold Breames I have delivered him and offered to give covert to what answear he pleased to Send but he promised to doe it some other way. Upon receipt of yo[u]r order I imediately dispatched the three Exemplificaions out of the Admir[a]lty Court concerning yo[u]r three Shipps bound for the Barbad[o]s to Mr Arnold Breames at Dover, to bee forwarded to Mr John Sparke aboard the *Black Horse* in the Downes, but by advice from him I understand said Ships sailed eight day before. Hee hath promised to forward them by the first co[n]veyance.

S[i]r, I perceive by yo[u]r last [word x out] that you have some Inclination to make a voyage into England for cleereing of the ships expected from Barbad[o]s but that troble to yo[u]r Selfe and inconveynience to yo[u]r other affaires may now be p[re]vented I haveing procured by meanes of a worthy persone, my freind S[i]r Tho[mas] Killigrew[1], groome of the Bedchamb[e]r to the King, upon my Petition a reference to the L[or]d Chamberlaine and by him granted that a writt or *Dedimus potestatem* Should be taken out of the Chancery and derected to two English m[er]chants at

Amsterdam impowering them, to take yo[u]r oath, Concerning the Shipps, you have dispatcht for Barbados and the reason you have itt not herewith is because by direction from Court the Petition, and itts grant was to be showne to the Com[missione]rs of the Customs that the[y] might take notice of itt to p[re]vent any Scruple that might follow att the Shipps Arrivall before whom itt now Remaines but I am promised itt tomorrow and then the procureing of the writt is what is to be donne which if not p[re]vented the approaching Holly dayes I hope to send itt p[er] next. As to yo[u]r ship which departed Amst[erdam] in August last, little cann be said, only that if shee cann bee Dispatcht thence before the first Aprill next, She will bee safe or possibly Security given at the Barbados that she unloade with us May be Satisfactory enough but to p[re]vent all danger, itt would ['be' x out] in my opinion be the Surest way to prevaile w[i]th those Gent[le]m[e]n at Amsterdam who take yo[u]r despositions for the for the other ships to adde for this alsoe which being here produced as occasion required might bee admitted by the Com[missione]rs of the Customs but I rather wish she be dispatcht from the Barbados as before the first of Aprill and their in probability all will be well. If you can hasten her homeward before the forementioned time, 'twil be much the surest way.

The dispatch of businesse att Court is not only troublesome but dificult and nothing without Larg[e] Gratuitys and although S[i]r Arnold Breames promised mee his assistance yet I found little benifit from him which made mee follow the other Courtier, S[i]r Tho[mas] Killegrew, and for the more speedyer [word x out] procureing a dispatch to yo[u]r businesse in which was noe small difficulty, I was forced to p[re]sent him £60 – for he being a person of quality and neare the King for w[hi]ch I hope the good Successe will abandantly Counteract the Charge.

1. Thomas Killigrew (1612-1683) 'dramatist, theatrical manager, rake and wit' (Pepys X p 213). More importantly in this context, he was Groom of the Bed-chamber to the King and had therefore special access to and influence with the latter. His father, Sir Robert Killigrew, was the grandson of John Killigrew of Arwenack.

192. M[essr]s Lytcott & Gascoigne

I make this addition only to confirme the above according to which pray pass al things in yo[u]r books what will then advance pray lett remaine upon my Cr[edit].

193. Mr Alex[ander] Travell London 21th Decemb[er] 1660

By the hand of the most beautiful Mrs Hubland[1] I have yo[u]rs of the 9/19th Curr[en]t from Paris. Glad to here of yo[u]r safe arrivall so farr of yo[u]r health wee question not because you say nothing to the Contrary. God prosper you with a Speedy and Safe voyadge the perticulars of w[hi]ch, I should gladly know when you are at Leisure that wee may read them with gusto at Paul's Wharf.[2] In our Letter you have the needfull of businesse to which referr you for other affaires first I was to acquaint your sister Young of the newes had from you who was very Joyfull of itt so were yo[u]r Aunt and Coaz[i]n King accidentily there, who all most Kindly Salute you. Yo[u]r Nephew James Young and his Sister are both at home & huge Lusty, yo[u]r bro[ther] Travell and the friends at Chiswick are in health. For publique news there is lately discovered a plott they say of Dangerous consequence if itt had not bin timely p[re]vented but itt's not said what is the bottom of itt, the effects wee See are the imprissonm[en]t of Divers Phenatiques amongst which is Overton[3], whome the King him selfe examined and found him much refractory and uncivill, so much that he refused to uncover [word x out] till he was forced by Compulsion for which and many other misdemeanours 'tis said a probability he will quickly be made exemplar. It's now the publique title at Court the Dutchesse of York, the grandest haveing yesterday been to Complement her and kisse her [inserted] hand kneelling in which posture shee is served att table.[4] The Chanselor 'tis said will be created Duke of Carlisle. The Parliam[en]t [word x o] Disolve the end of this month. The Court is sadd at the distemper of the Princess Royall who labors under the small pox which is growne dangerous and shee hath been bluded three times.[5] The Duke of Yorke and Princess Henerietta go Phisick itt for prevention, God keep them in health. If I mistake not you heard at yo[u]r departure of Mr Harrington's Sudden death,[6] which was a mistake for he is in good health and at the Exchang[e] the 10 Curr[en]t. My sister was safely delivered of a boy, since called Richard. Mr Mellish left us the Monday after you since which I heare not of him. He went alone. Our recreation at Gresham Coll[ege] is now in practice where wee want yo[u]r good Company.[7] The good friends you know are all in health & mighty glad of yo[u]r Welfare.

[in Italian] *The three ladies in particular remember you happily and I have presented your compliments. We have come together two or three times to dine and sup with music and [to dance?] with great joy. That Colonel Treswell [?] has returned here many a time to court the widow and she has a liking, unless she deceives me, but as far as accepting him as a husband I do not believe at all, though he profers he will give her for life an English Jointure of £1,000 sterling a year. However the widow lives like a queen & is courted by all and lives extravagently. My dear Aunt Maskeline[8] & Mrs Hublon are affected by the greetings of Mr Alexander. We three were at the comedy in the theatre where the ladies themselves were reciting wonderfully and ended the bill[9], but I must finish now with a thousand kisses of the hand. Your most humble, affectionate friend and servant.*

The [word x out] things that I would not like anyone to hear for the future I will write in Italian, if not too much trouble for you.[10] I hope that you have remembered to blow into Genoa because the ladies are awaiting you.

1. Mrs Houblon, born Sarah Wynne, was the wife of James Houblon. James and Sarah were special friends of Thomas (who left much of his estate to his goddaughter Sarah, their daughter, in his will) James Houblon who was, it would seem, introduced to Pepys by Thomas, later became a close friend of Pepys. (Pepys X p 193)
2. The Houblons would appear to have had connections with this area for James married Sarah at St Benet, Paul's Wharf. It could be also that the Maskelyne family had a house at Paul's Wharf.
3. This was a plot 'hatched by discontented sectaries and disbanded soldiers'. It included Major-General Overton. Its aims were said to include the burning of Whitehall Palace and the killing of the King and Albemarle. (Pepys I p 319 note 1.)
4. 'In early October, [the chancellor] Hyde's daughter Anne was discovered to be heavily pregnant, named the Duke of York as the father and claimed that they had been secretly married'. The Duke at first denied this and then confessed to its truth. (Hutton p 149) By

December Anne was publicly recognised as Duchess of York. Edward Hyde was created Earl of Clarendon in 1661, not Duke of Carlisle as mentioned here.

5. A further tragedy to affect the Court was the illness and then death of Mary, Princess of Orange, the sister of Charles II, on Christmas Eve.

6. Is this William Harrington, mercer, member of the Eastland Company? His death was rumoured again later. (Pepys VI p 296 note 1.)

7. The reference here to Gresham College is of interest for it would seem that Abraham Hill was not the only brother who attended lectures and meetings there. Thomas was accompanied by many of his friends including Alexander Travell when in England. One wonders if the next part of the letter refers to assemblies at Gresham College or in private homes.

8. I do not know who Aunt Maskeline is or how she fits into the Hill family.

9. During the Commonwealth professional theatre had been officially banned. At the Restoration in July 1660 Charles II issued an order for a royal warrant giving Sir William Davenant and Thomas Killigrew the exclusive right to raise companies of actors to perform in London. (Pepys X p 431) There was a problem as there were already three other companies performing. However the actors of two of these joined in with Davenant and Killigrew. By November 1660 these two companies were in operation together with a further one run by George Jolly who was also given a licence by Charles II. Jolly's was at the Cockpit Theatre, Killigrew's 'The King's Company' opened at the Vere Street Theatre on November 8 whilst Davenant's the Duke's Company was at Salisbury Court. Pepys went to the 'new Play-house near Lincolnes Inn fields (which was formerly Gibbons's tennis-court)'. (Pepys I p 297) There is no clue in this letter as to which theatre Thomas attended but it is interesting his reference to the ladies 'reciting wonderfully and ending the bill'. Actresses in a French troupe played in 1629 but were hooted off the boards. (Pepys II p 5 note 2) In 1656 a woman sang in the opera The Siege of Rhodes. It is possible that the first actress was in Killigrew's Othello on December 8 1660 but her identity is not known. Pepys first saw women on the stage 3 January 1661 (Pepys II p 5)

10. Thomas later explains to John Byam that the reason he writes in Italian is to prevent the person who copied the letters from understanding the text which referred to personal matters.

194. Mr W[illia]m Jennens Plym[outh] Lond[on] 25th Dec[ember] 1660

Sent him severall Debenters due to Ab[raham] Jennens his father Deceased.[1]

The Earle of Warwick's assignm[en]t for £321 to Walter Williams by a Privy Seale 1631

A debenter for £365-6-4 for Munitions d[elivere]d att Ply[mouth] to the Gunners store of the King's fleet und[er] the Earle of Dingby

Detto £17-14-3 for Provisions made att Ply[mouth] by ord[er] of the L[or]d Dingby

Detto £15-10s for three masts d[elivere]d att Ply[mouth] for the K[ing]s ships

2 Lett[e]rs of attorney from Ab[raham] Jennens to Ric[hard] Hill and Rob[ert] Westcombe

S[i]r,

Yo[u]rs of the 11th Curr[en]t I have rec[eive]d with the inclosed to Mr [word x out] James Thierry w[hi]ch was forwarded. Here was w[i]th mee yesterday yo[u]r sister-in-law, Coll[onel] Jennens Lady, very earsnett [sic] [word x o] that I should send you by the post Severall debenters belonging to Mr Abraham Jennens, yo[u]r father, which shee saith were given to her husband, that shee hath some hopes of recovering w[ha]t is due thereon.

Said debenters are herew[i]t[h], of there receipt pray a word at Leisure. There are some ould writings Likewise that have concerned yo[u]r father and mine too Jointly but of very antient dates and I suppose of Little or noe use and so not worth sending. The[y] are safe in a box with many Letters and acc[omp]ts that past betwixt them and I thinck itt best the[y] remaine where the[y] are, the[y] shall be always ready if you have occasion to make use of them.

Itt hath pleased God to ad a young sonne to my brother's family, since called Rich[ar]d, both hee & his mother are in good health which is w[ha]t wee wish to yo[u]r selfe, and Lady – with a merry Christmas.

1. These papers refer to occurrences in the 1620s and early 1630s at Plymouth.
   The Earl of Warwick. Robert Rich 2nd Earl of Warwick
   The Earl of Denbigh was nephew to the Duke of Buckingham and

this may refer to the La Rochelle Expedition. Robert Westcombe was possibly a former partner of Richard Hill.

195. **Mr James Thierry** London 28th December 1660

S[i]r,

Yo[u]rs of the 21 Curr[en]t I have received to w[hi]ch I cann now give you [words x out] answear by sending the inclosed Letter from the Commissi[one]rs of the Customes to S[i]r John Webster and Mr Jonas Ablees[1] intreating them to bee witnesses to the oath you make, which must be donne according to the forme herew[i]th. Now in case the two m[er]chants above mentioned to whom the Letter is directed on the inside only are not fitt I suppose any other may be inserted instead of Mr Abeels, who I am told is not English man, for yo[u]r better govenment I thincke itt the farr bett[e]r way if by your friendshipp with the above named English m[er]chants you could prevaile with them to Suffer you to make oath concerning what other Shipp you have aboard going to the Barbados, besides the three w[hi]ch wee have hitherto mentioned though not by their perticular names, the benifitt would be that which Shipps, of those abroad to the numb[er] of three first arrive, might [may x out] received the favour granted, to which end the oath for each Shipp must be made distinct to be the better produced as occasion shall require. I doe not conceive any great hast necessary for the Spedy returning of these oathes because as you have advice hereafter from the Barbad[o]s of any of yo[ur] Ships spedier dispatch or designe to any other plantation or that in probability may Suddenly arrive here, so you may returne mee the oath authentake to be produced in the Customes when I enter their goods, what answear these Gentle[men] give the Com[missione]rs must come under covert to mee.

S[i]r to the case you mention of English built Shipps Sailing from England to the Barbados af[te]r the first of Decemb[er], the act, as wee understand itt, makes no question, provided as you say the Shipps are of the built of England, for then itt is [word x out] supposed they belong to English men, and will soe passe but if foreigne built and belong to English men then itt required the proprietors make personall oath, which is yo[u]r very case, Unlesse favour cann be procured from the King as wee have for you. S[i]r, Since I writt what you have on the other Side, I received the inclosed for you from S[i]r Arnold Breames. Wee are sorry to heare of the great Losse w[i]th you by the late great Storme, God comforts the Loosers. On the 24th Curr[en]t Dyed the Princes of Orange to the great Griefe of the whole Court, itt's said shee will be privately intered tomorrow.

1. Sir John Webster and Mr Jonas Ablees were merchants in Amsterdam.

196. Mr Hugh Squier London 29 December 1660

I hope this will find yo[u]r selfe and friend in good healthe. Herewith is an inclosed for you. I suppose you have heard of the Princesse of Orange's Deathe, this day tis said Shee will be privately intered. Of Capt[ain] Bushell wee have noe newes but Suppose him gonne from the Downes, the wind continueing faire now three dayes together. My brother prays the relation you promised concerning the melting Gold with your noates thereon. Wishing you a merry Christmas & happie new yeare.

197. Rotterdam Mr John Sheppard[1] London 4th January 1660[/61]

S[i]r,
Yours of the 7[30 December] Curr[en]t directed to my deceased father I have received with the inclosed to Mr William Jennens which were duly forwarded and [advised x out] advice of the postage as you ordered. If for the future I may be serviceable to you please to command.

1. Mr John Sheppard was an English merchant in Rotterdam.

198. Mr James Thierry London 4th January 1660[/61]

S[i]r,
I have received yo[u]rs of the 7th Curr[en]t with the inclosed to Mr Bryan Rogers ['with' x out] w[hi]ch was duely forwarded. You will have perceived by my last that insteed of a Comission from the chancery to take yo[u]r oath concerning yo[u]r Barbados Shipps the Com[missione]rs of the Customes will be satisfied if itt be done by a publique notary and attested by two English m[er]chants of which S[i]r John Webster is one and you have Liberty to choose

another, so that both being yo[u]r friends you may probably prevaile with them to take yo[u]r oath for whatever Shipps of yo[u]r owne you have now abroad bound for England as you may Remember I hinted in my last. Herewith is a Letter from Mr Bryan Rogers.

199. (in Italian) Lucca **Sig[no]re Jacopo Baldinotti** On the 4th January 1660/61

Sir,

With the ship *Society* departed already 15 days ago for Livorno I have sent one box containing the caskets of silk and ribbons and buttons ordered by you and they go for the care of Mr Walwyn Gascoigne from which he will be able to pay the expenses that are here on the shirts and sent by the ship *Leister* which are not yet landed but will be in 2 days. I hope that Signor Gioseppe has received the boots and shoes sent with the ship *Providence* and that he has found them to his liking.

The casks of oil are already received but I am afraid spoilt in every way. I must thank you for them as if they had arrived perfectly with the kindest memories to you and the Patrons. I kiss your hands.

For you my Master etc.

Sig[nor] Jacopi Baldinotti owes:

4 pieces of ribbon colour of [fire?]	£5.12.00
4 pieces of [ditto] black ?	£3.02.00
12 dozen of large buttons	£1.12.00
2 dozen of small	£0.04.00
A [piece of ? of silk ?] mixed colour	£1.04.00
Two pair of black fleeces [?]	£1.02.00
	£12.16.00

£12.16 St[erling] @ 50 ½d per dollar makes	$60.16.8
	$56.05.0
	$117.01.8

[The $56.05 is from the previous account – see letter no 164)

200. Exon **Mr Bernard Sparke** London 6 January 1660[/61]

S[i]r ,

I have Received yo[u]rs of 26th past with Accompt of Sales of 40 Pipes Oile received by the *Swann*. I hope the buyers are punctuall paymasters, that soe you may suddenly be in Cash the whole proceed and be remitting what is for my proportion that so an end may be put to this Accompt. S[i]r I have obtained for Mr Thierry what hee [word x out] desired that is that hee might bee examined and deliver his oath in Amst[erdam] which shall be accepted of here, to cleere his ships when the[y] arrive notwithstanding the late act for Navigation. The dispatches I sent him 10 dayes since.

201.Mr John Sparke London 10 January 1660/61

S[i]r,

By ord[e]r of Mr James Thierry of Amsterdam, I inclose to you authentique Coppys of what I have transacted for him Concerning some Shipps of his bound for the Barbados, amongst which I suppose that you are aboard of is one. The intent of Mr Thierry in ordering mee to send you theise papers, is cheifly I conceive, to acquaint you with the businesse, that you being well informed you may better dispatch said Shipps from Barbados in convenient time. If I can be S[er]viceable to you pray Com[an]d mee, Wishing you a good Voyage.

202. Mr Will[iam] Newland[1] London 10th January 1660/61

S[i]r,

Inclosed is a packett of Letters for Mr John Sparke aboard the *Black horse* bound for the Barbados. If hee is Still with you pray deliver itt, or if departed I desire itt may be forwarded to him by the first Ship Pray excuse the trouble giving me a word of receit of said papers.

1. William Newland was a member of an Isle of Wight merchant family.

203. Mr James Thierry London 11th January 1660[/61]

S[i]r,

I have rec[eive]d yo[u]rs of the 14 Curr[en]t the inclosed to Mr Will[iam] Jennens shall be forwarded. According to yo[u]r ord[e]r I did Last night send Authentick Coppy of the petition to the King with the references thereupon to Mr John Sparke at the Isle of Weight and inclosed the Pacquett to Mr Will[iam] Newland desireing him to deliver them or in case Mr Sparke should bee departed then to forward them by the very first conveyance which I hope hee will doe, and advise mee the needfull. Of Late wee have had some disturbance in the Citty in the King's absence who went to attend the Queene to Portsmouth from whence he returned yesterday.[1] The tumult was made by a partie of the Anibaptists & oth[er] Sectarians but now thanks be to God Wee are all quiet, the party who appeared being all slaine, wounded or taken prisoners. By my next I intend to send the prices of Comodities for yo[u]r better govern[en]t. If I cann serve you in any thing please to Command.

1. This is a reference to the Venner riots of January 1661. Venner, a Fifth Monarchy Man, believed that the reign of Christ upon earth could only happen after an armed rebellion of saints. Only about thirty-five men took part. This occurred when the King was away from London escorting his mother to her ship for France. (Hutton p 150)

204. Mr John Sparke London 11th January 1660[/61]

S[i]r,

Yesterday I writt you the needfull, Since which I have obtained Coppy of the Letter sent to Amsterdam from the Com[missione]rs of the Customes for examining Mr Thierry by which you may perceive how [words x out] farr I proceeded if said oaths come p[er] next I intend you Coppies except I heare to the Contrary. The favour rec[eive]d from the King I hope will be benifitiall to Mr Thierry to make free his Shipps from the Barbados notwithstanding the late act for navigation which prohibitts all forreigne built Ships to trade from the plantations into England. I wish good Successe to this bussinesse and all yo[u]r undertakings resting.

The inclosed forme of the oath mentioned in the inclosed coppie being mislaid by the Secretary to the Com[missione]rs is here

wanting, but is not much materiall being only a forme by them used.
Isle of Wight

205. Mr Giles Lytcott & Mr Walwyn Gascoigne London 11 January 1660[/61]

S[i]rs,
Herewith I send you contents & bills of Lading for 51 h[ogs] h[ea]ds & 3 barr[el]s of Pilchards Laden aboard the *Agreem[en]t,* Will[iam] James Com[mande]r, which God sending in safty. Pray favor mee to sell them to the most advantage expecting my further order for dispose of the proceed. I question not their meeting a good markett, being a good sort of fish & you are to [word x out] endeavour itt because they Cost deere.

206. Mr Bryan Rogers London 12 January 1660/61

S[i]r,
Yo[u]rs of the 7th Curr[en]t I have rec[eive]d with inclosed invoice and bill of Lading for 51 h[ogs]h[ea]ds & 3 barrells of Pilchards dispatcht for Legorne and according to yo[u]r order I have drawne out a new Invoice and indorsed the bill of Lading consigning said goods to Mr Giles Lytcott and Mr Walwyn Gascoigne, freinds that I confide in, and make use of for my owne occasions so I doubt not of their endeavour for the hight of the m[a]rkett and a punctuall complyance [inserted] w[i]th what order you please hereafter to give, possibly you may be willing to sell some part of this fish, if so pray favour mee with advice upon what terms, and having consulted my freinds I shall give answear.

207. Mr Hugh Squier London 12th Jan[ua]ry 1660[/61]

S[i]r,
Yo[u]rs of the 4th Curr[en]t I have received, the inclosed to Mr Cook delivered, the other for wales forwarded. Mr H. Davies hath received the Parsell of goods Left for him, and promised to give you the needfull advise concerning the Departure of the fleet for India. The news with us is the late Disturbances made by the Phanatique

party but wee hope all is now quiet, his Maj[es]tie being safely returned. You have an inclosed from Leg[ho]r[n]e.

208. Mr Will[iam] Jennens London 12 Jan[ua]ry 1660[/61]

S[i]r,

By yours of the p[ri]mo Curr[en]t I perceive the Receit of the severall debenters sent you. I wish they may be of use to yo[u]r advantage. Those other papers you mention shall be Lookt out and sent you. Herew[i]th is a Lett[e]r from Mr Thierry.

[The beginning of a letter to Bryan Rogers is crossed out]

209. Mr Tho[mas] Trewolla Jun[io]r Lond[on] 15th January 1660[/61]

I have Received yo[u]rs of the 18th Octob[er] which a few dayes since Left for mee when I was when I was [sic] abroad but not by Mr Grosse[1], as you intended, so the advice of comodities which I might have had from him, I am without expecting itt from the Letters I may hereafter have from you at Leisure which if the give mee some encouragement that itt may be worth following, I shall be willing to doe something yo[u]r way and be glad itt may continue a good Correspondence. In the meane time pray our respects to yo[u]r good father & the freinds with you.

1. This Mr Grosse is most likely Mr Edward Grosse a prominent merchant in Truro at the time.

210. Mr Will[iam] Hill Lond[on] 15 January 1660[/61]

I writt you some weeks since but have no answear so shall be breife. I thank you for the barrell of Oisters you sent mee But why you Lett mee so long out of the proceed of Hops and Iron you sent mee in May last, I extreamely marvaile, or att Least you might send yo[u]r acc[omp]ts for the delay of which I think there cann be no reasonable pretence. I therefore expect itt p[er] the returne of this post. Mr James Nettmaker and Mr Haws do so much complaine of yo[u]r dealing with them that I know not what answear to make them when they lament to mee of you. Pray S[i]r minde yo[u]r owne Creditt & give men Satisfaction att least by Letters.

[beginning of the letter to Thomas Trewolla as 209 x out]

211. Mr Hugh Squier London 17th January 1660[/61]

S[i]r,

Accidentilly I met Mr Haxson yesterday who enquiered somewhat earnestly when you would returne of which I could not give him any certaine accompt. So hee entreated mee to advise you that hee departs in 14 dayes with the first fleet and if you have any businesse with him, as hee seemed to imply in discoarse, itt's necessary you suddenly beginn yo[u]r Jorney.

Wee have noe extraordinary news worth yo[u]r notice. With our Respects and the like from Mr Crodna who [dined x out] this day dined w[i]th us to yo[u]r good selfe and friends.

212. Mem[orandum] 19th January 1660[/61]

Sent Mr William Jennens p[er] the Carrier severall Papers vizt.[1] Indentures betwixt Ab[raham] & Hester Jennens dated 15th March 1629; Release of Ab[raham] & Hester Jennens; A writing und[er] the great seale; A writing und[er] the May[or] of Ply[mouth]; Mr Crosse bond by Arbitracon; W. Harby bond for £3.5.0; Geo[rge] Faulkner for £6 on demand; Geo[rge] Hamilton for £5; A debent[u]r[e] for £11.10.3; Rec[eipt] [? blot] Mrs Kettlebey for £50; Captain Steward's rec[eip]t for £20; Execution against Humphry Leate; Bond of Tho[mas] Symonds for £21 the 25th May 1634, £21 the 25 March 1635, £21 the 25 M[arch] 1636 & 1637.

1. These writings again appear to date from the 1620s and relate to the family and business affairs of Abraham, the father of William Jennens.

213. Mr Henry Mellish, Mr Henry Browne London 21th January 1660[/61]

S[i]rs,

I am indebted answear to yo[u]rs of the 12th November, the Volumes recommended to Mr Binion are received accordingly.

The 2 Jarrs of olives shipt by you on the *W[illia]m & Anne* (as I remember) for want of a bill of lading, were not demanded att the ships arivall, neither did I understand of any Concernm[en]t theire till from Mr Deth who w[ith]all tould mee the Purser had disposed of them to an Oileman, With others of his owne which purser is now in the same Capasitie aboard the *Society* – Capt. Bushell. So that if you cann without any trouble to yourselve receive of him the proceed I should gladly have itt converted into florence Wine, with some addition which I shall take care some way to reimburse you, and Imploy itt with Mr Lytcott to yo[u]r good healths. But if what I propound cannot be effected, Pray excuse the trouble already given you and take noe more Nay not so much as to answear this Lett[e]r.

214. Mr Tho[mas] Dethick & Mr Rich[ard] Browne & Compa[ny]. London 22th January 1660[/61]

S[i]rs,

By order of Mr Alex[ander] Travell wee herewith remitt you $500 att 50 ½ p[er] 3 mo[nths] in bill of Mr Giles Lytcott on him selfe and Mr Walwyn Gascoigne to w[hi]ch pray procure acceptance, and att day good paym[en]t observeing what orders said Mr Travell may have given you for itts dispose which wee suppose is to be sent downe by the *Greyhound* this being what the p[re]sent offers.

Gent[lemen] [at side]

I have this day yo[u]rs of the 31 of Decemb[er] takeing notice you have sould a Bale of Black Hounscotts to Sig[nor] Visini. I should gladly heare the rest were disposed that a Conclusion might be putt to that accompt which has byn prolonged to much, considering all things. I desire they may be dispatcht but att this rate the yeild not the first cost, which is small encouragem[en]t being in disburse a considerable time, the Capitall I leave all to your care.

215. Mr Hugh Squier London the 22 January 1660[/61]

S[i]r,

Yours of the 15 Curr[en]t is received for answeare the inclosed was delivered, and herewith you have owne from Mr Dethicks. Our onely news is the dayly [word x out] Execution of the late rebellious Phenaticks in the most principall places of the Citty. Mr

Croone[1] and Dethicke returne you their thancks for yo[u]r kind remembrance and good Counsell which they wish you & freinds to follow.

1. Mr Croone. William Croone (1633-1684). An anatomist, one of the original members of the Royal Society and 1st Secretary of the Society and Gresham Professor of Rhetoric 1659-1670

216 Livorne **Mr Tho[mas] Dethicke Mr Rich[ard] Browne & Compa[ny]** Lond[on] 25th January 1660[/61]

S[i]rs,

Our last was on the 21th past to accompanye a remisse on Mr Lytcott & Gascoigne for $500 for acc[omp]t of Mr Alex[ander] Travell, by error the first bill wanted our assignm[en]t to yo[u] rselves which is on the second inclosed. Besides wee here with send you first bill of Exchange for $719.1.1 at 3 mo[nths -word x out] on Mr Giles Lytcott [word x out] & Mr Gascoyne to which pray procure acceptance and at day good paym[en]t noteing itt for acc[omp]t of Mr Alex[ander] Travell, whose orders please to follow itts dispose which he tould us should bee to go downe in the *Greyhound* who is now expecting a faire winde.

217. Amster[dam] **Mr James Thierry** London 25th January 1660[/61]

S[i]r,

I have yours of the 21 Curr[en]t. From Mr Newland of the Isle of Weight I have advice of the receipt of the Lette[r]s I sent to Mr John Sparke, with all saith hee sett saile from thence with a faire wind the 29th Decemb[er] Last and that by the first convenience the[y] shall bee forwarded. I attend the Certificates about the Ships gonne for the Barbados that soe the[y] may bee registred in our Custome house.

Herewith is an inclosed from Mr Sparke.

The prices of Comoditys are putting into a new method and not yet printed which is the reason you have them not herewith. Since the above written is come to hand yours of the 28 Curr[en]t with the inclosed for Mr B. Rogers which shall be forwarded. I perceived you are expecting the writings concerning the *Dolphin* from S[i]r Hans Hanssen, when they are here I shall make the best use of them I cann.

218. Middleb[urg] **Mr John Lane** London 25th January 1660[/61]

S[i]r,

By the hands of yo[u]r freind Mr Pollexsen I have received yo[u]rs of the 11th Curr[ant] being Sorry to heare you are Likely to have a Suit of Law with Mr De pape which if could be prevented by a freindly composure, I believe in the end would bee to the good likeing of both parties. You desire a Letter of Mr De Papes to mee in August last that it might be sent you, which in my Opinion is not now convenient for mee to doe because I suppose you will endeavor to make some use of itt against himselfe, which posibly may prove to his damage, and if soe you cannot but conclude hee will come uppon the Security he saith is in his hands of my fathers, to save him harmeles in this case, so that to engage on yo[u]r behalfe is a certaine prejudice to the above mentioned Security, which hee most likly will come upon to the utmost rigour. However I shall be willing to give you all assistance posible if you will give mee a generall discharge the like I shall [word x out] to you excepting onely this businesse of Mr De pape for the bond given him at your unkle's request. What I desire I conceive to be very reasonable of which when you have Considered pray give me yo[u]r answear. The Coppie of the acc[omp]t you sent in part for ought I know is right, the other parte I should willingly have seene but you say itt's long, and long agoe, so that possibly some after Scruples may arise for prevention of which what I desire is the more Reasonable.

219. **Mr Bryan Rogers** Lond[on] 26th January 1660[/61]

S[i]r,

This is cheifely to give covert to the inclosed from Mr Thierry, the needfull about consignm[en]t of yo[u]r Pilchards att Livorne I advised in my last. S[i]r, I knowe betwixt yo[u]r Port & us here there are very often good conveniencys by sea which would encourage me to be doeing something, if by your advice and assistance, there were Liklyhood of making such a trad worth the following, formerly itt hath byn soe, and by quick dispatches and often returnes though small profitt I Suppose itt might give satisfaction. If you please to consider of itt and if itt bee not to the hindrance of your other affaire I should willing begin such a Corrispondence. What goods may finde sale with you [may x out] shall upon advice carefully provide and intrest myselfe halfe part. Tynn I suppose is the onely returns cann be made of further perticular wee may hereafter consult, if wee are Resolved in the Generall.

S[i]r Since the above written is come to hand the inclosed from Mr Tho[mas] Cox of Rochell.

220. Mr Will[ia]m Jennens London 19th January 1660[/61]

S[i]r,
This serves cheifely for advice that according to yo[u]r order I have this day sent by the Plymouth Carrier a small box directed to yo[u]r selfe Containeing Severall writeings belonging to you, Remaineing in my hands and if I meet any more I shall hereafter send them. This day were Executed four of the Phenatiques.
Ad[ded] 26th London S[i]r, The box above mentioned was not dispeeded till today. The Carrier goeing away last weeke sooner then ordinary.

221. Mr John Byam Naples London p[ri]mo February 1660 [/61]

I congratulate your safe arrivall & wish all good success to yo[u]r undertakeings. The last post brought mee yours of the 28th Dec[em]ber & 4 January with an inclosed Invoyce for 3 small boxes of strings aboard the *Alexan[der]* friggatt who is Safely arrived. What you say of manifesting but one bundle there is noe possibility att the Custome house to take up upon the same warrant more then is mentioned but because the parcel is fittley divided into three, I have ordered for you as I should had the Concernm[en]t bane wholly my owne – that is a freind experienced will endeavour to deliver them mee att home for a gratuity inconsiderable in respect of the Custome. I cannot yet give you any accompt of the successe but such like things are dayly practised, and I hope this will *riuscire* to Content, when the[y] are in my possession I shall doe in their dispose as for my selfe and advise the needfull. What you hinte concerning Mr Lampen shall be private. The bill of Ladeing for the strings I had from Mr Ephr[aim] Skinner. Those gloves and strings you recommended to Mr Mico I feare will not be received for the Mr Harris, the passenger on the *Jeremiah* to whome Mr Mico writes he delivered them, denies that he ever tooke them into his perticular charge but that he onely brought them aboard and delivered them to the m[aster]. The master saithe he never had any box at all from [the x out] Mr Harris onely at their arrivall in England, when he desired the Capt[ain] to put into his Chest a small box (which by many circumstances was ours) to bring itt the easier ashore which being donne hee had itt away, so that I being without any receipt, or bill of lading, am in the Darke and doe something strange att Mr Micoe's servants neglect the more, because in the Letter of advice from him he gave a very Suspicious character of this Mr Harris. Mr Stephkins is *mezzo rabbiato* for his strings & promises to have Mr Harris arrested. I shall endeavour to recover them if possibly I cann this Mr Harris is a p[er]son so hardly to bee found that I have Little hopes of any good successe for I feare he hath disposed of them, however w[ha]t cann bee shalbe done. I thanck you for yo[u]r severall advices as occasion p[re]sents the[y] shall be made use of. My due Respects p[re]sented & thankfull acknowledgem[en]ts for all favours.

Yesterday the Corps of Cromwell, Ireton and Bradshaw were hanged upon the Gallows at Tybourne & some say afterwards there buried.

222. Mr Philip De Pape London p[ri]mo February 1660 [/61]

S[i]r,

I have yours of the 12/22 past by Covent of yo[u]r freind and another by the post of the 2/ Curr[ant] both to the same effect. I could wish you might agree some other way as I gave for my opinion in my last to Mr Lane. In answear to yo[u]r desire I say that in my father's books I finde Mr Richard Lane his accompt hath Cr[edit] for £200 St[erling] Received of Leonard Wake p[er] bill from your selfe the 31th October 1639 alsoe for £200 received of Peter Mathew p[er] bill from your selfe [some crossing out in the text] 28 November, 1639. I forbore to make a certificate of this before a notary publique, first to save the charge to you and besides there needs noe such thing for Mr John Lane [word x out] lately [?] sent mee an extract of an accompt formerly given to his unckle in which hee is Cr[edited] the two summes above mentioned. I find Likewise that my father, Mr Richard Hill, did the 17th July 1639, or thereabouts, value him selfe on you £100 St[erling] for acc[omp]t of Mr Sampson Lane but I suppose this perticular hath no relation to what is now in dispute.

223. Mr Giles Lytcott Mr Walwyn Gascoigne Livorne London p[ri] mo February 1660 [/61]

S[i]rs,

I have received yours of the 10 January and a receipt for three Jarrs of Olives Shipt aboard the *Alexa[nder]* friggatt. I have not yet rec[eive]d them ashore but Suppose may in 2 or 3 dayes. I perceive the dispose of the 100 Piggs of lead p[er] the *Griffin* a $30¼ p[er] 1000 lbs I presume that was the highe of the Markett so are satisfied hath of the [word x out] proceed pray Carry to the Cr[edit] of my brother Mr Abr[aham] Hill, for whome I am to desire yo[u]r favour in procureing some Ruffe Loadstones of severall Sizes to the vallue of Twenty Dollars[1] . They may I suppose easily be had with you because of the great quantitys at Elva [sic] therefore pray take the assistance of some one that understands them. Besides I am Likewise to desire you for him the last part of the Duke of Northumberland's *Arcani del Mare* itt's the Sixth book and is a Collection of Sea Cards, [sic] the price is wholly unknowne to mee, I guesse itt to be about $15[?].[2] I thinck Mr Constable[3] hath this parte singly, and so may be willing to part with itt. Pray enquire the price of the whole worke, and if itt be reasonable possibly I may desire itt but of that more hereafter. I have ordered Sig[no]re Baldinotti of Lucca to pay you $117.1.8 out of which 'tis likely hee may Deduct 18 Livers Lucca money, the rest may passe to acc[omp]t. I perceive you have paid $100 to Capt[ain] Land upon the *Providence* acc[omp]t and charge mee 1/6 part which is well. Yo[u]r utmost Care, I hope, hath been used in dispose of our herrings, so that wee may not bee to great Loosers which I have reason to doubt if you arrive not to more then $7 p[er] barrell. I am confident of yo[u]r utmost Care in all things.

1. Both the rough lodestones and also the last part of the Duke of Northumberland's *Arcani del Mare* were for Abraham Hill. The Fellows of the Royal Society were interested in experiments with lodestones and on January 16 1661 (Journal Book of the Royal Society I 1660-

1664 p 8) it was reported that the King had sent two lodestones 'with a Message that he did expect an Account from us of some of the most considerable Exper[imen]ts of that Nature'.

2. Robert Dudley, styled Duke of Northumberland, was born 1573 at Sheen House, Surrey, and died in Florence 1649 He was the son of Robert Dudley, Earl of Leicester. When he failed to establish his legitimacy he left England and settled in Florence under the patronage of the Grand Duke for whom he performed many services generally associated with his naval expertise. His *Dell'arcano del mare* of 1646–7 was a major work on navigation and cartography. It was dedicated to the Grand Duke Ferdinand II. The final book (i.e. the sixth) was an atlas of 127 maps, the first to employ Mercator's projection. (*DNB* Vol. 17 p 117) Therefore it would seem that, by 'sea cards' 'sea charts' are meant. The interest of Abraham and his friends in these charts is understandable. (*DNB* Vol. 17 p 117)

3. Robert Constable was at Leghorn with George Northleigh. (Centre for Kentish Studies U234 Be 1667)

224. Mr James Thierry Amsterdam Lond[on] 8th February 1660/61

S[i]r,

This ordinary hath not brought mee any of yo[u]rs which causeth brevity, and for the present have onely to advise you that Mr Gifford Bale onely assured £200 to you on the *Dolphin* being sometime since retired as formerly advised you, hath att Length agreed with most of his Cr[editor]s t[ha]t they accept of 3s.4d p[er] pound ready money for their Debt upon which they give Generall discharges, to theise propositions. I could not consent (on yo[u]r behalfe) without yo[u]r Perticular ord[e]r which pray consider of and give itt fully in answear. Itts a small payment, but itts to be doubted that in case this be refused if any thing cann by law bee recovered, because hee is entred already prisoner in the King's Bench and against such person is Little redresse soe that in my opinion itt will be the best way to accept this, rather then put itt to the Chargeable & Hazardous tryall of the law, others in yo[u]r Case doing the Same. Inclosed is the price Curr[ant] of Comoditys in which, if I cann serve you freely, Comand.

225. Mr John Byam Naples London 8th February 1660/61

S[i]r,

My last was on the first Curr[ant] att Large, Since which I have yo[u]rs of the 18th past. For answer in my former I advised what course I had taken for landing the three small boxes of w[hi]ch I can now say No 2 q[uanti]t[y] 6 boxes is in my possession and one more I am tould is ashoare though not yet at home. I do for you, as my owne Concernment. The Sale I shall hasten and advance what's possible. You may be assured that had our freind Mr Lytcott byn Married, I should not have Committed soe great an Error as not to advise you for I am so Intimate in his Designes that such an accident could not happen without my knowledge upon Severall accompts when such matters growe to a Certainety you shall not want advice to give him opertunely the *buon pro.* For yo[u]r advices of Comoditys I thank you they shall bee for my Governm[e]nt as occation requiers. I wish good Success to yo[u]r intended *ragione* with Mr Eph[raim] Skinner, of whome I have heard a very good Character. [word x o] If I cann be Serviceable to you here frely Command.

226. Mr Bryan Rogers London 9th February 1660 [/61]

S[i]r,

I have received with yo[u]rs of the 4th Curr[ant] a full accompt of the trade in yo[u]r parts, which I believe to be managed by the tradesmen soe that yet little hope of Encouragem[en]t. However if, upon second thoughts, you resolve upon any thing I shall gladly engage with you, and be alwayes ready to serve you. My brother Mr Abr[aham] Hill will honour yo[u]r bill.

227. Mr Edward Bridgwood Lisbone Lond[on] 11th February 1660 [/61]

S[i]r,

I congratulate yo[u]r safe arrivall at Lisbone. Of bussinesse and Occurrances you have at Large from my bro[ther] so that I have little to say other then to p[re]sent you my Respect & Service. I could wish that you may hereafter give us good encouragem[en]t to be doeing Something yo[u]r way which might obleidge us to a strict Corrispondence which to mee would bee pleasing. All the freinds are (as you left them) in health. The Pretty Little Lady, I am tould, hath a Smart to the party formerly propounded by Mr Gardfoot, but of these matt[e]rs you cannot want perticular advice. The late disturbances made but the Anabaptists I suppose you have heard of and that about a douzen of them were executed, the Perticulars are large and wilbe better related by word of mouth. The 30th January being a Publique fast the bodyes of Cromwell, Bradshaw, Ireton & Pride were hanged att Tybourne & afterwards burryed there.[1]

Mr Lytcott & myself doe often rememb[e]r yo[u]r good health. S[i]r if I may be serviceable to you or yo[u]r good [selfe x out] Lady (to whom my very humble Service) pray freely Command mee.

1. Oliver Cromwell, John Bradshaw, Henry Ireton and Col. Pride had died before the Restoration. John Bradshaw had died in Ocrtober 1659 was Lord President of the High Court of Justice set up to try Charles I. Lt.Gen. Henry Ireton had died in 1651 and Col. Sir Thomas Pride in 1658 as had Oliver Cromwell.

228.(in Italian) Sig[no]re Gioseppe Baldinotti Lucca

My Master etc.

I feel pleased that you have received the chest with the boots and shoes in good condition [and that] those pairs sent to Livorno when they arrive will be yet as pleasing as the other pairs ordered. Today I have received the oil and olives in good condition and quite perfect, for these presents as for a thousand others I owe you infinite gratitude but I must not make more of this ceremony, certainly, Signor Gioseppe, I would not wish that you would not gratify me in this manner Truly it is too too pleasing. Now by trade we could easily sell the oil of Lucca here with us and for this reason I would be particularly grateful if you would advise me what price the aforesaid oil would stand if consigned by land to my friend in Livorno where the seller would be reimbursed for this with every punctuality without having to take credit, which is a thing to consider. I would wish to know how much is a pound of 12 ounces.[1] At Lucca perhaps you could sell [us] about hundred boxes [made] of silk. If you agree tell me which colours are the most common. Let me know at your convenience.

I have given to Mr Bowtell the two letters that you sent me. The olives of last year are arrived but all quashed as were those of Sir Ed.[Eliab?] Harvey. If there is anything I can do in this thing command me freely because I am your servant.
London 15th February 1660/61

1. The trade in Lucca oil with England predates 1633 but the earliest mention to date of Tuscan oil jars in England is 1652/3 only a few years before this letter. (With my thanks to Ronald Coleman for this information) The standard weights used of commodities varied between different towns in Italy.

229. **Mr John Byam** Naples London 15th February 1660/61

I have not any from you p[er] this ordinary which causeth brevity. Your Strings are most of them in my possession, the rest I hope will bee Suddenly for effecting which certaine oppertunitys must be taken. Of these I have, I offer to sale but meet no buyer to Content. The best is a person of acquaintance who would take the whole p[ar]cell and pay ready money but itt's so small a price that I forbeare to doe anything without yo[u]r perticular order Two shillings four pence p[er] bundle, one with one other. I tell him att that raite much money will be lost, and other argu[men]ts to advance, but itt's in vaine, besides the Comodity is not by farr the best as Mr Stefkins tell me. Likewise, upon his seeing them, and wee finde in the middle of many bundles an aparent difference of Strings, which must Certainely bee a mixture of ould w[i]th the new. I have prevailed with this freind of mine, and hee is content to [word x o] attend till you give answear to this Lett[e]r if att the above rate they shall be parted with but w[i]th all obligeth mee not to expose them to sale till then if wee agree not. You know best what's to bee donne. The Comodity walts in Lying and itts unlikely that any one person will take them all at any rate. A shop keeper would have had 20 bundles at 2s 6d [word x out] but I refused being in treaty with the other party for the whole. I Suppose the first Cost (being on soe Larg a quatity) might be lesse then Gailys [sic] 6½ p[er] bundle. Use S[i]r yo[u]r owne discretion, but really the towne is full and I dispare of attaineing any higher price or this if proffer bee refused. Out of this are expected those for watches which I gladly consented to for I have hopes to advance upon them having to begin disposed three bundles for 15s. and shall continue at such small *patititas* or Lesse to doe you service, Mr Stefkins nor my selfe cannot meet that Mr Harris w[i]th the Strings & Gloves nor I feare ever shall to Content.

230. (in Italian) Sig[nor]e Jacopo Baldinotti Lucca My dear . . . [Part of letter x out and then begun again]

Yours I have gratefully received. The table knives you ordered will be dispatched shortly and I will advise when sent. By the inclosed to Signor Gioseppe I have let him know that I have received the olives and the oil with many thanks and with great pleasure. The inclosed letter is not sealed so I can put in a sheet of paper as you know, here we pay very much so much for the outward journey and not so much for the return, truly it is too expensive. Please seal it and address it to Signor [word x out] Gioseppe if there is a reply I would dearly like for you to write it for I find the writing of Signor Gioseppe faint and difficult to read. Pardon the liberty that I put on you.

I will do my best to serve you in whatever you command me freely, with many salutations to all the Gentlemen patrons and friends of Lucca I remember you with my heart.

15th February 1660/1

231. Mr James Thierry Amster[dam] London 14th February 1660/61

S[i]r,

I have not [yet x o] any of yours p[er] this post and having written the need full with my last will cause brevity. This Serving cheifly to accompany the inclosed pacquet from Mr Sparke. The bill of prices is herewith w[hi]ch may Serve for advice in trade. My respects p[re]sented to yo[u]r selfe & Lady.

232. Mr Will[iam] Hill London 16th February1660/1

Inclosed is a Letter from Mr W[illia]m Blunden. Pray S[i]r, what's yo[u]r meaning not to send mee accompts of the Hops and Iron you have long since Disposed for mee such dealing as yours is not at all Satisfactory And for the future shall Serve as a warning. I have rec[eive]d Mr Peake's money. Pray dely mee noe longer but lett us even accompts or Say Something to contrary. I write often but you take noe notice of itt. I have noe more to say till I here from you.

233. Mr Bernard Sparke London 16th February 1660/1

S[i]r,
Yo[u]rs of the 18th Curr[ant] I have rec[eive]d, the inclosed to Mr Thierry forwarded. I have presented the two bill [sic] you Sent Mr Daunsy hath promised to Satisfy his this day, if otherwise shall advise underneath. Mr Menefie Smith cannot give answear nor accept that on him selfe till wednesday. Mr Daunsay hath not yet paid his bill not being within, but shall be called upon againe on Monday.

234. Mr James Thierry Amster[dam] London 22nd February 1660/1

S[i]r,
Yours of the 15/[5] Currant I have received, you may take your owne Conveniency for makeing the certificates, although the Custome house officer calls upon mee for them. For answear to yours Wee here understand that English built Shipps going from England to any of the plantations doe here give bond that the goods laden shall bee landed att the Plantations (the casualtys of the Sea excepted) and the Loading any Commoditys att the Plantations shall bee brought into England. This is the dayly Practice att our Custome house.

S[i]r, I presume you have heard that Lent is ordered to bee strictly observed which makes all Sort of fish in esteeme espetially white herrings (as they are Pact att Sea) And barrell Codd. The former yields 25 in 26s Sterl[ing] p[er] barrel, the latter 45 in 46s Sterl[ing] p[er] barrell. Eighty or a hundred barrel of each would find quick Sale & to Content. If you have any thoughts of makeing some tryall I shall be ready to serve you to the most advantage. I perceive the order you give mee concerning Mr Bale w[hi]ch shall be observed.

235. **Mr John Byam** Naples (no date) [Venice x out]

S[i]r,

Wee are the 22th detto not haveing any of yo[ur]s since the above, which is Coppie of my last in which you Perceive what was the heigh of the markett for yo[u]r strings which my freind was att first willing to give, but in the intrim mett with a Considerable parcell att 2s p[er] bundle and ['and' x out] was att our house to have tould mee before the post's departure but found mee not at home, So that being at better termes provided could not take Yours, nor could I force him to itt, nott coming to any positive agreem[en]t so that I offered them to others and disposed of one box q[uanti]t[y] 60 bundles att 2s.6d. The Shoppkeeper meeting mee since Laments very much & would have mee take them again att 6d bundle losse, and feares the badnesse of them will Loose his Custome. These things Considered and how Subject they are to decay makes mee use al diligen[c]e to put them of. I have this day come to an Agreement with a party for the whole Parcell att 2s p[er] bundle if you Consent. The perticular you may perceive from the inclosed Coppy. Now S[i]r consider what's to be donne. A better price I have noe hopes to attaine besides the hazard of wasts and the uncertainety of paymasters, if buyers should present of which I meet none, the towne being huge full of t[ha]t Comodity. If the parcell were mine whatsoever the Cost may have byn, I should take this offer therefore I hope you will give yo[u]r Consent. If there bee upon the whole accompt Small or possible noe profitt, I am sure itt will prevent an evident losse all things Considered. I sell the watch Strings by Single bundles att 5s. and usually carry some in my Pockett to proffer the watch-makers att their Shopps as I passe by. The King hath given strict order for observing Lent and two fish dayes a weeke all the yeare. Preparations are made for the Coronation to be Solemnized the 23th of Aprill. The box of Songs you mention Mr Skinner would send mee is a small p[ar]cell in oiled Cloth but possibly may be the same.

236. **Mr Alex[ander] Travel** London February 1660/1 [no day given]

My last in perticular was on the 21th December Since which I have yours of the 21th January & 5th Curr[ant], congrattulateng yo[u]r happy arrivall so Farr & oppertunely to enjoy the Convenicnce of passage with the *Defence* So I question not but this finds you in perfect good health at Aleppo.

I feare the losse of the long Letter you mention w[hi]ch I suppose contained the relation of your adventures through france, for as yet itt's not come to hand, itt would have beene very gratefull to some freinds. The inclosed in yours for Mr Hublon & Mr Maskelyne I have delivered & shall take care to give them notice when the *Hopewell* arrives to take upp the p[re]sents of wyne you make t[he]m for which by mee the[y] returne you hearty thanks, and besides will doe itt themselves in perticular Letters. Mr J.[?] Dethicke will Let mee have p[er]use of his bill Lading for the 4 Chests of wyne, if their bee occasion which shall be disposed of as you order.

I have the receipt for the 3 fanns aboard the *Mary Bonav[entur]e* which arriving Safe shall bee Lookt after, & presented as you order, takeing notice of that for Mrs Maskelyne. The other three arriveing shall be delivered, 2 to yo[u]r Sister Young & one to my Sister. You were happye in meeting soe pleasing entertainm[en]t att Genoa & Leg[hor]ne. In Operas, Mr Killigrew gives us hopes of one here.[1] This I send you by Mr Hen[ry] Hunter to whom must refer you for publique news, perticularly the disturbance lately made by the [word x o] phanatiques & the number of them taken and executed.

Yo[u]r acquaintance honest Mr Smith ['is surely dead' x out] the scrivener is lately dead. I know not if you have heard of the Princess of Orange's death of the Small pox, and that the Princesse Henrietta Maria being att Portsmouth and in departure with the Queene for france, had the Small Pox but recovered and safely arrived.

The 23rd Aprill is appointed for the Coronation, they are now att worke in Cornhill, fleet Street and other parts of the Citty makeing Tryumphall Arches[2] and our freind Mr Ogilby is the Poet.[3] The King hath Comanded that there bee a Strict observance of Lent. You will understand t[ha]t Mr Martyn Lee is chosen factor Marine att Scanderoone. The late differences amongst the Turky Company of the free and unfree men of the Cittie in that Corporation you will have a full relation from the Gentle[man] that comes with this to you. His Maj[es]tie appointed the 25th Currant to heare the businesse by Counsell for each party att the Privy

Counsell where himselfe was and many of the Company, and I Likewise went though upon noe other accompt then curiosity, and to heare the great champions plead which was aboundantly worth my paines, for the Cittie freemen were the Recorder Wilde, S[i]r Hennage Finch, and Mr Allen for the other party Sergeant Glynn, Maynard and Mr Churchill[4] all admirable Speakers & gave good reasons on both sides, but what the King's resolve is, I cannot yett advice but shall note itt under neath for at the hearing after two hours discourse the[y] were Comanded to withdraw, and no resolve of the King and Counsell declared.

1. The opera *The Siege of Rhodes* had been presented by Sir William Davenant in 1656. Because of its musical content it managed to evade the parliamentary prohibition of stage plays. It was presented again in June 1661 and ran for 12 days, which was a long run at that time. A few years later (August 1664) Thomas Killigrew told Pepys of a plan to build a play house in Moorfields and the repertoire would include four operas a year 'to act six weeks at a time – where we shall have the best Scenes and Machines, the best Musique, and everything as Magnificent as is in Christendom; and to that end hath sent for voices and painters and other persons from Italy'. (Pepys V p 230)
2. On the 21st February Pepys had seen scaffolding being put up for the Coronation. (Pepys II p 39) Several arches were erected. 17 April Pepys 'saw the Arches which are now almost done and are very fine'. (Pepys II p 77)
3. John Ogilby 'Originally a dancing master, he became an impresario, versifier, translator, publisher and cartographer'. (Pepys X p 305) He published several folios the best known being his second account of the coronation procession of Charles II which had engravings by Hollar. (Pepys II p 77 note 2)
4. Recorder Wilde. Sir William Wilde Recorder of London 1659–1668
   Sir Heneage Finch. Solicitor General
   Which Mr Allen is not known.
   Sergeant Glynn. Sir John Glynne lawyer d. 1666. At the Coronation his horse fell upon him and he was lucky to survive 'which people do please themself with, to see how just God is to punish that rogue at such a time as this – he being now one of the King's Serjeants and rode in the Cavalcade with Maynard to whom people wished the same fortune.' i.e. Sir John Maynard mentioned here. (Pepys II p 87) Both Glynne and Maynard were eminent lawyers who served Oliver Cromwell and then made peace with the King.

Mr Churchill. John Churchill, Duke of Marlborough was the grandson of John Churchill of Wootton Glanville, Dorset who was deputy registrar of chancery and MP for Weymouth in 1661. Possibly he is the person mentioned here?

In a petition six months later for the confirmation of their charter plus additions, the Turkey Company said that their trade had lately declined, that they were burdened with heavy expenses of £10,000 a year for the maintenance of their ambassadors and officials. They therefore did not wish outsiders to trade without paying fees. The charter was later renewed.

237. Mr Bernard Sparke London 28th February 1660/1

S[i]r,

Yours of the 20th Curr[ant] I have received with the inclosed to Mr Thierry which was forwarded. The two bills of excha[nge] you sent on Phillip Daunsy for £30 and Richard Minifie for £46.9.0 are satisfied for which I give you Cr[edit]. Att your convenience I should gladly shut up the Accompt of the *Swann*.

238. Mr John Byam Adi le p[ri]mo March 1660[/61] in London

S[i]r,

The above is Coppie of my last, Since which I have not received any from you, nor have to adde other then Confirming the above written.

239. Mr William Jennens London 5th of March 1660 [/61]

S[i]r,

I have not of late written you for want of occasion. This is Cheifely to desire your favour in forwarding the inclosed to Mr Ambrosse Jennens of Penryn, if no better & surer way p[re]sents I think itt may goe by the post. The Safety is what I ayme att rather then Speed, though itt should remayne with you 5 or 6 dayes after receit of this.

I hope you have received the box I sent you some weeks past by the Exon Carrier. If I cann be serviceable to you, pray Comand.

240. **Mr Ambrosse Jennens** London 6th March 1660 [/61]

S[i]r,

By this post wee send to Mr Will[iam] Jennens & desire him to send forward unto you, two writings which we have heare sealed & desire you to deliver unto Mr Walter Vincent he paying you £800 concerning the dispose whereof wee shall hereafter give you notice, the whole businesse you will understand by the said writings & Mr Vincent p[ro]mised the money should be ready by the end of this moneth. Wee have rather chosen to come to this conclusion, though much Lesse then our due, then to except any Longer the course of Law. Pray excuse the trouble we are forced to give you.

241. **Mr Alex[ander] Travell** London 8th March 1660 [/61]

S[i]r,

Wee are to [word x out] answeare yo[u]rs of the 21st and 28th Janu[ary] & 5 past, for the money you have taken at Livorne upon our accompt its very well & yo[u]r bills on T.H for his part are accepted & shall be well paid & those bills alsoe which you drew on Mr Pennoyer, Mr Davison[?] & Mr Squier have due respect[1]. Wee hope your selfe & this money are safe at Aleppo & ready to make returns by the *Society* which if you finde Galls or fine Silke to be had at reasonable terms [rates x out] will doe well, they both being in better demand then at yo[u]r Departure hence. By the inclosed accompt you will see what wee have done by Mr Dering[2] & in the remittes for Livorne, our intrest on the Last bill being $267.18.0 wee ord[ered] Mr Dethick (deducting the Charges att Livorne) to send w[i]th your money on the *Greyhound* which pray dispose to our best advantage, besides what wee have noted, Mr Dering has paid Mr Best but with yo[u]r Salters hee cannot come to an end, att p[re]sent, they p[re]tending damage, when hee cann receive any more [word x o] of them, or the money for yo[u]r bale of Silke (which is due in a moneth) wee may have itt & shall be better able then to Judge what's the best way to dispose of itt, for itt's now uncertaine what price Tynn will beare, itt's a Little risen in the west Country, & wee know not what will be done about Generall Ships, the difference betweene partys in the turky Company, being a hindrance to oth[er] businesse so that our next must acquaint you what we resolve ['to doe' x out] with yo[u]r next money.

We have made a pollicy for you on goods or moneys in the *Society* and (to be in the most Comprehensive manner) itt runs from Liv[orno] to any Ports whatsoever & to end at London, in trade, the rate being [words x out] 15s p[er] c[ent] p[er] moneth which will amount to little above 15s p[er] c[ent] as wee calculate, or not so much if the ship make a good dispatch, there is some danger feared, for wee are upon doubtfull termes with Argier, £450 is already underwritt & by men of good repute, the rest wee thinck to get done Suddenly, it's done by Valuation att £1000 to make all cleare. In a fish designe from Newfoundland it's p[ro]bable [word x o] wee may be intressed and when are resolved shall offer you a part. Last yeare produced a pretty good acc[omp]t & if Oyle continue in price as it now is & that the price of wine be sett, it may be the best way, to freight the Ship onely out or to have her p[ro]ceed from Spaine to Scanderoone.

1. Pennoyer. Possibly William? (Centre for Kentish Studies Kent U234 A2)
2. Dering. Is he Sir Edward Derring?

242. Mr Alexander Travel Lond[on] ditto

I writ you by Mr Hunter which suppos will arrive with this there is nothing to adde of news but the continuance four good health. The Ladys of yo[u]r acquantance, doe often remember you & promise to make visitt to yo[u]r Picture, yo[u]r pr[e]sent are as farr as Malaga so hope the next news will be of their safe arrivall.

243. Mr Tho[mas] Dethick, Mr Rich[ard] Brown & Compa[ny] Lond[on] 8th March 1660[/61]

Wee have formerly written you accompanying bills of Excha[nge] for $500 and $719.1.1. on M[essr]s Lytcott & Gascoigne which wee doubt not but finde due honour. Said bills are mentioned to be remited you by order of Mr Alex[ander] Travell & that wee supposed hee had left direction with you to send downe said money by the *Greyhound*. If hee have omitted itt, however we desire you to make use of that Convayance, first changing itt into weighty money, & if the bill fall not due in time pray discompt them which shall be allowed & of the Last Sume remited, there is for ourselves $267.18.6 which whether you noate or noe is not much materiall we writing him w[ha]t is necessary, here inclosed which pray forward onely Let him & us know what the Charge is on that Latter Sume of $719.1.1.

244. Mr Giles Lytcot & Mr Walwyne Gascoigne London 8th March 1660[/61]

I have your Severalls to mee in perticular taking notice of your paying Mr Alex[ander] Travell $1,250 ['way' x out] waighty mony for accompt of my broth[er], for yo[u]r ready complyance I thank you, & for what you may be in disburse for mee, please to draw itt on mee or possibly you may be imbursed out of the Pilchards p[er] the *Agreement* before this, which I presume may be disposed of to the most advantage. What you have rec[eive]d by assignm[en]t from Sig[no]re Baldinotti, I shall finde Cr[edit] in accompt. I am Sorry to put you to trouble by their means and must yett entreat further yo[u]r care in conveying a Case of knives which I send to him p[er] Capt[ain] Trelawny. The Receipt for the Jarr olives p[er] the *Hopewell* I have received and hope itt will come safe as the three former by Capt[ain] Nash. The acc[omp]t of the 100 Piggs of Lead p[er] the *Griffin* is rec[eive]d & upon pe[r]usal findeing itt right shall be noted accordingly. The herrings I perceive you goe disposeing I hope yo[u]r rec[eip]ts will prove better then was feared.

245. Mr James Thierry Amst[erdam] London 8th March 1660 [/61]

S[i]r,
Yours of the 4th Curr[en]t I have rec[eive]d. Haveing had your order I treat with Mr Bale and hope spedily to make an end with him. What passeth shall advise you. For answear Concerning the Ship you designe for the Plantations, though Shee be Dutch built, if sailed w[i]th English master & marriners and belonging to an English man as you are, Shee undoubtedly will passe free and all her loading. Now for proving said Ship to belong to English men as above said there is noe other way but yo[u]r personall appearance, and oath before the Custome house officer at Dover or here att London and there is noe Custome att all to be paid for what goods

are aboard except the Bulke be broke, nor any Necissaty the Shipp
come into England, except except [sic] you intend the Certifications
you make for her shall goe by her to the Plantations, which may
be the most convenient, Lest they otherwise miscarry and if you
resolve to come over yo[u]r selfe and can meet a good Convayance
before the Ship itt might doe well to have the Certificates all ready
so that the Shipp need not Come to Anchor in the downes but
have all necessary Papers sent of to her p[er] boate. If you please
to Comand mee I shall att yo[u]r coming ashoure upon yo[u]r
timely advice to be assistant in what yo[u]r occasions require. The
23 of the next month will be our King's Coronation, for w[hi]ch
are Large preparations and may be worth yo[u]r seeing if yo[u]r
affaires will p[er]mit yo[u]r Stay soe long. For prizes of Comodities
I refer you to the inclosed.

246. Liv[orno] **Mr Will[ia]m Mico** London 12th March 1660/1

S[i]r,
I have not of late written you, deferring itt in hopes I might before
this have given you some acc[omp]t of the receipt of the box you
recomened to Mr Bernard Harris but neither cann I yett nor I
feare ever shall, advice you that I have rec[eive]d itt. This This [sic]
Harris att first told mee hee had delivered itt to the Capt[ain] of the
Jeremy and many circumstances which made the story plausible
& Like truth with this answear I went to the Capt[ain], but he
denys that ever had any box from Mr Harris till his arrivall in the
Downes, which then he saith he had but upon no other accompt
then the most easy way to bring itt ['her' x o] ashoare, which being
done Mr Harris received itt back againe of the Capt[ain], this I
have under the Capt[ain]'s hand and returneing to Mr Harris so
well provided with the Captaine's answear I was earnest & prest
him heard which made him exclame much against the Capt[ain],
and A day was appointed for us to meet, and Mr Harris promised
as I thought seriously, but from that day, two moneths since, or
more, I have not seene him nor cann I heare the Least news of him,
att the place which hee said was his Lodgeing, many circumstances
make mee doubt the person, as Cheifly the Liberall distributing
Roman gloves which his necessity (as I have heard) abroad was
unlikely to permitt unlesse hee came by them at such easy rates as
I feare he hath mine.

247. Mr Bryan Rogers London 12th March 1660/1

S[i]r,

This Serves only to acquaint you that wee have advice from Genova of the *Agreem[en]t's* Safe arrivall att Legorne and, although my Letter from thence mentioned noe such thing, yet I Cr[edit] the news for the post from Genova hath wanted but few dayes thence and might bring advice from Legorne sooner then the ordinary Conveyance. The next post will bring the Certainety w[hi]ch shall be advised in due time. Herew[i]th is an inclosed for Mr Jennens w[hi]ch pray deliver w[i]th our Respects. The Pacquet last week I hope hee Received.

248. Mr Ambrose Jennens London 19th March 1660/1

S[i]r,

Yours of the 11th Curr[en]t wee have received, perceiveing you had the writeings wee sent Concerning Mr Vincent, and yo[u]r Readiness to afford us yo[u]r assistance, our desire is that you please to demand & receive of Mr Vincent the eight hundred pounds mentioned therein, and haveing paid yo[u]r selfe the ballance of yo[u]r accompt w[i]th our father, pray remitt up the remaineder in good bills of Exchange, payable to ourselves at the Shortest time may bee. What Convenience you have to doe this pray advise.

249. Mr Bryan Rogers London 19th March 1660[/61]

S[i]r,

Yo[u]rs of the 11th Curr[en]t I have received, the inclosed forwarded. What I said in my last Concerning the Shipp *Agreem[en]t's* arrivall att Livorne is not Since Confirmed so I suppose onely a report, when any good news comes I shall give you advice. Her passage hath binn som thing Long. Assurance on her is at 10p[er] C[en]t but I hope Shee may be well, other Ships meeting Some tymes with as Tedious passages.

250. Mr James Thierry London 22th March 1660/1

S[i]r,

Yo[u]rs of the 15/25 Curr[en]t I have re[eive]d for answear to w[hi]ch, what my formers have advised is according to the Custome house officer's opinion, w[hi]ch is thus, yo[u]r selfe coming into England as you formerly mentioned and make oath that a Certaine Ship & Lading designed for Barbados is wholly & properly yo[u]r owne, the officers here from the Custome-house will give a Certificate accordingly, which will make the Shipp free at the Barbados, as an English Shipp though dutch built. If you could come over before the Shipp & make oath as above, the Certificates might be sent p[er] post into Holland to the Shipp and then she need not Stop att all in the downes but keepe on her course for the Barbados or in Case this Cannot well bee, but that you come upon her, the Ship will not be Lyable to pay a Custome Provided shee doe not breake Bulke, w[hi]ch I suppose her occasions will not require. For yo[u]r takeing a house here thereby to be Lyable to pay taxes and other dutys, I doe not perceive any reason to put yo[u]r selfe to such [word x out] Charge, or what benifitt you could expect from itt. However I shall enquire more [four it x out] concerning itt, and give you a full accompt if you Continue in such thoughts. Itt will bee necessary you bring with you the Severall bills of Sale of the Shipps you make oath, with the perticular money you paid and the partys to whome and what else may cleere yo[u]r intrest in such Shipps, herewithy is an inclosed from Mr Rogers w[i]th the prizes of Comoditys.

251. **Mr Bryan Rogers** London 23th March 1660/1

S[i]r,

Yours of the 18th Curr[en]t I have received with the inclosed for James Thierry, which was the last night forwarded. Receit and invoice for 20 Slabbs of Tynn aboard the *Silence* for yo[u]r accompt, I have received att the Vessall's arrivall. I shall take Care to dispose them to yo[u]r best advantage. The price is now betwixt £4.18 and £5 p[er] c[w]t. This week's post hath not brought any Italian Letters soe I cannot give you any further advice of the *Agreement* the first that comes shall bee advised. Wee have not had any acc[omp]t how Pilchards have sould att Legorne, you may probably be informed att Large by the vessell arrived att mount's bay. Doubtlesse if they come before Lent they will doe well.

252 **Mr Bryan Rogers** London 30th March 1661

S[i]r,

Yours of the 24th Curr[en]t I have received, I should have observed your about makeing assurance on the *Agree[en]t* but that may now be spared for I have advice from my freind of her safe arrivall at Legorne, and that yo[u]r pilchards are sould att $25½ p[er] h[og] sh[ea]d which is a very good price considering halfe Lent was past. Some part of the fish was consigned by the last Letters and possibly by the next acc[omp]ts may come. I have given ord[e]r that the proceed bee remitted home, what further passeth shall be advised. Herew[i]th you have the prizes of comoditys. When yo[u]r Tynn arrives I shall endeavour for yo[u]r most advantage in itt's dispose, althoughe have noe hope to get more then £4.17s. The *Silence* I here is arrived in the river, and may may [sic] be up in two dayes.

253. **Mr Bryan Rogers** London 2 Aprill 1660[sic]

S[i]r

Yours of the 28th past I have received With an inclosed bill of Exchange on Mr Nich[olas] Bloy[1] for £30 w[hi]ch hee promiseth to pay out of the first fraight hee receives. His vessell is come to the Key, and may begin to discharge tomorrow and although yo[u]r 20 Slabbs are not yet in Warehouse I shall treat for their dispose and if possible, ready money, for the better Supplying yo[u]r occasions [word crossed out]. However yo[u]r bill for £80 when you please shall find due complyance. Herewith is Coppy of the acc[omp]t of yo[u]r Pilchards 51 h[ogs]h[ea]ds 3 barrells importing $1,068.16.4 and considering that there is small diference betweene drawing and haveing the pr[o]ceed remitted home in 3 moneths I have resolved to value my selfe on the friends at Leg[orn]e in $1,000 on this acc[omp]t[2] so you may draw on mee What you please, and the remaineder you shall be imburst out of the money Mr Vincent to pay us for your paines about which wee are obliged so that now there will be noe need [inserted] of overhasting the sale of yo[u]r Tyn.

1. Nicholas Bloy was a member of a prominent Penryn family
2. Hill wanted to keep the $1,000 in Leghorn for payment of his own bills. See Letter 257.

254. Lytcott 29th March 1661

Advised the rec[eip]t of theirs of the 11th March.

255. Mr Thomas Dethick, Mr Richard Browne & Compa[ny] London 5th Aprill 1661

S[i]rs

Yours of the 11th past I have received with the inclosed acc[omp]t of our Hounscotts which upon p[er]usal finding right shall be noted accordingly, the price they are disposed att will make us Loosers in the Principall, but being now ended I pray remitt home the ballance of what's in yo[u]r hands in good bill payable to mee att the most advantage. I perceive the Bill on Mr Lytcott for $719.1.1 is accepted. I hope good payment will follow. I formerly mentioned that there was an Errour in the waight of the lead you sould [word x out] which pray lett us have allowance for in the Acc[omp]t Currant.

256. Mr James Thierry London 5th Aprill 1661

S[i]r,

I have not any of yo[u]rs unansweared so that this will bee breif serving Cheifly to give Covert to the inclosed Price Curr[en]t of Comoditys. I attend yo[u]r comands and some advice if you intend a voyage into England, if soe please to take notice that the 23th Curr[en]t is appointed for his Maj[es]ty's Coronation for which there are huge preparations and if you occasions would permitt might be well worth Seeing for yo[u]r Lady.

257. Mr Giles Lytcott Mr Walwin Gascoigne Lond[on] 5th Aprill 1661

S[i]rs,

Yours of the 18th March I have received, with accompt of the 51 h[ogs]h[ea]ds, 3 barrells Pilcherds consigned you by the *Agreement* for yo[u]r care in the dipose I thanck you, yo[u]r accompt being right, I shall note accordingly. I have this day past my bill of Exchange on you for $500 payable to Mr Thomas Dethicke & Compa[ny] which I pray honour w[i]th yo[u]r acceptance and at day punctuall payment and (because I finde not that I have ordered the remitting home of the Proceed of the Pilchards I may draw $500 more in a weeke).

258. [$500 at side] London 5 Aprill 1661

Three moneths [dayes x out] after date of this my third bill of Exchange, first or second not being paid, Pray pay to Mr Thomas Dethick, Rich[ard] Browne & Compa[ny] Dollers five hundred Sivill & Mexico Effective for Value Exchanged herewith Mr Henry Regnier and Place itt to acc[omp]t as p[er] advi[ce]. Tho[mas] Hill

259. Mr Bryan Rogers London 9th Aprill 1661

S[i]r,

Yours of the first Curr[en]t I have received, with an Inclosed bill of Exchange on Mr Lucas Lucey for £9.11 which hee hath paid, and I give you Cr[edit] in acc[omp]t yo[u]r 20 Slabbs tynn by the *Silence*. I have this day rec[eive]d and have treated with the Shopkeepers but the[y] offer not above £4.17s p[er] hundred [weight] att w[hi]ch rate one hath this day bought a good p[ar]cell, as I am informed. However at that price, I shall not dispose itt without yo[u]r order, considereing yo[u]r occasions for money may be oth[e]r ways Supplyed. When yo[u]r bill of £80 is pr[e]sented itt shall be accepted & paid. Mr Bloy hath not yet p[ai]d yo[u]r bill of £30 but tells mee will Satisfie itt out of his freight which hee is [satisfied be x out] pr[o]mised tomorrow. Wee thank you for yo[u]r paines in Mr Vincent's businesse, who tould us in a few dayes after the 25th past hee would pay us, which wee hope hee will be punctuall in. So pray endeavour a speedy end w[i]th him. Wee have not had any Letters of this post as hee promised you, so hope he may bee by this time paying you some money.

260. Mr Bryan Rogers London 13th Aprill 1661

S[i]r,

Yo[u]rs of the 8th Curr[en]t I have received with the incloseds which shall be forwarded. I am glad itt so happily meets with yo[u]r occattions that I have drawne the Pilchards proceed att Legorne. I shall advise yo[u]r freind, Mr Rider, that hee may value him selfe on mee for yo[u]r accompt to £150 a 160 st[erling] which with yo[u]r other bill to Mr Depester for £46.10s shall find due payment. With us Newf[ound]l[an]d fish sells at 22 R[eal]s[1] p[er] Kintall itt hath bin sold at 23 R[eal]s by one man, but poole fishermen, I thinke will sell att 22 R[eals]. I am offered £4.17.6 p[er] c[w]t for yo[u]r Tyn att a moneth, but I refuse itt although if could get 6d more should accept itt. Mr Bloy hath not yet paid yo[u]r bill of £30 pr[e]tending hath not yett received his freight. I finde in the receit of the 20 Slabbs of Tin, no mention made of fraight and because I understand you are 1/4 p[ar]te owner of the *Silence* I suppose you may probably agree otherways with the parte owners, of which pray a word, although in the intrim, if Mr Bloy should demand itt, and insist thereon I cannot refuse [word x out] to pay him.

1. A real (Spanish currency) was generally equivalent to about 6d. see Roseveare p 635. kintall = quintal.

261.Mr Barnard Spark London 13th Aprill 1661

S[i]r,
Yours of the 8th Currant I have received, with the Severall incloseds which shall bee forwarded with the first opportunitys. I perceive the barter you have made for 100 p[iece]s serges against the remaineing Oiles with £100 Mony to which I answeare that I should gladly see an end to the *Swanne* Accompt, but I must pray excuse for being concerned in these Serges for upon my father's accompt I cannot doe itt and for my selfe, I have no acquaintance there, or other concernments that way and as I see by the last Serges, these may be [a x out] long a selling & because I suppose the bargaine was made to the best advantage, I hope itt will nott be any prejudice t[ha]t you take them yo[u]r selfe.

262. Mr Andrew Rider[1] London 13 Aprill 1661

S[i]r,
This serves Cheifly to accompanie the inclosed from Mr Bryan Rogers of Falmouth, who order me to accept yo[u]r bill of Exchange to the vallue of £150 a £160 which I shall punctuallly comply with. Only I am to desire you please to give mee to [sic] longest time you can for payment because monyes Mr Rogers ordered mee here are not paid, nor cann I att all depend on them.

1. Mr Andrew Ryder was a Penryn merchant

263. (part crossed out) **Mr Will[iam] Hill** London 18th Aprill 1661

My last was the 16th February, since which I have not heard from you, nor can I imagine what reason you have to deale so strangely uncivill with mee. Except you change yo[u]r practises and give mee the ordinary civilitys I look for from any man, you must pardon mee, if the respect I have hitherto paid you, be turned into the contrary. It's now neere twelve months since you had my goods and disposed of them, and not yet to give mee some Acc[omp]t is what I should scorne to deny any man. Besides the courtesies I did you (altho[ugh] I am loath to remember them) and the severall promises you made of speedy returnes should in my opinion engage you to some performance. S[i]r very unwilling I am to write such letters as these but you must know I am not so tame as to loose my right for want of speaking, or any other means which except you give mee some Satisfaction shall undoubtedly follow. Herewith is an Inclosed from Mr Blunden.

264. **Mr Bryan Rogers** London 20th Aprill 1661

S[i]r,

Yours of the 15th Curr[en]t I have received with inclosed Invoice an receipt for 37 Slabbs Tynn aboard the *Prosperous* God sending them in Safety. The[y] shall be disposed to yo[u]r most advantage. The 20 Slabbs rec[eive]d by Mr Bloy I have sold & delivered att £4.18s p[er] c[w]t to pay att a moneth which I hope will bee to yo[u]r good Likeing, being the hight of the markett. Some difference I finde in the waight itt makeing out here but 25[cwts] – 3[quarters] – 24[lbs] and yo[u]r Invoice mentions 26.1.10. I suppose the mistake is not with us haveing weighed itt twice for full Satisfaction. I perceive what advice you have from Mr Andrew Rider had his bill come should have found punctuall Complyance as in due time shall that to Mr Depester for £481. The Exchange for Legorne is advanceing so to the most advantage I shall advance my selfe of your effects there, that nothing may remaine behind. Mr Vincent deals not currantly with us haveing promised to writ us but forbeares. I hope is Speedy paying you for us, will make amend, however wee are obliged to yo[u]r care on our behalfe. Mr Bloy hath not yet paid yo[u]r bill of £30 pretending hath not rec[eive]d his freight. I have offered him my assistance but cann Seldome see him.

[At end] A small vessel with Pilchards from Falmouth arrived lately at Legorne and Cannot Sell att $10 p[er] h[ogs]h[ea]d.

265. Mr Ambrosse Jennens London 20th Aprill 1661

S[i]r,
Wee have yo[u]rs of the 8th & 15th Currant and according to yo[u]r desire wee have spoken with the Com[missione]r for Prizes, and are informed from one of them, yo[u]r freind, that as yet there is not any proceedings against in the Exchequer though that is the Course they make use of in Cases of diffirences upon acc[ompt]. Charges in the Accompts deliver into the office the Severall parties, Debto]rs to the King, which certainely is a troublesome businesse, if it should unfortunately proceed so farr for prevention of w[hi]ch the Com[missione]rs say they have sent objections to your accompts expecting yo[u]r answear and tell then they for bare desireing itt may finde some Conclusion peaceably, and because the distan[c]e of place and by correspondence much time will be required to answear & object etc. they desire some freind may be imployed by you to make an end with them, in w[hi]ch if wee cann serve you please to Comand us. For the bond you mention itt's not in our possession, if itt were ['you' x out] should doe you any service. Wee have resolved upon the advice of the above mentioned freind to forbeare paym[en]t of the ['money' x out] £55.7.3 to the Com[missione]rs till some Conclusion bee putt to this busines for 'tis but paying att Last, and till then Surely best in yo[u]r owne hands. [signed] A.H. & T.H.

266. Mr Bryan Rogers London 23th Aprill 1661

S[i]r,
My last advised the Sale and delivery of the 20 Slabbs Tyn and received by the *Silence* since w[hi]ch I have not any of yo[u]rs. This serves Cheifly for advice that the *Prosperous* is safely arrived with us, and comes this day to they key soe I hope my next may advise the receipt of yo[u]r 37 Slabbs Tyn by her, which being in my Custody shall be offered to sale for yo[u]r most advantage I hope that Comoditie will advance in the Price being dearer w[i]th you. I shall doe my utmost for yo[u]r Interest.

267. Mr Edward Bridgewood London 24th Aprill 1661

S[i]r,

I am to begg the favour of you to procure a Safe conveyance for the incloseds in behalfe of a freind. The kind token of China Orranges you sent us, wee received from our freind, Mr Lytcott, in very good condition and returne our harty thancks, him selfe, I suppose, writs you by this Conveyance and gives you an account of an affaire now in agitation, and I hope [brought ?] to a certainety which doth nerely concern him, if itt bee the fashion to give gloves you will be Saluted w[i]th the first.

268. Mr John Byam London 26th Aprill 1661

S[i]r,

Yours severall I have received, the last of the 5th Curr[en]t with yo[u]r order to dispose of yo[u]r lute strings att 2s p[er] bundle, according to the agreement formerly sent you, which is now donne and when imburst the proceed shall attend yo[u]r order for itts dispose. The watch strings I goe selling as best I cann. I perceive the poor accompt, this Comoditie is like to produce which you seeme to impute to my discovering the great parcell I had to dispose, which (under favour) was not donne tell I met this Mr Felgate, that hath them all, nor was there exposed to sale other then one box, which was sold at 2s 6d p[er] bundle. How unwillingly the buyer was to be obliged to accept them, you may judge from his offering mee a Couple pair of silke stockings, to be released. And farther offers mee halfe the profitt provided I will equally share in the losse, which hee greatly feares. S[i]r I did for you the best I could, and had not this party taken them off I question if ever should have arrived to that price. I should thinck itt betters meddling w[i]th this Com[modity] by Commission then otherwise. You mention some small Things you are provideing from Naples which I beleive may doe well, I shall send you a particular of some things for yo[u]r governe. Roman gloves will sell if you finde conveniency to send them. The 21st Curr[en]t his Maj[es]tie roade through the Citte atten[d]ed by Nobility which made a magnificent Cavalcade.[1] In the Citty wee have 4 Tryumphall arches. A larger acc[omp]t I shall send you p[er] the first Conveyance to Leg[orn]e. The 23th was the King's Coronation performed with high Solemnitie. The *Hannibal*, Capt[ain] Haddock, was unfortunately cast away coming about the King's Channell and all her cargo of Currants lost, esteemed worth £50,000. There being likewise aboard some fine Bologna silke.[2]

1. Cavalcade through the City. Pepys wrote 'So glorious was the show with gold and silver, that we were not able to look at itt . . .'(Pepys II p 83.)
2. I cannot find any other reference to the loss of the *Hannibal.* If the cargo were worth as much as £50,000 it would have been an enormous loss. Currants were a very popular commodity in England.

269. Mr James Thierry London 26th Aprill 1661

S[i]r,
Yours of the 29th Curr[en]t I have received with an inclosed accompt of the Sugars & Cottons sould which upon perusall findeing right shall be noted accordingly. I perceive you have the *Dolphin* papers back againe from Mr Hans Hansen without any hopes of restitution from those of Gottenburgh so that some other way must be taken which wee must Consult about when you arrive, which I see you have now thought convenient to make voyage into England, and then may be dispatched the businesse depending about these Shipps at the Barbados. The above mentioned Papers if you please may bring with you. I pray S[i]r give mee timely notice that I may attend yo[u]r arrivall and be some way serviceable to you. The last weeke was cast away the *Hannibal* Capt[ain] Haddock Comander, from Zant with his lading of Currans and some [word x out] silke to a Considerable value – Coming about the King's Channell mett with a Storme so that nothing of the goods was saved. The Ship's compa[ny] had byn Likewise lost had not they byn mett accidentily by one of the King's friggatts as they were in the long boat & Schiffe. For Prizes of Comoditys I referr you to the inclosed.

270. Mr Ambrosse Jennens London 27th Aprill 1661

Our last gave you an acc[omp]t what wee had done in order to yo[u]r bill of Excha[nge] payable to the prize Commissioners since which wee have not had any of yo[u]rs, this serveing cheifly to give covert to the Inclosed coppie of the objections w[hi]ch the Com[missione]rs have made to yo[ur] accompt. As Concerning the

Sallary, after the rate of 12d p[e]r pound wee from discourse gather
that no such allowance hath byn made to any nor will they passe
yo[u]r acc[omp]t being so made up – And because they are willing
to shew you all respect posible they allow severall sumes ['which'
x out] which should [by] Law be made. They judge 'twould be
difficult to obtaine as perticularly the £180 for warehouse keepers.
They Com[missione]rs in short time will be oblidged to give in
their acc[omp]ts to the Exchequer and if, by that time they shall
not have ended with the out ports they must there returne the
Severall Sub Com[missione]rs Debters to the King according to the
Charges themselves put on them, and the dificulty to come out of
the Suit there, is easy to imagine so that upon the whole if there
Can be an end put to these objections 'twill wee conceive be the
best Course in w[hi]ch if wee can be s[er]ving [?] you [word x out]
pray Comand us. Wee take notice Mr Rogers is takeing a Jorney
for London, wee wish him well & intreat you to receive w[ha]t Mr
Vincent is to pay us, either all or p[ar]te & remitt itt up in good
bills as soone as you can.

271. Mr Thomas Dethick, Rich[ar]d Browne & Compa. London 29th Aprill 1661

S[i]rs,
Yours of the 15th Currant I have received with inclosed bill for
$400 at 54d. That on my brother Mr Ab[raham] Hill is accepted,
for $200 and I question not but Mr Squier will accept, and satisfie
that on him, for the other $200 though I have not yet presented
itt to him. The accompt of all I desire as soon as may bee and that
what rests may bee remitted home, the like is what my brother
entreats and that they may come together, because severall p[er]
ticulars therein doe jointly concerne us. The rec[eip]t for three
fanns by Capt[ain] Hart, I have likewise & att his arrivall shall
demand them.

272. Mr Giles Lytcott Mr Walwyn Gascoigne Detto

S[i]rs,
This is Chiefly for advise, and Confirming a draught of mine on
your selves for $500 payable to Mr Dethick & Compa[ny] formerly
made, which was upon the proceed of pilcherds the rest on the

accompt being $568.16.4 I pray passe to the Cr[edit] of my brother Mr Abraham Hill and as then you finde my acc[omp]t Curr[en]t please to vallue yourselves on mee or if in my Cr[edit] remitt of ballance. Yo[u]r Mr Lytcott nor my selfe have not byn of late so punctualls as usuall, *the intrigues of love are tedious,* but I hope itt's almost past, and few dayes may bring him to *Consummatum est.*

273. Justinion Pearde London 30th Aprill

S[i]r,
Yours of the 12 Curr[en]t I have received with your Accompt inclosed which shall bee perused and what errors may appeare shall bee rectified. Mr Timothy Alsop[1] p[re]sents mee yo[u]r bill of Exchange for £14 telling mee yo[u]r occations required a speedy supply for that summe, which I paid him being assured t[ha]t if upon adjusting the acc[omp]ts if you remaine D[ebto]r I shall be reimbursed.

1. Mr Timothy Alsop was brewer to the King. Thought to be a Plymouth merchant who moved to London.

274. Mr Bernard Sparke London 4th May 1661

S[i]r,
Yours of the p[ri]mo Curr[en]t I have received with the inclosed for Amsterdam, which are forwarded. The barter you made against the Oyles I suppose a good bargaine and would willingly concerne my selfe in itt, but because its for our greater conveynience to end all acc[omp]ts depending I am Content that you make our parte yo[u]rs allowing in acc[omp]t according to the market price in w[hi]ch I am confident you will doo us right which donne I pray that w[i]th the first conveniency all acc[omp]ts may be adjusted. Mr Thierry adviseth mee that hee intends shortly to take a voyage hither to us, to dispatch some businesse of Concernment.

275. Mr William Hill London 4th May 1661

I have received yo[u]rs of the 29th past, which I hoped would have accompaned the acc[omp]ts you so Long Since promised but what ever I desire or you promise, I see Little Complyance. A post or two Longer I shall attend, but must advise you that itt's now a yeare since my goods have byn in your possession and I think sould. Should I deale so with anyone I feare might quickly Loose my Correspondence. I beg a Conclusion of this tedious businesse.

276. Mr Ambrosse Jennens London 2d May 1661

S[i]r,

Since our last we have not rec[eive]d any of yo[u]rs. This serves cheifly for advice that yesterday wee past a bill of Exchange on your selfe, in the name of W Hill for £48 att 5 days sight payable to James Corey which wee intreat you to satisfye not doubting but before this Mr Walter Vincent will have paid you a Considerable Summe for our accompt. At instant is come to hand yo[u]rs of the 29th past and, according to yo[u]r desire therein, wee have spoken w[i]th some of the Com[missione]rs who promise that all things shall bee in a readinesse against Mr Rogers comes up to put a Conclusion to yo[ur] accompt depending. Mr Samuel Wilson is yo[u]r freind and wee are Carefull to Engage him to be p[re]sent when any meeting shall bee and wee ourselves will attend also to facilitate the businesse what may bee. Wee hope Mr Vincent will be punctuall. Pray let him be called on to remember his promise.

277. Mr James Thierry London 10th May 1661

S[i]r,

Yours of the 3/13 Curr[en]t I have received with the inclosed for Mr Bernard Sparke which shall be forwarded. With the assurer, Mr Giffard Bale that fayled, I have made an end according to yo[u]r orde[r] and as others have done att 3s 4d p[er] pound and in yo[u]r accompt I give you Cr[edit] £22.7.0 received of him for the Losse of £200 assured by him on the *Dolphin* after the rate of the rate of [sic] £65 p[er] cent as the other assurers paid. I pereceive you resolve for England by way of Dover about a moneth hence. I wish you a good voyage and Safe, if I cann serve please to comand mee. Here is arrived the *Comerce* from Scanderoone with galls and two more expected dayly so that Comodity may be bought reasonable I suppose att £3.12s p[er] c[w]t. If with you the[y] will turne to accompt I shall gladly serve you. The 7th Currant sat the new Parlament, where his Maj[es]tie declared the Match with Portugall which makes the Spanish Embassador Angry[1] and 'tis said hee will suddenly depart without takeing leave of the King. For prizes of comodities refer you to the Inclosed.

1. Charles, King of Portugal offered with his daughter, Catherine, 'one of the richest dowry ever brought by an English queen' it included Tangier, Bombay and trading privileges together with £1,500,000. (Hutton p 188) Spain was not pleased with this alliance and war was a possibility, hence the comments in Thomas Hill's letters.

278. Mr John Byam Detto

S[i]r,

Since my Last of the 26th past I have not received any of yo[u]rs which will cause brevity this serveing Cheifly for advice that yesterday I sould the remaineing Watch Strings at 4s p[er] bundle, to pay in a moneth, which was the height of what I could obtaine for the whole parsell and I hope will be to your good likeing. Altho[ugh] I sould a bundle [a bundle x out] or 2 att 5s yet that price Could not be gott for more and my feare that they might wast by keeping as some began to mould I thought itt best to dispatch them. When I am imburst the money for their proceed I shall attend your ord[e]r for itts dispose. I yesterday met Mr White of Rome who is safely arrived and Left our freind Dr Bacon att Paris intending to follow suddenly. On the 7th Curr[en]t sate the new Parlam[en]t where his Maj[es]tie delared to them the Portugall match at which the Spanish Embassad[o]r seemes huge angry and intends speedily to depart without takeing leave of our King. What the Successe will be, is uncertaine, whether warr or peace, a breach with them is talkt of but not much feared. The Spanish Embasador hath spread abroad some papers in English representing how much more benefitiall it had byn for England to have byn allied to Spaine in a match, then to Portugall, and how prejuditiall to our Comonalty a warr with Spaine will prove, and more perticulars of this nature, tending somewhat to Sedition and is resented in our Court.

279. Mr Thomas Dethicke, Mr Richard Browne & Compa[ny] Detto

S[i]rs,

Yours of the 22th and 29th past I have received with first (and second) bill of Exchange on S[i]r Will[iam] Gardiner for $300 att 54¼[d], 3 mo[nths] in £67.16.3 which he hath accepted and good payment following shall be noted upon acc[omp]t of Hounscott says together with the former remisses of $400 on my brother Mr Abr[aha]m Hill and Mr Hugh Squier. I desire that you please to continue still remitting till all acc[omp]ts be ballanced. What may be due to Mr Groves upon acc[omp]t of calico I shall satisfie him att his arrivall. His Maj[es]tie hath declared in the Parlament his Concluding a match with Portugall, which occasions discourse of a warr w[i]th Spaine but wee hope the Contrary. I have received foure Chests of wine from yo[u]r brother Mr Henry Dethick upon acc[omp]t of Mr Alex[ander] Travell.

280. Mr Ambrosse Jennens London 11 May 1661

S[i]r,

Yo[u]rs of the 4th Curr[en]t wee have received and delivered the inclosed to Mr Rogers. Wee are ready to assist him in Ending yo[u]r accompt with the Com[missione]rs of the Prize Office, and hope in a few dayes may doo itt to yo[u]r content, of all which wee suppose Mr Rogers writs you at Large, and of the new trouble from the Exchequer which wee are informed will come to nothing else but the Charge of s[er]ving forth a *Quietus est* which wee hope will be done without much Charge. However it's an inconvenience to be subject to such disturbances. Your bill of Excha[nge] for £22.4.0 payable to Mr Will[ia]m Glanvill hath not yet byn p[re]sented. Itt shall in tyme find due honour. Mr Vincent deales not well by us, wee must have a little more patience, and are engaged to yo[u]r care in the businesse.

281. Mr Ambrosse Jennens London 14th May 1661

S[i]r,

Yours of the 9th Curr[en]t wee have received. The inclosed delivered to Mr Rogers, with whome wee have byn to adjust yo[u]r accompts of the Prize Office and wee suppose all things are agreed unto, tomorrow is appointed to have them past, when we intend to be p[re]sent and take Care to advance what may be resting to balance itt. We hope the p[re]sent Trouble from the Exchequer will passe over, there being so much Equity and reason on yo[u]r side. What wee may be assistant to Mr Rogers, wee doe readily offer him. The inclosed is all wee have understood from Mr Vincent & till wee heare further can say but Little, wee suppose itt m[a]y bee well to receive some of the money if hee will pay itt in the meane time.

282. Mr Ambrosse Jennens London 21 May 1661

S[i]r,

Yours of the 16th Currant wee have received w[i]th the inclosed to Mr Bryan Rogers which was delivered. Wee have this day satisfied yo[u]r bill of £20 to Mr John Hunkin, and shall give the Like honour to the other of £22.4.0 to Mr Glanvill. Wee expect Mr Vincent according to his promise on the 25th Curr[en]t and require a ready Complyance of what is due to us, though his delay hitherto hath byn to our inconvenience. Mr Rogers has thoughts Speedily to begin his Jorney, what hee leaves w[i]th us to ac[comp]t in his absence, shalbe carefully lookt after.

283. Mr Philip De pape Lond[on] 24th May 1661

S[i]r,

I have understood from a freind of Mr Lanes that yo[u]r selfe and said Mr Lane have put a Conclusion to the businesse formerly betwixt you which I am glad. Hee now desires that I would deliver him up the security his relation gave to my father, when hee requested you to Engage in the businesse of Colwell etc. which I have not yet done, but for answear told him that when I was satisfied from you that the businesse was wholly ended, by the Consent of both partys, and had received from you the Security in your hands of my father's I should doe what was reasonable. Pray S[i]r in answear Let mee understand on w[ha]t termes you are agreed and what else may be necessary to the Concluding this businesse. Whether the Security you have bee bond, or Letter, or what else itt's Conveynient I have itt up for my Discharge.

284. Mr James Thierry London 23th May 1661 [Ditto x out]

S[i]r,

Yo[u]rs of the 17th Curr[en]t I have rec[eive]d the inclosed for Mr Bernard Sparke shalbe forwarded I hope the *Paragon* is arrived and by y[ou]r Care the 14,000 lb Sugar on acco[mp]t of the Ship *Dolphin* will finde quick dispatch. I give you thanks for the present you favour mee w[i]th, I shall take Care at the vessell's Arrivall to gett itt home, and study some requitall for yo[u]r many Courtesys. There is here a fleet ready to goe for Portugall to attend the Queene. The Covenant[1] formerly [made x out] taken, was by the Parlam[en]t ordered to be burnt by the Comon Executioner w[hi]ch was done accordingly. For Prices of Comoditys, I refer you to the Inclosed.

1. The Covenant (the Solemn League and Covenant of 1643) was ordered to be burnt by the common executioner. (Hutton p 155)

285. Mr Ambrosse Jennens May 25th 1661

S[i]r,

Yours of the 18th Curr[en]t, wee have received, w[i]th the inclosed packet for Mr Bryan Rogers, but he haveing begun his Jorney homewards on the 23rd you have itt inclosed. The Letter to you from Mr Vincent wee have perused and hope to see him here, that so wee may make an end of our businesse, on his part has byn delay w[hi]ch in reason must be Considered for Satisfaction. Wee are so well satisfied of the Justnesse of yo[u]r accounts past w[i]th Mr Rogers, for which you now are troubled that wee shall be Carefull to Vindicate you on all occasions. Such Troubles as these frequently happen to persons that have had Publique imploym[en]t and therefore no strange thing if itt fall on you, but wee hope itt will passe over without any further p[re]judice. Mr Rogers will give you an accompt what hee hath done in itt. Yo[u]r bills to Mr Glanvill for £22.4.0 and to Mr John Hunkin for £20 are both satisfied, so shall t[ha]t of £25 to Mr John Rowe.

286. Mr Ambrosse Jennens Lond[on] 28 May 1661

S[i]r,

Being without any of yo[u]rs unanswered shall be the briefer, this serving [word x out] onely for advice that I have this day paid Mr Nicholas Gibbons £5 upon yo[u]r bill of Exchange. By a freind of Mr Vincents wee understand that hee is not yet come to towne as hee intended, but is Expected this weeke. I hope Mr Rogers is in safety with you. Pray let him have the Inclosed.

287. Mr Bryan Rogers Ditto

S[i]r,

I hope this will finde you in safety returned home. This serveth cheifly to accompany the Authentique Translation of the Dutch Chiptye[?] for the Com[missioners] of the Prize office I have not heard any thing nor doe I further Solicitt them to signe the accompt supposeing their occasions for money will make them send to mee first, which possibly may be the best way. As you shall direct I shall act. I have not mett Mr Hodges since yo[u]r departure but I intend to goe to his house for information concerning yo[u]r businesse. Wee have noe news worth your notice. I have not yet heard of Mr Beake & Jacobson.

288. Mr John Jackson London 29th May 1661

S[i]r,

I have understood from Mr Phillip Jackson, yo[u]r brother, of some difference that was betwixt yo[u]r selfe & my father Rich[ar]d Hill concerning £40 paid to Mr John Barker. It was long before my time So that our bookes are my only direction where upon perusal I finde that by yo[u]r order £875 was paid John Barker. So that if after yo[u]r said order was given you supplied him with £40 which should have byn Defaulitt [sic] out of the above said some, Yet I suppose it was not. The coppie of m[y] Father's Letter I have p[er] used, in w[hi]ch he mentions somewhat of an Error in the acc[omp]t Sent, which certainely would at that time have byn made good. If upon second thoughts some sufficient reason appeared not to the contrary, nor doe I find by yo[u]r correspondence for many yeares after, any mention of this businesse and doe suppose had appeared otherwise then I state it, would you have left money standing owt. S[i]r, Itt's my desire to doe what is equity and therefore pray that if you can say anything may better [word x o] cleere this businesse. I shall be alwayes ready to give answear and satisfaction where 'tis due.

289. Mr Alexander Travell London 30 May 1661

Under this date wee writt jointly to w[hi]ch referr you, my Letter Serving onely to give some hint of pasages with us. The first remarkeable is the King's Coronation and passage through the Citty[1] which was Highly magnificent, passing foure tryumphal Arches designed by Mr Ogilby who intends to Cut them In Copper[2] w[i]th the Cavalcade which when perfected shalbe sent you. The Nobility were gallant w[i]th foot cloaths to a great Value, but the p[ar]ticulars I leave to the [?] relation. For the Solemnity were made Knights of the Bath, of which S[i]r William Gardiner[3] is one, and the[y] say two dayes Marryed a great fortune w[i]th a widdow, and now I speake of Knights – S[i]r Will[iam] Rider[4] hath rec[eive]d that honour & Sir Joseph Throckmorton[5]. The Letter of yo[u]r Jorney in France that I Lamented the hope of, is since come to hand giving us a very pleasant acc[oun]t of yo[u]r self, which I did you the right to Comunicate to yo[u]r freinds. Wee had lately w[i]th us the Florance Embassador, who Entered very handsomely and was accompanied to his Audience w[i]th score of Coaches. The Turky Compa[ny], espetially our friend Mr Lytcott, Entertained[6] and the Prince of [word x out] Parma who was then Here, first w[i]th the Sight of Hampton Court & in their returne w[i]th a Stately Dinner and banquet at his Cousin Carlisle's in new parke to the Intire satisfaction of his Excilency and his retinue.[7] *Sig[nor] Giglio* hath byn happy in p[re]senting his service to a young Lady by name Mrs Sarah Culling rarely handsome without Complement.[8] Her age not Sixteene, tall allmost as I am, her vertue as other Ladys', and something more haveing an Estate bin £7,000 st[erling] and has in Jointure from him, not so much as may p[re]judice his Estate. The marriage is not Solemnized but I Looke on itt as a Certainety. It's a Strang great fortune, and though wee found great & many difficultys -for I have byn engaged since the beginning- yet I think all is now past. Will Vannam is this day marryed to Mr Wild's daughter the druggest in Lombard Street and for her portion hath under £2,000.

The King's match w[i]th the Infanta of Portugall is the great news, a fleet of 20 Sale are in a readinesse to fetch her over. The Spanish Embass[ador] Seemes much troubled att It, but in probability wee may not fall out w[t]h that Crowne, though it hath byn Spoken of. The Parliam[en]t is now Sitting. The things of note done are the ordering the Covenant, and Oliver's instrum[en]t of Governm[en]t to be burnt by the Comon w[hi]ch was done accordingly. Mr Crafton for Seditious preaching is Close prisoner in the Tower & Care takeing to prevent Such things for the future. G.Richard's man, Richard, was unfortunately killed by the goeing off of a pistol in Mr Butler's shop This weeke dyed ould Mr Harvey in the Country, so probably Mr William Harvey may not come abroad. Pray my Service to Mr M. Harvey. I am to give you the thanks of the friends you obliged w[i]th the Present of wine, w[hi]ch proved rarely good thoug[h] after a long passage. The 3 Fans I have delivered as you ordered perticularly, that to Mrs Maskelyne. [word x o] Wee never meet but yo[u]r good health is remembered accompanied w[i]th many good wishes. The Widdow remaines Still as Shee was although entertaines Severall upon acc[oun]t of matrimony but I think *more for passing the time than anything else.*

All yo[u]r Kindred are well. Yo[u]r bro[ther] Travell I saw today & yo[u]r Brother Young every day. Your Cousen Mal Travell as I take itt wants you to promise as Compare to her great Belly.

1. The Coronation held on April 23 is described in detail by Evelyn (Evelyn p 273) and Pepys (Pepys II p 83)
2. Evelyn spent part of the evening of the 22 April 'seeing the severall arch-triumphals built in the streets at severall eminent places thro' which his Majesty was next day to passe, some of which, tho' temporary, and to stand but one yeare, were of good invention and architecture, with inscriptions'.(Evelyn p 273)
3. Sir William Gardner. London merchant (Woodhead p 75)
4. Sir William Rider. an important Baltic merchant. (Pepys X p 354). He died 1669.
5. Sir Joseph Throckmorton. a merchant trading to the Mediterranean.(Pepys X p 446)
6. This entertainment of Giles Lytcott shows his importance as a merchant.

7. Cousin Carlisle? Charles Howard was created Earl of Carlisle on the 22nd April the day before the Coronation. Lt.General of the Kingdom in 1667, Governor of Jamaica 1677-81. FRS 1665. (Pepys X p 197)
8. Sarah was the only daughter and heir of Richard Culling, a merchant of Exeter

290. Mr Tho[mas] Dethicke Mr Rich[ard] Browne & Compa[ny] Lond[on] 27th May 1661

Yo[u]rs of the 13th Curr[en]t I have received w[i]th the inclosed acc[omp]t Curr[en]t w[hi]ch upon p[er]usall findeing right shall be noted accordingly. The bill of $262.14.7 at 55¼d on Mr Will[iam] Williams he hath accepted and I question not but good payment will follow.

291. Mr James Thierry London 31th May 1661

S[i]r,
Being without any of yo[u]rs unansweared shall bee the Breifer. This only Serveing to accompany the inclosed from Mr Bernard Sparke and give Covert to the bill of prizes [i.e.prices].

292. Mr James Thierry London 7th June 1661

S[i]r,
Being without any of yo[u]rs unansweared shall be the Briefer. This is Cheifly for Covert to the inclosed papers Received from Mr Richard Jones, the master of yo[u]r *Dolphin* the trouble he is in, you will p[er]ceive from their p[er]usal. There are Large instructions to his wife, how shee should proceed in procureing his release and Satisfaction for the damages he hath Suffered. I wish hee may obtaine what he desires, in which if I cann be Serviceable I Shall be always ready. The Vessell by which you send the taken of biskett is arrived, and I hope to have itt up to morrow.

293.Mr Bryan Rogers London 8th June 1661

S[i]r,
I congratulate your Safe returne home, where I hope you found all our freinds in good health. Since your departure I have had

Severall meetings with those of the prize office, and till yesterday the[y] Resolved not to signe Mr Jennens' accompt insisting upon his giveing them Security to make good what might be objected to the accompt in the Exchequer. To which I gave them Such reasons t[ha]t the[y] [might x out] are satisfied w[i]thout itt, and so to continue them in a good mode I paid them £50, and am provideing the rest t[ha]t so the acc[omp]t may be I hope Speedily Sent you. The papers of Mr Hodges shall be delivered him and yo[u]r businesse recommended to his Care. I have observed your order not to pay Mr Jacobsons the money formerly you desired mee to doe [word x out], and Such answear I have tould them, so I Suppose you heare from them p[er] this post. Two pounds of Spanish Tobacco Shall be Sent you p[er] the first conveyance. I have paid Mr Leacher £10. Mr Vincent is in towne & wee have appointed a meeting w[i]th him. I have this day paid £25 to Mr John Rowe, yo[u]r father's bill. Pray advise the late draughts he hath made are to be placed to yo[u]r acc[omp]t.

294. Mr John Lane Ditto

S[i]r,
I have understood from Mr Philip De pape that the businesse formerly depending betwixt your selfe, and him is now [ended x out] concluded. The like was tould mee by Mr Pollexfen to whome I perceive you Recommended the adjusting the acc[omp]t betwixt my Father and yo[u]r Unckle. To that Gentl[eman] yo[u]r freind I have not to object but Suppose itt would be more Convenient that it were done by yo[u]r selfe, both for takeing and giveing [word x out] necessary discharges after wee Shall have agreed, and other p[ar]ticulars, w[hi]ch I Suppose a third p[er]son cannot so well doe. Upon yo[u]r answear I shall doe what shall be reasonable.

295. Mr Bryan Rogers London 11th June 1661

S[i]r,
The want of yo[u]rs causes brevity, This Serveing only to accompany the Inclosed accompt from the Com[missione]rs of the Prize Office Signed by them all and the note I gave Mr Walter Barnesly for £200 with his receipt upon itt, in w[hi]ch though he mention £150 by my note Upon Ald[erman] Backwell, that Somme is Since

Complyed w[i]thall I am Glad this troublesome businesse is att Last ended. I wish a good Conclusion to the others depending, to the effecting of w[hi]ch if I cann bee any wayes Serviceable.

296. Mr Hillary Hill London 12th June 1661

In August last I writt you, and therein was willing to forebeare six moneths, for your more Convenient paying of the £26 you owe by bond, expecting to have heard from you, but not onely that Lymitted time is past, but some moneths Longer and I am Still w[i]thout that money. I writ therefore to put you in minde of itt, entreating that you would take some Speedy Course to Satisfie itt and thereby prevent any further Inconvenience.

297. (In Italian) My dear Sig[nor]e Jacopo Baldinotti,

In conformity with your orders given me I have had made six pairs of shoes which will be dispatched with the first ship for Livorno. The letter with a song inside sent with the *Good Hope* I can in no way find. This accident, truly unfortunate and disagreeable to me being a song as you say which is very beautiful. But show patience, there are others. The pewter sells at higher prices. I would like to say a few words about this. Big plates of every sort if they are plain as always well made [cost 13 *Pennini* ?] thanks to the pound of 16 ounces. Pewter as candlesticks and other large weighty objects as decanters [*boccali*] and similar cost once twice and three times, according to the work on them.

New Signor Jacopo command me freely, with all my fond remembrances to Signor Gioseppe and all my patrons of that my dear Lucca I remember with my heart.

14 June 1661 London

298. Mr James Thierry London 14th June 1661

My Last accompanied Severall Writings rec[eive]d from Capt[ain] Rich[ar]d Jones, I hope the[y] are Safe w[i]th you. Being Still wanting yo[u]rs causeth my brevity, this Serving only for Covert to the inclosed from Mr Rogers and the Price Curr[en]t of Comodities, if in ought I can serve you please to Command mee.

299. **Mr Bryan Rogers** London 15th June 1661

S[i]r,

My Last was on the 11th Curr[en]t accompaning the Acc[omp]t from the Com[missione]rs of the prize office w[i]th the Severall sumes which I hope to is to the good Likeing of Mr Jennens & yo[u]r self. According to your order I refuse to pay the £90 demanded by Mr Beake & Jacobson. Yo[u]r Severall Papers I have delivered to Mr Hodges who Saith is mindfull of yo[u]r businesse, but Cannot yet give any further acc[oun]tof itt. I shall be carefull to call upon him to bring itt to a Conclusion. I shall in a few dayes send acc[oun]t of the Tyn sould, that so all thing may be sett right. The Letter to Mr Tho[mas] Cox Shall be forwarded by the first post. I perceive the price of Tyn is w[i]th you very High with us itt's worth £5.1.0. p[er] c[w]t. If in any thing I can Serve you pray Comand mee.

300. **Mr Bryan Rogers** London 18th June 1661

S[i]r,

Yo[u]rs of the 13th Curr[en]t I have received takeing notice of yo[u]r draught on mee for £25 payable to Mrs Elizabeth Peters, which Shall finde punctuall Complyance and past to acc[omp]t where you shall have Cr[edit] for the ballance of Mr Ambrosse Jennens's acc[omp]t. I have made enquiry Concerning the *Providence* of new England, John Sprye m[aste]r, but Cannot have any news of her. I shall be mindfull of itt hereafter and advise you. Wee are endeavouring Some Conclusion w[i]th Mr Vincent Whilst in towne and I hope to bring itt to some good Issue.

301. **Mr John Byam** London 21th June 1661

S[i]r,

Being without any of yours Causeth brevity, This serveing Cheifly to accompany the acc[omp]t of yo[u]r Lute strings, 19 boxes rec[eived] p[er] Capt[ain] Nash. You will p[er]ceive 6 bundells wanting of what the Invoice mentions which wee found to bee in those Consigned to Mr Felgate which had in each 60 or 66 bundells so twas Easie to make an Error in markeing them. Wee Counted out every box for [word x o] the more certainety.

Adi detto

S[i]r,

Since the above written is come to hand yo[u]rs of the 7th Curr[en]t for answear, Strings for watches will sell w[i]th us, the evener they are wrought so much the better, if anything to be gotten by them att 4s p[er] bundle, I suppose may arrive to it at any time, if more you may bee assured I shall doe the best I cann. For Roman gloves ⅔ for women of a Sadd colour, the Longer the more in Esteeme, one ¼ to be of Principani skins, ¼ half principani, the rest the ordinary sort. The Like Sortment for men. Some whole Skins may doe well w[i]th the Cost noted perticularly for my Goverm[en]ts. Oiles & Esenses may doe well but Cheifly Roses, because those Sorts keep best & if they once decay are not in esteeme, and will not sell at any rate. Of late wee have been disturbed w[i]th doubts how wee stand w[i]th Spaine but at p[re]sent thers no reason to suspect the Continuance of a good Correspondence. The fleet of twenty Sale in Cirea were variously discourst of in relation to their designe but itt now generally beleived they are ordered for the Streights to Looke after the Turks motion.[1] Our Spanish M[er]chants goe on still in their usuall trade for Spaine and till wee p[er]ceive some reason to the Contrary wee need not feare. The Spanish Embassador is still here, & keeps a faire correspondence w[i]th his maj[es]tie. The Princesse of Portugall that is to be our Queene will shortly be attended w[i]th a Royall fleet. Aatt [sic] home thanks bee to God wee are all quiett. The Marquesse of Argile was lately Executed in Scotland by the Comand of that parliam[en]t.[2] The King's Judges remaine in the Tower still, the parliam[en]t not haveing yet taken any notice of them. *Our dear Mr Lycott is not yet married but will be soon his wife being very beautiful and very much to his liking. I wish them every happiness.*

1. There were worries, which occurred frequently, about Turkish pirates, and also some fear that war might break out with Spain because of Charles II's marriage to a Portuguese princess.
2. Marquess of Argyle. See note to letter no. 103

302. **Mr James Thierry** London 21th June 1661

Being w[i]thout any of yo[u]rs unansweared causeth brevity this Serving cheifly for Covert to the inclosed from Mr Bernard Sparke.

I am againe to returne you my thanks for the barrell of Dutch Rusk w[hi]ch is come to hand in Safety. I hope may shortly bee able to serve you here which I shall bee alwayes ready to doe.

303. Mr Bryan Rogers London 22th June 1661

S[i]r,
Being without any of yours causeth Brevity, this being cheifly to accompany the inclosed accompts of the Tynn consignmed mee vizt.
20 Slabs p[er] the *Silence;*
18 Slabs p[er] the *John*
37 Slabs p[er] the *Prosperous*[1]
[word x out] All which I hope upon perusall you will finde right. Att present said Comodity is worth £5.1s. [per cwt]. I am mindefull to Enquire after the *Providence*, but Cannot meet any of her assurers that are Concerned in her. Pray advise who she is Consigned to, if here or to what port, that I may know the best way to bee advised of her. I have Spoken w[i]th Mr Hodges who gives mee no further accompt of yo[u]r businesse but saith will take care to prevent any inconvenience. My Respects to yo[u]r selfe and all freinds w[i]th you I Remaine.

1. There are references in the Falmouth port book for 1661 TNA: PRO E 190/1037/3 to these three ships. The *Silence,* Captain Nicholas Bloyes re a voyage London to Falmouth; the *John,* Captain Angel Corbin, in April 1661 loaded tin for London and the *Prosperous* Captain George Pomeroy, also loaded tin for London including 188 cwt for Bryan Rogers. See Appendix A re accounts for the Silence, *John* & *Prosperous.*

304. Mr Bernard Sparke London 22th June 1661

Yo[u]rs of the 19th Currant I have received, yo[u]r Letter to Mr James Thierry forwarded. By the last Letter from him I p[er]ceive had resolved to beginn his voyage for Engl[and] in a moneth. I wish wee ['then' x out] might then thinck upon some meanes to procure restitution for the *Golden* ['*Fleece*' x out] *Dolphin*. I have your Accompts ot the *Swann*'s Oyle w[hi]ch shalbe perused & being found right, shalbe noted accordingly. In the meane [while?]

your bill of £100 on Mr Lawrence Blancart, he hath promised to Satisfie. The rest on the acc[omp]t I desire may be remitted up w[i]th yo[u]r conveyniency.

305. Mr Bryan Rogers London 29th June 1661

Yo[u]rs of the 24 Currant I have received with the inclosed for Bilboe which Shall be forwarded with the first oppertunity. I am mindfull to inquire after the *Providence* but have yet noe news of her if the master have embraced freight for Spaine itt may doe well, for at pr[e]sent is no more discourse as formerly a breach with that Crowne, because the fleet Lately departed is beleeved to be gonne for barbary. If you think fitt to have assurance made I shall doe itt to the best advantage. I perceive you have drawne £33 payable to Mr John Hopkins, Which shall be satisfied as that of £25 is to Mrs Peters. I am promised the Tynn money the next weeke. I hope the Party will be punctuall, that Comodity now worth £5.1.0 to £5.2.0 p[er] c[w]t. Mr Delmier[1] was w[i]th mee, earnest to have bought a good p[ar]cell. I suppose the rather, because Likely itt may be brought under a farme.[2] Some say already done, so that if you think of dispatching up any quickly, may bee well. Some thoughts wee have for a Pilchard Shipp therefore yo[u]r full advice will be welcome, if 6 in 700 h[ogs]h[ea]ds of the first fish can be Secured. I call upon Mr Hodges but hee gives mee no farther acc[omp]t of your businesse only Saith, will be Carefull that no further prejudice follow.

1. Mr Delmier. Peter Delme [?] was an important London merchant of Huguenot descent.
2. Before the Civil War the 'farmers' of tin enjoyed a monopoly for the purchase of tin. There was a suggestion that this should be revived.

306. Mr Bryan Rogers London 6th July 1661

Yours of the p[ri]mo Curr[en]t I have received with an Inclosed for Mr James Thierry which I for bare to forward (because, calculating from his Last advice, he is now upon his Voyage for England). I have been mindfull of the *Provid[ence]* & shall so still but from new England hath not come any vessell in the last 3 moneths nor any yet expected. When any Shipp arrives I shall take up yo[u]r

Lett[e]rs & forward them. To give any certaine advice w[i]th our accord with Spaine I cannot nor is it now much Spoken of because the fleet Lately departed is gone for Barbary. A breach w[i]th that Crowne is not feared. If I understand further shall advise you. The bill of £50 you have drawne payable to the order of Mr W[illia]m Harper shall finde due honour, and I shall supply Mr W[illia]m Rogers what he wants for yo[u]r use but he saith will be £26 or £28. I suppose may doe itt w[i]tho[ut] yo[u]r approbation. In few dayes I hope to cleere the accompts of Tyn and be in Cash to accomodate yo[u]r occasions. Herew[i]th is an inclosed from Mr Tho[mas] Cox, and our price Curr[en]t of Comodit[ie]s.

307. Mr John Jackson Lond[on] 9th July 1661

S[i]r,
Yours of the 10th [word x o] past I have received. The £40 in dispute, paid on Mr Barker, I know not what more to say, but that it was really paid him, and to pay itt twice is not att all reasonable. Possibly this Sume should have been deducted out of the £875 but I suppose the not doing itt, is not suffitient reason to make ill our lose. However I am Content to prevent farther trouble to imbursse you this Sume of forty pounds provided I receive yo[u]r obligation to repay itt in case (upon perusall of the Accompts to which I am a Stranger, being a businesse transacted Long since) I finde itt and make itt appeare already made good. This I more readily Consent to, in respect to yo[u]r selfe and yo[u]r brother, Mr Phill[ip] Jackson, who discourst to me of this businesse before he left the Citty, although the soe doing is wholy to our p[re]judice.

308. Mr Bryan Rogers London 13th July 1661

S[i]r
Yours of the 7th Currant I have received with the inclosed for Nantz, which is forwarded. If any Letters from the *Providence* for you, shall be lookt after you will have by this post, yo[u]r Joint lett[e]r Confirmed, so I pray be very carefull to comply w[i]th our desire it happ[en]ing so opertunely and I hope wee may have the fish upon the better termes supposing wee are the first buyers and although wee Limit no price yet wee must not pay the dearer, because you are at liberty. This I write as the sense of the Interested, for my

part I am assured you will doe the utmost for our advantage. I must farther note to you, that the Larger our fish is, its for our advantage, so that if a h[ogs]h[ea]d might containe 5000 small tale fish, 'twould be to our great satisfaction. The fish must be well cured and the Cask tyte, for our designe is for Leg[orn]e and passages are uncertaine, Sometymes Long. Dispatch is certaine gaine and neglect as Certain Losse. You know this sort of trade so sufficiently that I shall not enlarge.

I am not yet in Cash for the whole of yo[u]r Tyn money however shall give honour to yo[u]r bill of £105 to Mr Richard Sleeman etc. Mr Thierry is arrived in England and remaines at Dover about the dispatch of a ship of his there outward bound, he intends to bee here w[i]th us Shortly. I forward yo[u]r letter to him p[er] this post. Tyn worth something about £5. The trouble you have about that Comodity I suppose is in order to the farming of itt. S[i]r Will[iam] Vincent & S[i]r George Smith had some such discourse & thoughts to doe itt, but 'twas six moneths since, but now have layd itt asyde. Herewith is Coppie of what wee writt you, and should now have confirmed but besides that some of our number are out of towne, wee have not to ade only that our agreem[en]t of the fraight is so much by the Tunn of 4 h[ogs]h[ea]ds so that bigger or smaller itt [tis?] the same thing. But this is not to be understood to make any alteration in the usuall bignesse of the Caske, only what is before mentioned the larger fish & consequently the fewer in each h[ogs]h[ea]d is what wee desire. Yo[u]r punctuall advice of the needfull will be welcome.

309. **Mr Bernard Sparke** London 16th July 1661

Yo[u]rs of the 10th Curr[en]t I have received w[i]th the inclosed accompt Currant w[hi]ch shalbe p[er]used. Yo[u]r Remisses of £218.6.5½ I have received & have promise of payment (that on Mon. Coronell Chalon is at long time, however am Content supposeing itt will be punctuallly Complyed w[i]th). Mr James Thierry is arryved at Harwich and gone since for Dover to dispatch a Ship afterwards intends for London [in margin] [where?] I shall gladly see you.

310. **Mr Bryan Rogers** London 16th July 1661

By the last post I writt at large to which and the former Joint Letter wee attend yo[u]r answer. I have now yours of the 10th Curr[en]t w[i]th the inclosed to Mr Thierry which at his arrivall shall be d[e]l[iver]ed [to x out] him, and if he discourseth Concerning you, I shall doe you all the service I cann doe. As yet I have not received any Letters from the *Providence* when I doe they shall be forwarded. Yo[u]r bill of £50 payable to Col[onel] Arundell shall be accep[te]d. Mr Willi[am] Rogers shall be supplyed according to yo[u]r order. Besides what I formerly writt about a fish designe if there be hopes of plenty and a Nimble Vessel of 100 t[on]s would load to discharge at Alicant or Legorne to be had w[i]th you, my brother and my selfe would Concerne o[ur] selves and you might have ¼. Pray Consider of itt and give us yo[u]r full advice.

311. **Mr Bryan Rogers** London 17th July 1661

Your Severalls are Received to which the Intressed have desired mee to answear. Yo[u]r discretion in not giveing so extravagent a rate as 11s.6 p[er] m[ille]. for Pilchards they very well approve of, and by this are well satisfied that though they have not Limited you, you will endeavour in all things for their most advantage, and hope that the hopes & probability of plenty will much abate the price. Large fish and Carefully Cured is what wee againe Recommend to your Care because our Voyage will be as farr as Legorne. For your Provision with money some part though wee cannot say how much will be paid your order in Plymouth, the rest for the first payment, your freind Mr Ab[raham] Searle may for your acc[omp]t Value him selfe on mee, I being promised timely imbursement from the Intressed, but I supose will nott be necessary to draw till fish secured. What convenient time may be for the bills will suite best w[i]th our occasions. I have paid yo[u]r £105 bill to Mr Sleeman & £30.17s for 2 Cables aboard the *Willing Minde* as p[er] the inclosed note.

Wee Continue w[i]th thoughts of a small Vessel with fish when the come in plenty and Cheape in which you may have a parte, so that I think you may Looke out for a fitt Shipp and advise us the needfull. Your Severall incloseds for Mr Thierry shall be delivered when hee Comes hither, at p[re]sent is att Dover about the Dispatch of a ship Herewith the price Curr[en]t.

312. Mr James Thierry London 29 July 1661[1]

At instant are Come to hand yo[u]r severalls, altogether which I strange att. Surely have byn deteyned somewhere. I perceive the Care you have taken to arrest the Shipp that tooke our *golden Dolphin*,[2] w[hi]ch is very well and I hope so much may Come of itt that itt fully repay the losse and charges wee have been at. I shall use all diligence to finde out the Command[er] though I suppose will lye hid to p[re]vent trouble, but possibly may be found by as good fortune, as you mett the Shipp, my endeavour shall not be wanting. Tomorrow I shall writ the needfull to Mr Sparke and Jennens & forward the incloseds. Mr Sparke will be here to meet you. If yo[u]r advice had come Sooner I had wayted on you at Dover, but now itt's to late. I hope to kisse yo[u]r hand in 2 or 3 dayes in London.

1. James Thierry arrived in Harwich on the 17th July (new style) He twisted his foot and sprained his ankle shortly after arriving which made travelling difficult for him. (Schellinks p 31) When they arrived at Dover Thierry's ship *The Seven Star* came into harbour to meet up with Mr Thierry. It had come from Barbados with a cargo of sugar and cotton.
2. On the 3rd (NS) a privateer from Dunkirk tied up next to Mr Thierry's own ship It was recognised as the ship which, under a Swedish Commission, had captured the *Dolphin* and James Thierry arranged for it to be impounded. [There is some confusion here as Hill mentions the *Golden Dolphin*]

313. Mr Bernard Sparke London 30th July 1661

Herewith is an inclosed from Mr Thierry, I Suppose adviseing the arrest he hath laid upon the Ship that tooke the *Dolphin*, which hee mett accidentally in the Downes. It's necessary wee Consult about improveing this good fortune for our most advantage and repareing o[u]r Losses. Mr Thierry may be here in 2 dayes soe that Since you have resolved to meet him here the sooner the better to prevent Losse of tyme.

314. Mr W[illia]m Jennens Ditto

Of late I have not written you for want of occasion. This serves Cheifly for Covert to the inclosed from Mr Thierry who I suppose adviseth the arrest hee hath Laid upon the Shipp that tooke our *Dolphin* meeting her accidentaly in the Downes. Hee desires wee may consult how itt best to proceed for improveing this good fortune & Repaireing our losses, yo[u]r advice will be welcome.

315. Mr Bryan Rogers London 3rd August 1661

Yours of the 29th past is received, by which the Severall intressed in the *Virgin* p[er]ceive that since yo[u]r formers there hath not beene taken any more fish but that w[i]th the first oppertunity their p[ar]cell shall be secured. Upon notice of which for the first payment one Will order £200 or thereabouts to bee paid att Plymouth, as you hereafter direct, which will pr[e]vent Mr Ab. Searle valueing himselfe upon mee. You formerly desired two pounds of Spanish Tobacco which I intended you out of a p[ar]cell of my owne, but that not proveing very good I send itt not and pray to know if you are otherwise Supplyed, if not, other shall be sent p[er] the first convenience. Mr Thierry I expect In London to day when yo[u]r Severall shalbe delivered. Mr Delmier and others enquier after Tyn. I could wish had a p[ar]cell – itt's worth about £5.1s a £5.2s. p[er] c[w]t.

316. Mr Bryan Rogers London 6th August 1661

I have rec[eive]d yo[u]rs of the p[ri]mo Curr[en]t. Yo[u]r 2 draughts for £50 & £8 shall finde due honour. Wee hope yo[u]r next will bring us good news of fish. The Dutch Greenland fishing hath failed and besides 24 Sale are there Cast away. Yo[u]r Severall are delivered to Mr Thierry now w[i]th us.

317. Mr Arnold Breames London 8 August 1661

The businesse of arresting the friggat in yo[u]r Port Mr Thierry hath recomended to my Care. I have byn at the adm[ira]lty Court for more Certaine advice where the Procters tell mee, That the

Procter who there assists you must proceed to have her Condemned w[i]th what Speed may bee, w[hi]ch will [inserted] question[less?] bee if noe one in the behalfe of the owner Mr James Splading [sic] putts in bale to the action. If there should bee baile then wee cann send you downe all necessary proofes, which are here by us. Pray advise the Capt[ain]'s name and what you cann understand from the Shipp's company, whither that Mr James Spalding be Sole owner, or if his father, one Spalding of Gottenburgh, be not Concerned and who is their Correspondent in London, and what else you Suppose may give us Light in the businesse. Tomorrow I shall send you a Letter from o[urselves] to yo[u]r Procter for his Goverment.

318. Mr Arnold Breames London 9th August 1661

Yesterday I writt you the needfull since w[hi]ch I have understood by yo[u]rs to Mr Thierry that Mr Dela Vall had given order to baile the action against the Shipp *Robino.* If it be accordingly done, pray advise, and if said Shipp be departed, as yo[u]r answear is, soe will proceedings be governed. Pray lett itt be full and the needfull. Till I have yo[u]rs to answear I shall not enlarge.

319. Mr W[illia]m Hill London 13th August 1661

I have rec[eive]d yo[u]rs of the 5th Currant w[i]th the inclosed to my Cowz[i]n W[illia]m which is delivered to him as I have hitherto. So I shall continue to Supply his occasions for necessarys. I note to you D[ebtor] £3 upon acc[omp]t of goods I recommended to yo[u]r Care though I might better have imployed my money, however I make noe more words of itt. Pilcherds, I p[e]rceive, fall not in to Content, when doe I wish yo[u]r dealings may encourage others more then my selfe.

S[i]r, I had [inserted] forgott to note that you allowe £10 upon acc[omp]t of my coz[e]n Thomas Howett, and then I shall be in disburs for you as underneath w[hi]ch pray appoint mee.

Mr William Hill	D[ebto]r	Cr[edit]	
to cash lent him	£ 6.01.00	By Mr Peake	£70.00.00
Paid his Son	£ 7.01.02		
to the proceeds of hops etc	£51.05.00	By Ballance	£ 4.06.02
you allow for Tho[mas] Howett	£10.00.00		£74.06.02
	£74.06.02		

320. Mr Bryan Rogers London 13th August 1661

Yo[u]rs of the 8th Curr[en]t I have rec[eive]d and Shewed the Cont[en]ts to the interresed, who are not willing to give so great a price as 12s p[er] m[ille].as itt seemes some have done, but leaving itt to yo[u]r discretion, hope you will doe for them as ['for' x out] yo[u]r selfe, although nere the price is beyond what they are willing to give, but if Plenty of fish fall in, and the Price abate, then wee pray be as forward to secure our p[ar]cell, as may be, and because the first payment must be advanced, you or yo[u]r freind may value yourselves on mee & Compa[ny] which shall finde due honour. You shall have 2 lbs of the best Spanish Tobacco with the first conveya[nce].

321. Mr Arnold Breames London 15th August 1661

S[i]r,

Yo[u]rs of the 10th & 13 Curr[en]t I have rec[eive]d takeing notice how our Cause is going forward. Your next may give the certainety if the Shipp be bailed, when not please to make use of the Sev[er]all authentique writings made here by my deceased Father, Mr W[illia]m Jennens, Mr Bernard Sparke & Thomas Waterfeild m[aste]r when our *Dolphin* was taken. They are questionless sufficient to prove our intrest. Mr Thierry will make his againe here if itt be needfull, though I believe may be spared, the others declareing his Concernm[en]t espetially Mr Waterfield. Pray S[i]r give us yo[u]r utmost assistance in this businesse.

322. Mr Alex[ander] Travell Lond[on] 15 Aug[us]t 1661

The three Fans you Sent p[er] the *Rose & Crowne* are received and delivered according to yo[u]r ord[e]r. My Sister's pleaseth her well and shee gives you her thanks. Yo[u]r Couz[in] Bullivant hath received yo[u]r Sena, but saith itt's very bad however will make the most of itt. Yo[u]r shee freinds are all very well and give you theire respects. Wee are here in a sickely season, a new distemper, my sister being very ill, wee hope the best, and pray o[ur] next may give you better news.

323. Mr Bryan Rogers London 20th August 1661

Yo[u]rs of the 15th Curr[en]t I have received. The inclosed to Mr Thierry delivered. I p[er]ceive that pilchards Fall in but slowly, and those already taken are Sould at such high rates that for my part I am unwilling to give and I suppose the intressed w[i]th mee are of the same opinion of which you shall have more Certaine advice p[er] next so pray in the interim dissist proceeding farther. Although lett us have yo[u]r continuall advice, for iff plenty fall in itts probable wee may be doeing somew[ha]t. When the Com[missione]rs of the Prize office send to me for £24.12s upon acc[omp]t of Mr Amb[rose] Jennens they shall have itt. The two lbs of Spanish tobacco you desired is delivered to Edw[ar]d Tinckler aboard *Rob[er]t Morrell* at whose arrivall pray demand itt of him, for such a small p[ar]cell they would not give a rec[eip]t.

324. Mr John Byam London 23th August 1661

Yo[u]rs of the 2nd Curr[en]t I have received, p[er]ceiving you had with Satisfaction received mine which accompanied the accompt of yo[u]r Lute strings. I wish wee may hereafter thinck upon some Comodities, that will give better encouragem[en]t. Yo[u]r Cousin Hatsell is now become housekeeper here in London, haveing lately marryed a widdow, whose former name I cannot yett give you an acc[omp]t of, nor whether or noe shee were a fortune. I sometymes meet him and mind him of you, and that should bee very willing to come in for a fish Shipp to you but the truth is this season hath produced but small quantitys of Pilchards in so much that some freinds w[i]th ourselves having designed a shipp for Liv[orn]o imploy her another way meerly for want of Pilchards and those alredy taken are in Severall hands that have paid for them 12s p[er] m[ille] which is to extravagant a rate. Wee are still in good posture w[i]th Spaine and noe feare of the Contrary. I have been sometimes in Company w[i]th Mr White from whome I understand Dr Bacon hath taken a Jorney into the north. Since his arrivall I have not seene him, although much endeavoured itt. Of Mr Bernard Harris I have not heard [formerly x out] any thing more then what have said formerly soe I feare that businesse is desperate.

Our Mr Lytcott is at his Villa 7 miles off, where besides the delights of the [in Italian] *country, he enjoys the well-beloved company of the lady fiancee although not yet married for she is unfortunately subject to the cursed whims of one of her uncles of poor birth who, controlling a good share of her dowry does not wish them to marry. He gives no other reason except certain interests such as that they have begun a lawsuit God grant it soon [?] The young lady is with her aunt who is her guardian and also stays with Mr Giles in the country, and the aunt is always with her even in bed. So may God sort it out quickly.*

I write in Italian because of the young man who makes the copies of my letters so that he does not understand. If he does not do it properly I apologise. Yours I have not.

325. **Mr Bryan Rogers** London 24th August 1661

Yo[u]rs of the 19th Curr[en]t I have received. The small quantitys of fish taken, and the Price so high as 12s p[er] m[ille] discourageth the freinds concerned w[i]th myselfe to proceed any further in that designe att least for the p[re]sent, although if plenty should hereafter Fall in, wee may engage againe but as now itt is, Pray desist from doeing any thing for secureing the p[ar]cell of Pilchards formerly desired. Three of our number being out of towne, you want their firmes but itt's their sence.

The Letter to Mr Grigg w[i]th the bill of £50 inclosed is now sent him (answear you have underneath). Since the above written answear is t[ha]t the bill will be paid.

326. **Mr Bryan Rogers** London 27th August 1661

I have not rec[eive]d any of yo[u]rs since my last w[hi]ch being the needfull cau[s]eth breavity And have only now to accompany the inclosed Received from Bilboa. The late stormy Weather wee suppose may have brought in store of Fish, of which pray a word for o[ur] Governm[en]t.

327.Edw[ard] Bridgwood Lond[on] 15th Aug[us]t 1661 –

Sent him bill lading for 100 p[airs] silke stockings by the [*London?*]

328.Mr Edward Bridgwood London 28th August 1661

Being well assured of yo[u]r frindship and Confident I may freely entreat yo[u]r utmost asistance, as occation requires, makes mee now earnestly request you, in the behalfe of my esteemed good freind, Mr James Thierry (under whose Covert this will goe) to be helping in a businesse depending in yo[u]r Court at Lisbone. The Severall papers you will have the Perusall of, by which is evident that his desires are full of equity, and nothing but reasonable, soe hee hopes haveing such freinds on his side and by yo[u]r assitance (in which an extraordinary maner I desire) hee may finde justice and quick dispatch in the King's Court. And the rather because his businesse is in a peculiar manner recommended by o[ur] King to S[i]r Rich[ar]d Fanshaw his Maj[es]tie's minister there[1], to whome yo[u]r frequent addresse is [required x out] desired, and offers as yo[u]r experience shall direct for his speedy obtaineing what my freind prays. Could I urge more argum[en]t for the Stronger Recommending this businesse, I would but all are included by the Confidence I have of yo[u]r best endeavours, which being shewed in this will further oblidge.

1. Sir Richard Fanshaw was ambassador to Portugal in 1661/62. (Pepys X p.129)

329.Mr Bryan Rogers Lond[on] 3rd Sept[emb]er 1661

S[i]r The last post I was accompanying Mr James Thierry at Dover who from thence tooke passage Satterday last for Ostend so I did not writ you. I am now w[i]th yo[u]rs of the 26th past to which I p[er]ceive my brother gave answear and I have not to adde other then Covert to the inclosed from Mr Heverland. Yo[u]r £100 bill shall finde punctuall Complyance. The £21.12z is p[ai]d to the Prize Com[missione]rs as you ordered.

330. **Mr James Thierry** London 6th Sept[ember] 1661

By yo[u]rs of the 2d Curr[en]t from Bruges I gladly understand of yo[u]r Safe arrivall soe farr and hope this may welcome you home to Amst[erdam]. For yo[u]r great care of my brother I give you my harty thankes and shall be here alwayes ready to serve you, as him selfe will bee there, when by yo[u]r grave directions he shall be any wayes capeable. Yo[u]r cousin Bullen and my Selfe after yo[u]r departure attended S[i]r Rich[ard] Fanshaw in ord[e]r to the more earnest recommending your businesse to him, of which he hath promised to take an extraordinary care, besides wee lett his secratary know that, if hee assisted, wee should be Civill to him. Pray S[i]r be mindfull to procure Mon[sieur] Selio Marcellis' Letter of Attorney to receive our agreem[en]t w[i]th the *North Lyons* assurers who scruple p[ro]ceeding any further till I have Such an authority, w[hi]ch pray lett come as soone as may bee. Herew[i]th is a Pacquett from Mr Bryan Rogers.

331. **Mr Samuell Hill** London 6th Sept[ember] 1661

By a letter of Mr Thierry I understood of yo[u]r arrivall att Bruges and hope will finde well at Amst[erdam]. Pray bee carefull of what Mr Thierry counsells you Stricktly to observe itt, and hasten yo[u]r settlem[en]t in the Country to Learne the Language w[i]th the utmost Diligence. Avoyde the Dut[c]h vice of Drincking, and thinck often of what I tould, which I hope in a few moneths you will confesse to be true. The improvem[en]t of yo[u]r time will bee to yo[u]r owne advantage. What you want Mr Thierry will furnish you w[i]thall, pray respect him as you ought. Here[i]th is a receit for yo[u]r Trunck, w[hi]ch att the Shipp's arrival, pray a s[er]vant of Mr Thierrys to take up for you.

332. **Tho[mas] Killigrew** Londo[n] 6th Sept[ember] 1661

S[i]r,
A freind of mine hath p[re]vailed with mee to give you the trouble of this Let[te]r, in behalfe of a Gentle[man] of whom itt's necessary

you be informed this Charecter. That hee was a Created Knight of the Bath by his p[re]sent Maj[es]tie and is fated for any other honours, (besides other qualitys) w[i]th Seaven thousand pounds p[er] annum. His humble Request he desires may be P[re]sented to his Maj[es]tie that hee would gratiously bestow on him the honour & title of a Viscount in Ireland which by yo[u]r acceptable interceeding hee doubt not of, because hee lieth not under any censure in Relation to the late distractions. Acknowledgem[en]t of yo[u]r assistance I am informed is in ready Cash, on purpose at a short warning. The name is for some Reasons yett kept from mee, but when itt's necessary shall be knowne. Some indisposition by a late violent Jorney keeps mee from waiting on you but I shall Suddenly doe itt and endeav[our] for yo[u]r pardon in thus troubling of you.

333. Mr Tho[mas] Killigrew London 7th Sept[ember] 1661

I conceive a larger discourse (then is fitt for this paper) to be necessary for the better Carrying on the businesse my former Letter acquainted you w[i]th. I therefore desire if this finds you not att home, that I may by some meanes understand the most convenient time for my attendance on you, for in my opinion, the businesse is feasable, and worth the Consideration for a few minutes. Yo[u]r owne time shall comand my attendance.

334. Mr Bryan Rogers London 7th Sept[ember] 1661

Yours of the 2d Curr[en]t I have received w[i]th the inclosed Pacquet for Mr Thierry, which was forwarded and I hope will finde him safe att Amst[erdam]. I am glad the Letter from Bilbao brought you good news. I have rec[eive]d £50 by the bill y[o]u sent on Mr Tho[mas] Griggs which shall bee noted to yo[u]r Cr[edit]. Your bill of £100 at 6 dayes to Mr Arthur Spry hath not yett byn p[re]sented, in itts time shall finde due honour. Of late wee have not heard from Mr Vincent, pray therefore doe us the favour, at yo[u]r conveniencie to enquire of him his resolution in o[ur] businesse.

335. [in Italian] **My dear Sig[nor]e Jacopo [Baldinotti]**

I have received yours very welcome of the 16 August with the order for a parcel of wrought tin in '*Real*' plate etc. which I acknowledge and within eight days will be ready to enjoy the convenience of the first ship for Livorno and I hope it will please you. A dictionary Italian and English with a certain *libretto* I am sending you together with the aforesaid commodity.

Much to my dismay I have heard it said that at Livorno they suffer very much from a deadly disease therefore I hope our friends are well and that they enjoy perfect health. The new hint of my getting married is in no ways true. God grant that there might be ladies young, rich, beautiful but they cannot be found in the streets so easily. To my dear Piccini I send good wishes. Remember to ask him kindly if he had ever received a letter of mine through Signor Santini, if not I must remember him another time. Now, my Signor Jacopo, you can command me freely as also Signor Gioseppe whose hand I kiss with the greatest affection. Mr Samuel has gone to Holland to learn that language and French and it is possible he will be able to come to Rome and kiss your hand at Lucca. Again all my best wishes my patron and I remember myself to you.

336. **Mr James Thierry** London 13th Sept[ember] 1661

My last was the 6th Curr[en]t. Since which I have not received any of yo[u]rs but suppose you safely arrived at Amst[erdam], haveing understood from Mr De Peyser of yo[u]r being w[i]thin a daye's Jorney of itt. My former Requested yo[u]r speedy procureing Monsieur Sellio Marcellis' Letter of Attorney for, till I have that, nothing more cann be done w[i]th the assurers on the *North Lyon*. Our East India Compa[ny] have appointed a Sale the 18th Octob[er] for all sorts of Comoditys if I can be serviceable to yo[u]r selfe or freinds please to comand mee. Herew[i]th is our Price Currant.

337. **Mr Arnold Braemes** London 19th Sept[ember] 1661

S[i]r,
I give you many thancks for your civilitys when I was at Dover, for which please to command mee freely. By Letters from Mr James Thierry I understand his safe arrivall att Amst[erdam].

Hee mentions the Looking after the Law suite depending w[i]th you and because I have not Lately heard from you I cann give no acc[oun]t of proceedings but Suppose little done otherwise should have heard from you. Your utmost care for us in the most advantageous manadgeing of this businesse I am Confident off but for the better Satisfying the other intressed pray give mee advice of what passeth.

338. Mr James Thierry London 20th Sept[ember] 1661

Yo[u]rs of the 23th Curr[en]t I have rec[eive]d with the Severall inclosed w[hi]ch are forwarded according to Direction onely that to Mr Peter Harvey I know not where to Deliver. I thanck you for mindeing the procuration from Mons[ieur] Sellio Marsellis, the sooner itt comes I shall give the quicker dispatch to his businesse. Pray S[i]r have you heard any thing about Mr Spalding at Dunkirke. I have written to Mr Arnold Brames and shall give you his answear though I beleive Little done else should have heard from him before now. I thanke you S[i]r for the Care you have of my Brother, pray continue itt and Command us freely. I herew[i]th write him which pray lett him have. Some pewter you ordered the workman saith is ready graved and desires you give direction how itt shall be disposed. In what I can serve you please to Comand mee. Herew[i]th is an inclosed from Mr Bryan Rogers.

339. Mr Sam[uel] Hill London Ditto

I have gladly understood yo[u]r safe arrivall att Amst[erdam]. Pray be carefull to settle your selfe somewhere as soone as you can to avoid the Losse of time. Mr Thierry will furnish you w[i]th what you may have occasion for. Your nurse Siggons is very well and p[re]sents you her service. In yo[u]r Roome shee hath both Franck and Richard.[1] I have little to say more then the very earnest recommending to you to very hard study, both to the Language and writing which as I formerly said lett be an Italian Hand being most in use and best for all Languages. Be sure to study and p[er]fect your selfe in the French tongue, the Dutch you must necessarily learne. Although att ['seeme' x out] first itt seems tedious Industry will quickly [inserted] make itt plesent, and the benefitt will be yo[u]rs. Wee are all well thanks be to god, who I pray keepe you soe too.

1. Frances and Richard were the children of Abraham.

340. **Mr Jonathan Parker** London ditto

I owe answear to yo[u]r Courteous Letter of the 28th March and have been prevented answearing itt by some occations and what I can say now is onely that in requitall of yo[u]r Civilitys I shall continue alwayes most ready to serve you and t[ha]t I desire some comand from you is evident from the trouble I herew[i]th give you (that our acc[omp]ts may Ballance) in praying the favour that w[i]th the first conveyance you please to provide and send mee what works of Sig[nor] Giovanni Batt[ist]a Hodierna[1] are published and the *History of Insects* by Pietro Castelli[2] a Phisitian of Messina and, if not yet published, to know when itt will be because *certi vertuosi* here w[i]th us are huge desirous of itt. I hope for some better occasion of trobleing you which I should willingly embrace and is now in designe w[i]th our *Sig[nor]e Gilio* [ie Lytcott], Mr Hopegood, my br[o]ther and myselfe. If itt *succeeds* well if not, you I know will pardon the present troble because in the Like occation or ought elce [word x out] you may freely Command.

1. Giovanni Battista Hodierna (1597–1660) A priest who was an astronomer and mathematician. The Dukes of Montechiaro gave him a house and funded his publications. He studied light passing a prism and formulated a vague explanation of the rainbow. He developed an early microscope and studied the eyes of insects etc. and meteorlological phenomena. His work was little known outside Sicily because his publications had little circulation. These included *Protei caelestis vertigines sev. Saturna systema* (1657) (he produced drawings showing the planet with its rings); *Meidaeorum Ephemerides* (1656) – the first published ephemeredes of the Galilean satellites, *De Admirandis Phasibus in Sole et Luna visis* (1656) a treatise on the appearance of the Sun and the Moon including sunspots and eclipse and *De systemate orbis cometici; deque admirandis coeli characteribus*. Only recently has his work become acknowledged. ref. http:/seds.lpl.Arizona.edu/messier/ xtra/Bio/hodierna.html. seen 24/02/2005. In the *Familiar Letters* (p 39) James Alban Gibbes writing on June 29 1661, told Abraham Hill that he

had met Signor Hodierna by accident. 'His book is printed at Naples (his own country) and treats of the laws and customs of Naples'.

2. Pietro Castelli Italian physician and botantist (1574-1662) He laid out the botanical gardens at Messina where he cultivated many exotic medicinal plants. He was equally distinguished as a botanist, chemist and surgeon.

Ref. http://www.newadvent.org/cathen/03409a.htm seen 24/02/2005

341 .Mr Bryan Rogers London 21th Sept[ember] 1661

Yo[u]rs of the 16th Curr[en]t I have rec[eive]d. the inclosed for Mr Thierry forwarded, and one from him I send you p[er] last post. Yo[u]r £100 bill hath not yett byn pr[e]sented, w[hi]ch I wonder att, being drawne soe long since. Wee thanke you for speaking w[i]th Mr Vincent and for answear pray at yo[u]r leisure lett him know, that the Sume wee agreed on, should have byn paid in March past, and because others complyed not w[i]th him, hee disapointed us, and then came to a new offer of giveing halfe money and bond for the rest att Midsomer next which wee must not consent to but if att one paim[en]t itt may soone bee done and accounting interest from March Last (although something possibly may be abated as to that) Wee are ready to order the delivery of all writings to him and what is fitt in such Cases. If not wee conceive ['of' x out] our selves most free to treat w[i]th others of which there are Choice. Thus much please to acquaint him, and us his answear. For John Pascoe pray gett his rent as soone as you cann. I have been with Mrs Poxton who hath promised to pay your bill of £29 which being rec[eive]d shall be put in yo[u]r Cr[edit]. Wee would gladly make an end w[i]th Mr Vincent to avoid troble, espetially at law to w[hi]ch wee suppose him addicted,. so t[ha]t as above wee might make a perfect conclusion. I would to effect itt make a jorney downe if otherwise itt could not be done. Of yo[u]r £9 bill I cannot yet give any acc[omp]t. I sent this morning but the party was not at home, I shall say more in my next.

342. Mr Arnold Breames London the 24th Sept[ember] 1661

S[i]r,

Yo[u]r courteous Letter of the 19th Currant I have rec[eive]d With the Inclosed claime of S[i]r Rob[ert] Harly and Mr Thomas Delavall, to which I cann say noe other then to endeavour the most advantagous way of yo[u]r Court for strict proofes, that they & no others are and have been the sole proprietors of the Shipp *Robino*. The Procter you imploy must be often called upon, that no oppertunity bee Lett passe to o[ur] damage, but that a conclusion may bee put to the Suite to prevent charges and thoughfullnesse & wee may after endeavour some way of redrese by other meanes. The Continuance of yo[u]r Care I desire and advice of what passeth. S[i]r I am engaged to yo[u]r selfe and Kinsman Mr Breames for the Civilitys showne to my freind, Mr Stones. He is gonne for Legorne to settle some concernm[en]ts, if hee may there be serviceable to yo[u]r selfe or friends I cann assure you hee wilbe most ready. You see, S[i]r, the freedome I have used w[i]th you. Pray doe the same w[i]th mee, and in [word x out]what I cann Serve you pray Comand mee.

343. Mr Bryan Rogers Ditto

Haveing written you att Large under the 21th Curr[en]t and w[i]thout any of yo[u]rs, have onely to advise that Mr Robert Ginn on whome you drew £9 is gonne for Parris and the answear wee have was from his mother, whose habitt and some other circumstanses make mee doubt she will scarce pay her son's Debt, what you order to be done w[t]h the Bill shall be observed. From Argier wee have advice That the fleet is retired from Lisbone, the Gennerall haveing made an attempt on the towne, but not succesfully as was hoped for. Before itt are the friggatts under the comand of Vice Admiral Lawson.[1] A few dayes may give us a more perticular accompt but wee are now in open hostility and the Turks are strong, badd news for us m[er]chants.

1. 24 September. Sandwich had bombarded Algiers 5-8 August but he had broken off because of bad weather. He then left a squadron under Lawson there and set sail for Lisbon. A treaty was later made with Algiers. (Pepys II p 184 note)

344. Wors[hipful] Mr Justinian Pearde Ditto

I writt you the 30th Aprill past Advising that in conformity to yo[u]r desire I had satisfied yo[u]r bill of £14 to Mr Timothy Alsopp, notw[i]thstanding the acc[omp]t depending betwixt yo[u]r selfe and my father in w[hi]ch as you have stated itt. wee finde some Errors, a perticular whereof is here inclosed which pray p[er] use that t[ha]t accompt may be shutt upp and I should be glad of some good occasion to begin a new one.

In the accompt Curr[en]t rec[eive]d [letter x out] from the Wor[sh]ip[fu]ll Justinian Pearde for ballance whereof he makes resting to him £118.14.00 are the errors following:

A mischarge not being any way allowed us	£75:00:00
1651 Oct. paid p[er] bill to John Bathurst and J Martin	£25:00.00
omitted their Charge on a draught of £70	£00.10:00
1651 Feb[ruary] paid Wymond Cliffe	£05 00:00
November paid Tho[mas] Fletcher	£05:00:00
1656 June paid Will[iam] Paul and James Marshall's bill	£20:00:00
1657 June paid Nicholas Dipford	£05:00:00
So much charged & paid Mr Trewolla which wee know nothing of	£10.00:00
	£145 10: 00

345. Mr Eustace Budghill[1] Lond[on] 24th Sept[ember] 1661

Att the request of Mrs Hill I am to acquaint you that both her self and Mr Lytcott have written you in order to the settlement of Mrs Culling's businesse to which your presence would much Conduce. Therefore they by mee doe desire to know (being all out of towne) when yo[u]r occasions will p[er]mit yo[u]r coming up, and pray itt may be as soone as you cann, for their greater convenience. Not haveing answear to their Letter [word x out] they suppose them miscarryed which giveth the occasion of this to w[hi]ch pray afford answear, and oblidge

1. Eustace Budghill – There is a reference to him in CRO CF 248 (1657)

346. Mr James Thierry Lond[on] 27th Sept[ember] 1661

Yo[u]rs of the 30/20 Curr[en]t I have received w[i]th the inclosed for which I thanke you & for your care of my Brother. Herew[i]th is an inclosed from Mr W[illia]m Jennens. S[i]r According to your order I am provideing twenty clothes for Smirna. I have lately re[eive]d [words x out] a good sortment from thence of the coulors most in esteeme, which shalbe punctuallly observed and all necessary care taken to procure them at the best hand. Wee finde itt the best way at this time of the yeare, not to buy whites and stand the Hazard of dyeing which for want of hott and faire weather, Sometymes makes not so perfect coulors, but take choice of large parcells ready drest, in doeing of [blot] I shall endeavour yo[u]r most advantage, and intend to Load them on the Shipp *Virgin* bound for Legorne consigning them to Sig[nor] Gio. Sabe & Ca [Company]. to follow yo[u]r order which ship I suppose will have Convoy. Tyn is lately risen worth att p[re]sent £5.10.00 to £5.13.00 p[er] c[w]t. Lead in esteeme att Legorne £16.12.00 to £16.14.00 p[er] fodder. Pepper in request likewise, the price uncertaine because of the intended sale att the East India House the 8 Oc[tober], I being concerned in the stock, have convenience and some advantage in buying there, if I may be serviceable to you pray Command mee. Mr Tho[mas] Delavall hath laid claime to the *Robino*, but not yet produced proofe. I have recommended the businesse to Mr Breames who hath assured mee to be carefull of itt.

347. Mr W[illia]m Jennens London 28th Sept[ember] 1661

Yo[u]rs of the 24th Curr[en]t I have rec[eive]d w[i]th an inclosed for Mr Thierry which is forwarded. I thank you for the advice of Capt[ain] Stockes his arrivall, and am sorry to understand the bad Successe they have had att Gambo. Wee are prosecuting att Dover the Condemnation of the *Robino* the last from [word x out] Mr Arnold Brames advised that Mr Delavall had put in a claime but not being sufficiently proved nothing more was done. What father I heare, shall advise you. Mr Thierry hath likewise undertaken to arrest Mr Spalding at Dunkirke but if anything yet acted I expect his next may advise. Wee thancke you for the Remembrance of yo[u]r Respects the like wee hartily returne you. It hath pleased God to lessen o[ur] family by the death of my Dear sister. Wee must all patienly Submitt to such providences.

348. Mr Bryan Rogers London Ditto

Being w[i]thout any of yours unansweared causeth breavity, This being onely to entreat you that the first good english Shipp bound for Livorno puting into yo[u]r port you would buy for us Tyn in the blocks the best sort, at the best advantage you cann, to the value of £250 or £300 St[erling] Consigning itt there to o[u]r selves or order, the freight as cheape as you cann. This order wee desire may lye Dormant till such an oppertunity as above mentioned do pr[e]sent.

Mrs Poxton hath not yett paid that bill of £29 although faithfully pr[o]mised to doe it as this day.

349. Mr James Thierry London 4th October 1661

Yours of the 7th/[27 September] Curr[en]t I have received with the Severall incloseds which shall be forwarded. I have, according to your order, bought 20 Peeces that is for 2 bales of cloth fitt for Smirna, the Sortment is herewith which is the Latest received thence and I hope they will turne well to acc[omp]t because they are cheape bought as any and choise Coulers and the full measure, which I caused to be done in my sight. They are now Packing and shall be dispatcht w[i]th the first opertunity, consigned att Le[gorn]e as formerly ordered.

The *North Lyon's* Paper I have put together. You shall have them p[er] the first conveyance. I am expecting the procure, till which no money will be paid. Mr Peter Harvey's Letter shall be given him att his arrivall. I have already written Mr Brames the needfull about the *Robino* and shall again advise him what you write. S[i]r I returne you and your Lady due thancks for your respects to my Brother, the way you intend to dispose of him is very well, and I doubt not but will be much for his improvem[en]t.

Here lately arrived the Sweedish Embassador, att whose landing at Tower wharfe there were Severall Coaches as is usuall, to accompany him, through the Citty among which were those of the french and the Spanish Embassadors, the both resolving before to strive for the Precedencie, came w[i]th many attendants Armed which occasioned a notable Sckirmish in which some few were killed on both sides, and many wounded. In Conclusion the Spanish obtained the Place Partly by force, partly by Pollicye, haveing att the first encounter disabled the french Coach by killing the Postillon and 3 of his six horses. This accident hath bred Ill blood and tis feared will not end soe.[1] The price Curr[en]t will informe the necessary about [word x o] Commoditys.

1. 'Our King, I heard, hath ordered that no Englishman should meddle in the business, but let them do what they would'. (Pepys 11 p 187)

'The truth is, the Spaniards were observed not only to fight most desperately, but also they did outwitt them; first in lining their owne harnesse with chains of iron, that they could not be cut – then in setting their coach in the most advantageous place, and to appoint men to guard every one of their horses, and others for to guard the coach, and others the coachmen. And above all, in setting upon the French horses and killing them, for by that means the French were not able to stir.' 'I got a coach and home – where I vexed my wife in telling of her this story and pleading for the Spaniard against the French'. (Pepys II p 189)

350. Mr Bryan Rogers London 5th Octo[be]r 1661

Yours of the 30th past I have received and forwarded the inclosed to Mr Thierry from whome and from Mons[ieur] Haverlant are letters for you. Yo[u]r bill of £9 on Robert Ginn I keep by mee till use may be made of itt. That of £29 upon Mrs Poxton I'me promised shalbe paid this day. Mr Samuel Wilson hath paid his brother's bill of £3 which I give you Cr[edit] for. S[i]r I thanck you for your paines and care about o[ur] businesse depending with Mr Vincent, and the freindly advice you give, which hath much reason, but on the other hand, wee are Credibly informed that Mr Vincent hath in other cases of this nature paid parte of the Sume agreed on, upon which the writings necessary to cleere the Title are delivered up, and given security for the rest, but, before the second payment falls due, Hee finds or makes some ground for a scruple to Comence a Law Suite and make benifitt by an after Composition, or att least longer time. Such trobles would disturb our imploym[e]nts and are what he desireth and delights in, for these and other such reasons wee pray and endeavour a Conclusion at once to p[re]vent after claps. What he saith of the title, Persons such as Lawyers as him selfe give Contrary opinions. Hee speaks much and loud I suppose to scare others from coming on but he will faile. When your freind Mr D[?]enogell comes to towne I shall tender him yo[u]r respects and bee serviceable to [you x out] him in what hee may have occasion for.

351. Mr Will[ia]m Jennens London 8th Octob[er] 1661

Yours of the 4th Curr[en]t I have received with yo[u]r inclosed for Mr Foote which is delivered him. Herewith is one for your selfe from Mr Thierry. I doe often minde Mr Arnold Breames of Dover to hasten [ye ?] suite in t[ha]t Court [inserted] for the Condemnation of the *Robino*. What is at p[re]sent acting there is Mr Delavall's proofe of the Clayme hee [inserted] puts in which I suppose will prove noe worse then to a prolonging the sentence. I am now attending the Successe of our admiralty Court's monition to M[essr]s Spalding and Jacobson at Dunkirke. What passeth shall advise you. Wee returne you harty thanks for your friendly resentment of our Losse. I have given your respects to Mr Hugh Squier who hath lately Labored under the danger of a violent feaver, hopefull symptoms there now are of his recovery, but his distemper was very dangerous.

352. (in Italian) **Jacopo Baldinotti** Lucca

Dear Signor Jacopo,
Since my last of the 12th September I have received your very welcome one of the 21 September with the order to add more to the order for tin first ordered which is now on the point of departure with the first ship which will be the *Leister*. I do not doubt at all that you will be pleased with the aforementioned goods being carefully wrought. I will give you more information when I send you all the account in the future. Thank you for the watch of small cost three or four pounds sterling but is more esteemed than those of silver for it shows the days of the month and is of a very beautiful make and will cost less than those that do not. Those that show the days of the month are very valuable and cost from £6 right up to £10 sterling according to the workmanship [No-one has bought one until now a friend was interested and wishes to make a purchase and gives me an order. I would like to help my friend by having it sent it by land.?]
To all friends I give dutiful salutations especially to Signor Gioseppe I remember you with all my heart, etc.
London 11 October 1661
Please would you send me a few melon seeds of the best sort.

353. **Mr James Thierry** London 11th October 1661

Yours of the 4th Curr[en]t I have received and forwarded the incloseds. I minde Mr Arnold Brames often of the businesse of the

Robino and am attending the Successe in that court, but I feare there will bee dalayes. I shall continue still to Remember him on yo[u]r behalfe. S[i]r Arnold Brames is at p[re]sent in towne. Wee Remembered you and hee presents you his Respects. S[i]r, What you say of buying Cloathes white hath much Reason, but then tis necessary that bee done in the Spring that there may be faire wether for dyeing and through drying the want of which makes cloth change colour and spott being at Sea which those Drest in the Summer are not subject to. And should I have bought this p[ar]cell of 20 p[ieces] white they could not have been [word x o] time enough dispatcht. I question not but you will finde these as Cheape as any and Turne well to acc[omp]t. If hereafter you please to order a Larger p[ar]cell in the Convenient time of the year I shall take all possible care for your most advantage. I have M. Selio Marcellis' Letter of attorney of which I have acquainted the assurers, and they promise the next weeke to give mee a meeting for the Concludeing that businesse. The *N. Lyon's* Papers I have laid out to send you, but conceive shall have occasion to make use of them against [word x out] Mr Gifford Bayle, one of the assurers who will not att all Comply by faire meanes. S[i]r you have very well Resolved how to dispose of my broth[e]r, for your care therein I give you many thancks.

354. Mr Bernard Sparke London 22th Octob[e]r 1661

S[i]r,

Yours of the 16th Curr[en]t I have received With [word x o] the inclosed for Mr James Thierry which was forwarded. Herewith is one from him. The prosecution of the friggatt arrested att Dover upon the *Golden Dolphin's* acc[omp]t is left to the management of Mr Arnold Breames Juni[o]r at Dover from whome the last advice was that Mr Thomas Delavall had put in claime to the Shipp So itt Remaines on the [adversary ?] party to prove there intrest. I this day writt Mr Brames, what answear I have shall advise you.

The 17th Curr[en]t Mrs Sarah Culling was married to Mr Giles Lytcott an intimate freind of mine by whose meanes I have the happinesse of her acquaintance.

355. Mr Bryan Rogers London the 22th Octob[e]r 1661

Yo[ur]s of the 10th Curr[en]t I have received With the inclosed bill of Exchange of £5 which is satisfied and past to o[u]r Cr[edit]. Wee thanck you for your advice and assistance in Mr Vincent's Businesse. We shall consider of itt and Resolve. The Guns you desire shall be sent you But I doubt the Lengths mentioned cannott be bought att yo[u]r Limited prices. I shall doe the best I cann. Wee have little news worth notice.

356. Mr Arnold Brames Ju[nio]r London Ditto

This serves cheifly for Covert to the inclosed Pacquett of Mr James Thierry, who Continually minde mee to Rememb[er] your earnest following our Suite depending in yo[u]r Court. I do it not oftner being assured of yo[u]r Care and that ought happening of note I should heare from you. But because the intressed expect advice of itts p[ro]ceeding from mee pray favour mee w[i]th the needful.

357. Mr James Thierry London 25th Octob[er] 1661

Yo[ur]s of the 28/[18] Curr[en]t I have received and forwarded the inclosed to Mr Arnold Brames earnestly recomending the prosecuting our suite at Dover of w[hi]ch I am expecting some accompt from him. [Sir x out] S[i]r, according to yo[u]r order I have laden [words x out] for yo[u]r acc[omp]t 2 bales containeing 10 Peeces Cloth upon the *Leister* friggat bound for Legorne, Invoice and bill of Lading are inclosed. I hope they will prove to Content, and encourage yo[u]r larger Comissions, I haveing used all diligence for your most advantage. That you Suppose itt the Cheaper way to buy Clothes white and dresse and dye on yo[u]r owne accompt and hazard that is in Relation to the Colours few have found it the Most advantageous and, excepting one I know, noe merch[an]t on the exchange that uses itt and he haveing a brother intressed in his trade and stock though by profession a Dyer they may doe good on itt, when others Cannott. Besides the Spring and Summer being the proper seasons for Dyeing, provision of White Clothes must be made every weeke and Markett day in the winter by w[hi]ch meanes a Large stock must unavoydably lye dead till Spring that they may be fitted for exportation. Whereas on the Contrary wee now buy Clothes Ready Dyed and have the Benifitt of Chusing the perfectest Colours. However if you please to order any quantity I shall serve you to the most advantage and carefull as any.

S[i]r, what I said of the *North Lyon's* businesse assurers would give mee, in a few dayes, twas intended to have them bring in their Money and have a Collation, but now they [inserted] will that I send to their houses, which I am now doeing but have not yet received any money of them, they shall not want often Calling upon, what passeth shall advise you. According to yo[u]r order I have made a pollicye in yo[u]r name on the *Golden Fox* from Amsterdam to Barbados to touch at Madeiras, itt is begun att £5.10s p[er] cent w[i]thout Rebate in case of Losse. I conceived itt somewhat to Deare so have the Liberty, if you approve itt not, the Subscription shall be Cancelled but I am Confident will not be done Cheaper because of touching at Maderas which t[he]y [inserted] Value above 1 p[er] c[en]t.

S[i]r, I give you many thanks for the great Care yo[u]r selfe and Lady have taken on behalfe of my Brother in placeing him abroad at schoole. Whatsoever Charge you are a for him shall be thankfully Repaid & wee Remaine Oblidged to serve you and yours. If you please that yo[u]r sone, Mons[ieur]. Jacopus and Mr Sckelling shall be in London this winter they shall be very welcome to our house and Command the Conveniences it affords and I shall be ready to afford them My best assistance in all things. I writ my brother herew[i]th with some advice about the Most advantageous imploying his time. Since the above I have gotten assured on the *Fox* the £600 you ordered. I hope itt will be to yo[u]r Likeing.

358.[in Italian]) **Sig[no]re Jacopo Baldinotti**

My dear Signor Jacopo
This serves solely to advise you that I have loaded the pewter you ordered on board the ship *Leister* frigate, Captain Aron Wallis. The ship will depart in about eight days and perhaps in company with other ships. But this I cannot tell you in any way. It is a good ship well armed. The invoice will follow the next for you.
I kiss your hands. From London 25 October

359. Mr Bryan Rogers London the 26th October 1661

Yours of the 21th Curr[en]t I have received perceiving the great care you had taken in our businesse w[i]th Mr Vincent. I wish that by yo[u]r meanes a good end might be put to itt. The often delayes that hee hath made and disappointments appeare not handsome no very good construction cann be made of such proceedings. Upon advice of [inserted] what effects follow the intended meeting w[i]th my Couzen Trewolla, if not what reasonably expected some other Course must be taken. The former order wee gave for Tyn wee pray may be [not ?] the occation that then p[re]sented being otherway supplyed but possibly upon the fall in the Price something may hereafter be done, of which shall advise. As yet have not any advice what price Pilcherds have found in Spaine and Italy what passeth shall advise you.

The 3 fowling peeces you ordered I have bought and shall put them aboard the first Vessell for yo[u]r port. Will Rogers I thinck is gonne.

360. Mr Arnold Brames London the 26th Octob[e]r 1661

I have yo[u]rs of the 25th Curr[en]t w[i]th Coppie of what y[ou]r freind at Dunkirke writs you. I wish his forbearing to publish the Monition prove not to o[ur] great pr[e]judice had that been timely done in probability o[ur] businesse might before this have been brought to some Conclusion. Now wee must doe as well as wee cann, in w[hi]ch I depend on yo[u]r knowne care. I suppose Mr William Jennens of Plymouth to bee Mr James Thierry's Cheif Correspondent because weekely I give Covert to and from each of them to Divers Lett[e]rs.

361. Mr Alex[ander] Travell London 26 October 1661

The other side haveing advised the needfull as to businesse I have to adde the telling you the Great Losse wee have had in the untimely death of my most Deare Sister,[1] but few dayes after my Last mentioned her sicknesse. I cann not enduer to dwell upon such unpleasant a Subject so hasten to tell you, that Mr Lytcott hath now ended all his wooing and Solemnized his Nuptials about 14 dayes since. Harry Browne is I presume upon the like design and Harry Mellish too has at last gotten a Mistr[ess]. Last friday night yo[u]r good Company was wished for at Paul's Wharfe where among Divers freinds I was entertained at the baptising my aunt Maskalyne's sone and heir with aboundance of joy. Mrs Hublon's turne is next who looks very bigg. Her brave boy Wynn thrives lustily and is ready to prattle[2]. Those freinds Designed you some Canary but the above said accident put it out their thoughts. Mr Squier hath undergonne a very dangerous fitt of sicknesse and not yet quit recovered. Tomorrow is the yearely show of the Lord Mayor which is now p[er]formed by S[i]r John Fredrick.[3] Great preparations thier [word x out] are of pagions. His maj[es]tie was invited but not knowne if hee will dine w[i]th him. Mr W[illia]m Harvy is gonne out of England w[i]th Mr George [Hayles ?] through Holland and Jermany and intends Travell for some time. I suppose Mr Mathew Harvy now thinks of returneing. Pray give him my Respects.

Wee have now many divertisem[en]ts. S[i]r W[illia]m Davenant gives us Comedys with Fine scenes. Two other play houses wee have, the Patentee, Mr Tho[mas] Killigrew, wisely Considering the charge of Coach hire to the Cittizens, is p[re]pareing a stage at the Glasse house[4] in Broad street & Besides a french Company plays here dayly. St Paul's is lately Reformed and now addorned w[i]th a new and Glorious Organ to w[hi]ch the Grave Aldermen are very attentive. The churchyard to hath suffered Reformation, the Herb markett usually kept there is now removed to Broad street & AldermanBury. You see w[i]th [word x out] what triffles I am forct to p[re]sent you but tis for want of Better.

Mons[ieu]r Sam is gonne to Holland where hee intends to obtaine the Dutch and french tongue & makeing himselfe capeable of serveing yo[u]r selfe and friends.

1. This refers to the death of Abraham's wife.
2. Mrs Houblon, the wife of James Houblon. see note to Letter 191. Her son Wynn and his wife were to become special favourites of Pepys several years later.
   Pepys was all prepared to go to the Lord Mayor's feast he put on his 'half-Cloth black stockings and my new Coate of the fashion, which pleases me well; and with my beaver I was (after office was done) ready to go to my Lord Mayors feast, as we are all invited' but others were loathe to go because of the crowds so none of them went. (Pepys II p 203)
3. Sir John Frederick, knighted June 1660, MP Dartmouth 1660. London 1663-79 (Woodhead p 73)

4. The Glass house was the place in Broad Street where Venetian glass was made earlier in the century. The building later became the Pinners' Hall and then a Dissenting Chapel. Walter Thornbury *Old and New London* (London etc not dated but *c* 1880) p 165

362. Mr John Byam London p[ri]mo November 1661

Yo[u]rs of the 4th past I have received and according to yo[u]r former desires was allwayes ready to have intressed you in what Designe could have been carried on for Naples But the great reates and Small quantitys of Pilchards put my selfe and freinds quit of from buying any this yeare, Supposeing those that have will scarce finde then turne to Accompt. If you please to Value yo[u]r selfe on mee or order the investment of yo[u]r effects in my hands, itt shall be punctuallly complyed w[i]th but if itt were my owne case I should not wish it had been laid out in fish.

Wee have not the least suspition of difference w[i]th Spaine, though the Reasons you give are Considerable. How that Crowne and France may understand one another is the discourse because the two Embassad[o]rs here did forcibly strive for the place at the Reception of the Sweeds Embassador in which 5 or 6 were killed but in conclution the Spaniard gott the place which is highly resented in France. Our freind, Mr Lytcott, is now married. I shall give him yo[u]r Respects. The Like to Mr H. Browne when hee returnes out of the Country. Little news only the Fleet p[re]paireing to attend the Queene.[1] Yesterday departed 8 of the Nobles to congratulate the birth of the Dauphin of france.

1. The fleet were preparing to escort Catherine of Braganza to England.

363. Mr James Thierry London p[ri]mo November 1661

Haveing writt you at Large on the 25th Curr[en]t have not much to add. Herewith is what answear I have from Mr Arnold Brames about the Monition out of o[ur] Adm[ira]lty Court, the neglect of serveing itt on Mr Spalding and others I feare much pr[e]judice our businesse. My Last accompanied Invoice and Bill of Lading for yo[u]r 2 Bales of Cloth in the *Leister* friggatt w[hi]ch I hope is to yo[u]r Content and that I have pr[o]cured £600 to be assured on the *Golden Fox.* Yo[u]r sonne, Mons[ieur] Jacopus and Mr Skelling, are att pr[e]sent w[i]th us,[1] they came to see the L[or]d Mayor's Show in which I served them the best I could att so short warning for the arrived but the very morning. Although the[y] Returne to Bridge w[i]th S[i]r Arnold Brames yet I hope their stay will not be long there, that so wee may enjoy their good company here. In what I cann Serve them I shall be always Ready thereby to show the great Respects I have to you.

1. William Schellinks and Jacobus returned to London on the 8 November (New Style) 29 October (Old Style) for they returned to see the Lord Mayor's Show. Thomas Hill would seem to have arranged a viewing place possibly at his relatives' or friend's house at Paul's Wharf. (Schellinks p 65)

364. [in Italian] Sig[nor]e Jacopo Baldinotti

My dear Signor Jacopo,
With this I send you the invoice and bill of lading for the 4 barrels of pewter aboard the ship *Leister* God send her in safety although she has not yet departed only stops a little in order to enjoy the company of other ships. [As to the terrible damage from the Turks I have not heard and you are in a better position to judge than we are andif you could insure more easily at Livorno. When you have the commodities I will make the accounts.?] . . .
    London primo Novemb[e]r 1661

365 [in Italian] Sig[no]re Jacopo Baldinotti

My dear Signor Jacopo
With my last I sent the invoice and bill of lading for the 4 barrels of pewter aboard the ship *Leister* which I hope you will find to your liking. Now this serves to accompany the advice that today I have drawn the costs made for your charge to Mr Edward Mico to whom I have given my bill of exchange for $362.16.01 at rate of 53½[d] per dollar for you to pay in your own time. With kind remembrances to all friends.

On the 4th Novemb[e]r 1661 London
The cost of the pewter as per invoice [1]   £80.08.08
Provision and Commission on the
transaction @ ½ %   £ 08.10
                                                 £80.17.06 @ 53½d makes
$362.16.01

. . . .

$362.16.01   On the 4th November 1661 London
Three months after date paid by this my second bill not being
followed by the first or third pray pay to Mr Edward Mico or
his order in Livorno reals of Seville and Mexico effective three
hundred sixty-two, sixteen soldi and one denario for the value of
himself to said Mr Mico and place it to account as per advice.
For Signor Jacopo Baldinotti Lucca

1. The invoice which goes with this is given in Appendix A

366. Mr James Thierry London 8th November 1661

Yo[u]rs of the1/11 Currant I have received With the Severall
incloseds. That for your sonne, Mons[ieur] Jacobus I delivered him
being then on Departure for Bridge with S[i]r Arnold Brames. I
suppose haveing your order will shortly returne with us hee shall
bee very welcome and for his improvem[en]t shall not want the
best masters in whatsoever he inclines to. Hee already speakes
good English and hath gotten a good pronontiation. What hee
may have occation for shall bee supplyed him. S[i]r I thank you
for the incloseds from my Brother, whome both your selfe and
Lady have much Oblidged, I am sorry to heare of her sicknesse.
Pray God restore her health. My brother I perceived haveing need
of some small things hath made bold to trouble you but I write
him to provide himselfe for the future if you please to let him have
what mony may bee convenient which shall thankfully bee repaid.
I perceive you had made assurance upon the *Golden Fox* in the
intrim your order Remained with mee so what I have [word x out]
donne you would should [sic] be onely the one halfe which I have
[prevailed?] w[i]th the Assurers to alter, although the pollicye was
entred in the publique Register so that there will be assured to you
onely £300. Here inclosed I send samplers of the Clothes shipt
for yo[u]r accoumpt. The whole Cloathes show much better, and
besids [sic] are hott pressed which these are not. I hope this Small

begining will give you encouragem[en]t for Continuance of the trade in which my Diligence shall not be wanting for yo[u]r most advantage. Herewith is an inclosed from Mr Edward Bridgewood of Lixa [Lisbon] with some Acc[omp]tt of yo[u]r businesse. I am confident hee will use his intrest in that Court for yo[u]r satisfaction.

367. Mr Bernard Sparke London 9th Novemb[e]r 1661

I have unansweared yours of the 30th past. The inclosed for Mr James Thierry was forwarded, herewith is one from him. The Monition sent from our Adm[ira]lty Court to Dunkirke to warne Mr Spalding and others into the Adm[iral]ty the Correspondent of Mr Brames there, who was desired to publish itt, made the Governour first acquainted with itt (who was wee Suppose to be concerned in the *Robino*) and he desired for some reasons which are not declared, that the monition might be for some time be respited which the Correspondent, one Mr Cullen, consented to. How to understand this I know not, but Certainely itt hath retarded our businesse. This was what last I had from Mr Arnold Brames. I did your Respects to Mr Lytcott and [Lady x o] his Lady, who returne theirs to you, it is the same person you concluded on, brother to Mrs Upton.

368. Mr Bryan Rogers London the 9th November 1661

I am [word x out] without any of yours. Herew[i]th is an inclosed from a servant of yo[u]rs att the Barbados, and one from Mr Thierry. I have bought the three Gunns you ordered and putt them aboard the *willing-Mind* the Master Refused to give any Receit But I suppose him honest and that att his [inserted] arrivall hee will safely deliver them. They Cost together £3 yours the Shortest Reconed att 18s. I hope the[y] will prove to yo[u]r Likeing & I wish you good sport in useing them. S[i]r I hope in this intrim Mr Vincent hath given you some other Answear then his Last meeting. Our Desire is to have a final conclusion with him and therefore intreat you to favour us to give him a meeting & timely notice that hee may not faile principally because if you cannot agree wee may may have the benifitt of this Terme. So pray itt may bee with all Conveniant speed you may perceive he was to pay £800 Lady Day last now for t[ha]t time is since past its wholly left to yo[u]r care, for agreeing w[i]th him for the intrest of the said Summe in which rather then lett it rest longer [word x o] unsettled, something of strict intrest may be abated him, for prompt paym[en]t. Hee offered to pay £400 long since, and give his owne Bond and Mr Trewoolla for the rest. The latter wee cannot much depend upon, and to take onely his p[er]sonall security is not Discretion, therefore you may offer him the Contents of the inclosed paper which a freind of ours learned in the law [inserted] thincks reasonable, and for what writings are Convenient to bee delivered up, and the Letter of Attorney hee expects all shall bee delivered to the persons hee orders here to make his warrant of Attorney, if he thincks fitt according to the inclosed instructions.

In case that Mr Walter Vincent will not pay in the eight hundred pounds then I doe conceive that it is not reasonable for Mr Hill to part w[i]th the Mortgage. But in case Mr Hill shall bee willing to take foure hundred pounds of itt downe and to take Security for the Remaineing foure hundred pounds I doe thincke itt very reasonable that Mr Hill should have a judgement from Mr Vincent for six or eight hundred pounds Deffeazanced for the payment of £400 w[i]th interest And to that purpose that [word x out] warrant of Atturny bee made from Mr Vincent, directed to Mr Thomas Seaman, Mr Dutton Seaman, and put in the name of some other Atturney in the King's Bench of that Country, and to any other Atturney of the King's Bench or any of them to appeare for Mr Vincent at suit of Mr Hill and Confesse a Judgement for the said Summe, for this £800, being but for Redemtion of the Mortgage, ought in Reason to be paid downe or if a further day be given for any part of itt that the Sume should bee secured in the best manner Mr Hill cann desire, for else he departs w[i]th a Certaine Real Security for an uncertainety.

And when such a warrant of attorney is made lett it be sealed and delivered in presence of three or foure Credible witnesses, & if it may bee of some person who is Coming up to town who canne testify the same.

369. Mr W[illia]m Jennens London 12th Novemb[er] 1661

This is onely to entreat yo[u]r favour in forwarding the inclosed, And in what I cann serve you please to Comand mee.

370. Mr Hugh Crocker London 12th November 1661

It hath beene the desire of my brot[he]r and myselfe to end the businesse depending betweene Mr Walter Vincent and o[ur]selves, in a freindly way, but hee is little inclineing, nor have wee hopes that hee will doe otherwise. My desire is to know how wee are to proceed if he Comply not to the Propositions already offered him. Yo[u]r full direction I desire for my Regular proceedings That the benifitt of this Terme may not Be lost.

371. (In Italian) Sig[no]re Giovanni Sabe & Compa[ny] Livorno

16 November 1661 London
By order and account of the Illustrious Signor James Thierry of Amsterdam I have loaded on the ship *Leister* frigate two bales of cloth consigned to you, as you will see per the inclosed bill of lading, God grant that it arrives in safety, [you following the orders?] of Signor Thierry etc.

372. Mr James Thierry London 16th November 1661

Being without any of yo[u]rs causeth breavety. Inclosed is a letter from Mr Bryan Rogers. I am attending the Returne of Mr Jacobus and Mr Skelling. The cold weather will I suppose drive them to the Citty Where they shall have my utmost Assistance in what they have occati[o]n for.

I have sent bill of ladeing for yo[u]r 2 bales of Cloth to Sig[nor]e Gio[vann]e Sabe & Compa[ny].The *leister* is now Fallen downe and will goe along with Convoy so I hope she will arrive in safety. Mrs Jones hath been severall times w[i]th mee to inquire for news of her husband and to know if you had given mee order to furnish her w[i]th money which shee Earnestly expects. The assurers are slow in paying thier Mony, but p[ro]mise to doe itt by Christmas. I wish they Prove Punctuall.

373. Mr Bryan Rogers London 16 Novemb[e]r 1661

S[i]r,

I have yours of the 4th Curr[en]t, but not in itts due time, the inclosed forwarded. That part of itt w[hi]ch concerns Mr Walter Vincent, you will perceive already answeared in my last, to which referr you, hopeing you have p[re]vailed w[i]th him to comply w[i]th what was there propounded. The Candles and hops you order shall be sent p[er] first. Yo[u]r bill of £100 to Mr Arthur Spry was not p[re]sented till the last weeke and is satisfied. Munday's post may bring news from Legorne of the Sale of Pilcherds and something of Algeere. What news wee have shall advise you.

374. Mr Jacopus Thierry London the 18th Novemb[e]r 1661

I hope the Cold weather will cause yo[u]r speedy returne hither. Herew[i]th is a letter from yo[u]r father who supposed you here, att yo[u]r owne [leisure x out] conveniency I shall be glad to see you. Pray my *Devoir* to S[i]r Arnold & my lady.

375. Mr W[illia]m Jennens London 19th Novemb[e]r 1661

Yo[u]rs of the 15th Curr[en]t I have rec[eive]d w[i]th the inclosed for Mr Crocker. I shall take Care to speake with him here And thank you for Returneing my Letter. I am expecting some accompt from Mr Arnold Brames what is donne in o[ur] businesse att Dover but of late not heard from him w[ha]t passeth shall advise you. I have [given yo[ur ?] Respects to My brother [Squier x out] and Mr Squier [Brother x out] who both returne theirs.

376. Mr James Thierry London 22th November 1661

S[i]r,

The last post brought mee yo[u]rs of the 18th and 25th Curr[en]t with Severall incloseds which were forwarded. That for yo[u]r Sonne, Mr Jacobus, I sent to Bridge[1], where hee still remaines but I hope will shortly come to us, the Winter now begining and the Cold weather will drive them to the Citty where I shall be always ready to serve them. According to yo[u]r order, I have Caused £500 sterl[ing] to be assured for yo[u]r accompt aboard the *Parragon*, John Barefoot m[aste]r at & from the coast of Guinny in trade, and soe to the Barbados at the Rate of £4 p[er] cent without Rebate w[hi]ch was at the lowest rate I could doe itt and I question not yo[u]r approveall. That you may the better perceive the expressions of the policy, to p[re]vent scruples in case of losse and some other name that you inserted in the Bill of ladeing. You have herewith Coppy of the pollicye soe that if you mislike any thing itt may timely be remedyed by a memorandum but I hope there will not be any such occation.

The bill you have drawne for £150 St[erling] at 2 Usa[nce] payable to Mr John Cooke or his order shall finde punctuall Complyance. The Assurers on the *N[orth] Lyon* are very Backward in paying their due so that from them I am but little in Cash.

S[i]r I have writt to Mr Brames about o[ur] businesse of the *Dolphin* but have not any thing from him, more then I formerly advised. I shall againe minde him and upon his answear resolve whats fitest to bee done. I hope hee will deale fairely although I know not well how to understand his letting the friggatt you arrested at Dover goe away as by accident I understand hee hath donne, att least some of us should have heard from him [inserted] if security had been given, that so good an oppertunity might not be wholly lost. I p[er]ceive S[i]r Arnold Brames is goeing for Portugall. There are ships now departing. I shall Engage to serve him by Mr Edward Bridgewood And I hope hee may likewise bee Assistant and helpfull to yo[u]r Businesse.

1. For a description of Bridge, the home of Sir Arnold Braems, which was a spectacular house and one of the largest in East Kent, see article by P.C. Elgar in *Bygone Kent* Vol. 18 No 9

377. Mr Bernard Sparke London 23th November 1661

Yo[u]rs of the 20th Curr[en]t I have received, the inclosed for Mr Thierry forwarded, so shall the other w[i]th the first opertunity for the Barbados. I this day write to Mr Arnold Breames at Dover recommending earnestly our Businesse to his Care, but principally to know the Certainety of the friggatt arrested there by Mr Thierry be departed, as I heare shee is. I hope wee are Fairely dealt with although Mr Thierry is something dissatisfied w[i]th proceedings. Till I have Mr Braems answear I forbare to Conclud anything but I have prayed him that notwithstanding the delayes of the

Governour of Dunkirk, who tis supposed may Be Concerned, That the Monition sent thither may Be published, w[ha]t answear I have shall advise you.

S[i]r, Since the above written I have Rec[eive]d the Monition Formerly sent for Dunkirke w[i]th attestation that it was publiquely served on Capt[ain] Jacobson, Mr Spalding being deceased. I shall now proceed according to the orders of our Adm[ira]lty Court, and advise w[ha]t passeth.

378. Mr Arnold Braems London 23th Novemb[e]r 1661

Att instant I have yo[u]rs of the 21th Curr[en]t With the inclose monition w[hi]ch I perceive hath been personally served upon Capt[ain] Jacobsen, and am Glad yo[u]r freind hath effected soe much, because Mr Thierry writt often to mee and supposed some neglect but now I hope will bee better satisfied. Pray afford the Continuance of yo[u]r Care and advise w[ha]t passeth.

379. Mr Bryan Rogers London 23th Novemb[e]r 1661

Yo[u]rs of the 18th Curr[en]t I have received the inclosed for Amst[erdam] forwarded. I thank you for speaking w[i]th Mr Vincent, to which wee [word x out] forbare to give positive Answear, because in a day or two wee intend to have a meeting w[i]th Mr Crocker, and then hope to Conclude what's best to be done. I am glad the letter I sent you brought you good news, pray God send the ship safe hither, but if you have thoughts of makeing assurance I suppose may bee done att better termes here then att Amst[erdam] because I doe assure often for Mr Thierry. If I cann serve you in any thing I hope you know w[i]th w[ha]t freedome you may command mee. From Barbados hither the assurers aske £5 to £6 p[er] cent. If you Resolve any thing itt shall be done to yo[u]r most advantage. Pilcherds have this yeare been sould att $27 to $28 p[er] h[ogs]h[ea]d. Wee have advice that the algier men of war have taken the *Pelican* a small vessel from the Streights. Wee here not of any Publique action [inserted] p[er]formed lately by fo[ur] [shipps x o] friggatts but only the Better secureing m[er]chants shipps w[hi]ch questionlesse would otherwise be in great danger. The Parliam[en]t have voted the King £1,200,000 for paying his ould debts.[1] S[i]r according to the burden and force of yo[u]r ship,

· so will yo[u]r assurance Be and upon punctuall advise of that I shall be able to answear you more perticular.

1. Hutton says £1,260,000 (Hutton p 158)

380. Mr W[illia]m Jennens London 26th November 1661

Since my last I have received from Mr Arnold Breames of Dover the Monition formerly sent to Dunkirke to be served there upon Capt[ain] Jacobson which was accordingly donne and certified on the backe side in due forme and withall noted that Mr Spalding Lately deceased. I have now returned the Monition into o[ur] Adm[ira]lty Court and shall consult w[i]th the procter what Course wee are to proceed in. Nothing of Care on my part shall be wanting to Conclude this businesse.

381. Mr Cyprian Sawdy London Ditto

Wee have seldome any thing here worth or fitt for yo[u]r notice [word x out] w[hi]ch hath made mee soe long Silent w[hi]ch I hope you will excuse. I have now to acquaint you that my being Execut[o]r to my father's estate Oblidgeth mee to Looke after the Debts standing out among w[hi]ch my uncle Mr Hillary Hill owes by bond £26. I have often written to him of itt, to take Care to discharge it, to my first letter hee gave some answear but nothing else to Severall others I have had none, which I strange att. [word x out] I therefore entreat you to acquaint him what I write and p[re]vaile with him to minde itt by a speedy payment nor cann hee expect any favour that itt should bee released as hee seems to Imagine because I stand Charged w[i]th itt, and must be responsible to the estate for that Summe. Pray S[i]r doe mee this favour, & I hope itt will produce his Complyance.

382.Mr Arnold Breames Jun[ior] London 27th Novemb[e]r 1661

My last of the 23th Curr[en]t advised the needfull since which I have received the inclosed for you from Mr James Thierry, who in his letter accuseth mee by advice from you, (as he saith) that since his departure from hence I never writt any thing Concerning the Friggatt arrested att Dover, w[hi]ch to mee seemed strange because I well remember and my Coppy booke tells mee, I have done itt, and earnestly recommended the prosecution of the Suite depending to yo[u]r care, and you must certainely have taken notice of itt. Although by the way twas accidentall that I understood the Friggatt was Baled and departed I hope their is a right understanding on all Sides. It shall be my Care to Continue itt. But to our Businesse, upon p[er]usall of the monition returned wee finde that the time limited for [for x out] Capt[ain] Jacobsens appeareing, was elapsed before hee was served, so that what hath been hitherto done, is altogether ineffectuall w[hi]ch pray advise yo[u]r freind Mr Cullen that hee may informe the Governour how pr[e]judiciall his intreatie or rather Comands have byn to our private businesse in hindring the timely serveing o[ur] Warrant.

383. Mr Bernard Sparke London 28th November 1661

My Last of the 23th Curr[en]t advised the receit of the monition from Dunkirke, since which I have consulted w[i]th the Procter how wee are to proceed But upon p[er]usal of the endorsements made there Wee finde that the Limmitted time [for x out] in the monition for Capt[ain] Jacobsen's appeareing was elapsed before hee was p[er]sonallly Served so that what hath now been done is of noe Validity. So much I have advised Mr Braems that hee may acquaint Mr Cullen his Correspondent at Dunkirke how p[re]juditiall his neglect hath byn to o[ur] businesse. Although for the delay w[hi]ch hee acknowledgeth he pleads the Governour's desires, that the monition might not be published. Wee in the meanetime are loosers. Pray S[i]r Consider whats now to bee done, if to take out a new monition but in probability Capt[ain] Jacobsen Relateing to the Sea upon this Alarme will quickly remove him selfe, The *Robino* friggatt Arrested att Dover is departed, upon Baile given for £95 being what shee was [words x o]appraised att.

The above is likewise Coppy of a letter sent to **Mr W[illia]m Jennens** bearing the same date.

384. Mr Bryan Rogers London ditto

My Last was on the 23th Curr[en]t since which I have not any of yo[u]rs. This serves to give Covert to the inclosed from Mr James

Thierry. I am attending [words x out] your advice of the burden & defence of the [your x o] shipp you expect from Barbados, that soe I may answear more positive how assurance Governs. Wee have Spoken w[i]th Mr Crocker who manages o[ur] businesse w[i]th Mr Vincent and shall in few dayes resolve how to proceed of w[hi]ch you shall have advice.

The Candles and hops you ordered are ready and expect onely a convenyance.

385. **Mr James Thierry** 29th Novemb[e]r 1661

Since my last of the 22nd Curr[en]t I have received yo[u]rs of the 2 Dec[emb]re with severall inclosed which are Delivered and forwarded according to Direction. Herewith are Letters from Mon[sieu]r Jacobus and Mr Skelling who are now w[i]th us where the[y] are very wellcome and may Command as att home. I take Care to procure the most esteemed Masters for yo[u]r sonne, the Better to improve his time this Winter and in whatsoever I cann be serviceable to him I shall be always most ready and to furnish him with whatsoever hee may have occation for.

S[i]r, I haveing att [Length ?] received from Mr Breames the monition formerly sent to Dunkirke w[i]th endorsements upon the Backside that it was personally Served upon Capt[ain] Jacobsen but to little purpose for the time Limited that hee should have appeared in our adm[ira]lty Court was elapsed before the warrant was Served. Thus our business is prejudiced by the Governor there who itt seemes desired Mr Cullen (Correspondent to Mr Braems) that the monition might not bee for some time published for Reasons [word x o] best known, as hee said, to him selfe. Now S[i]r pray Consider if itt's best to take out another monition although in probability Capt[ain] Jacobsen, upon what hath already been done, will remove, which hee may easily doe relateing as he doth to the Sea. What you order shall be observed. I strange Mr Braems should say I never writt him about this businesse since yo[u]r departure when him selfe knows the Contrary and I have from him Answear to Severall letters of mine – but I lett that passe – and wish wee could finde a way to redress the pr[e]judice wee are like to suffer through the neglect of itt.

When Mrs Jones comes to mee next I shall give her the Answear you ord[e]r mee. That sort of money made in the Common Wealth's time is now recalled by a proclamation of the King. Tomorrow is the last day that its Curr[en]t. The assurers on the *North Lyon* are still delaying payment but promise to cleere by Christmas. One or two have paid mee some part of their losse in the new Coine, and I dispose itt againe as Best I cann and will make the Losse on itt as Little as may bee. I shall suddenly draw out yo[u]r acc[omp]t that wee may Begin a new & a Larger if the Clorh Bought for you sell to Content, of w[hi]ch I make no question because I used much care in provideing itt. Herew[i]th is a Letter from Mr Sparke who desired mee to enquire and advise you if the King had granted a Patent to a perticular Company for the whole Guinny Trade, as yett there no such thing donne but itt's endeavoured by some p[er]sons, of which I shall further enquire and give you an accompt.[2] Likewise Mr [Ab xo] Ambrosse Jennens of Falmouth expecting a shipp from the Barbados and hopeing shee might be among [word x out] a fleet lately arrived, desired mee to give you advice to save the insurance, But as yett shee's not arrived. But I have advice that 7 weeks since she had good part of her loading, and would have the company of 2 English shipps of 20 and 24 Gunns.

1. Schellinks wrote 6 December NS ie 26 Nov OS 'went to our lodging at Messrs Abraham & Thomas Hill in Lime Street. This was to be our winter quarters for the next two months, and we were there well boarded and lodged.' On the 9th 'we went with Mr Hill by coach to the King's playhouse and saw there the play 'Love the first'. They moved from the Hills' on 13 February NS (Schellinks p 70)
2. The third English African Company re 'The Royal Adventurers Trading into Africa' was constituted in 1662.

386. **Mr Samuel Hill** 29th November 1661

I have received yo[u]r Letter with the inclosed for my Brother which I have delivered him. I am glad to see you make so good progresse in yo[u]r writing. Pray Continue yo[u]r diligence. You had best follow yo[u]r master's advice, altho[ugh] I think you might make French yo[u]r study for the Dutch Language you must of necessity Learne that, if ittselfe itt will gett into you.

When you practise the pipe [words inserted] which I thinke should be thee flajolett[1] and not the Dutch Flute, bee sure looke out to yo[u]r fingers. It may unhappily draw downe yo[u]r sight and make an irricoverable b[l]emish, to which if you finde yo[u]r selfe the least inclineing by all meanes leave of Drawing pictures. I could wish you to Bestow some time in the Benifitt you will prize in yo[u]r after Travells which may probably be many to take the Discription of places to yo[u]r after satisfaction and reward for the present paines w[hi]ch will but small. Mr Thierry is desired to furnish you w[i]th w[h]at you have occation of. I pray God continue yo[u]r health.

1. a whistle flute with four holes at the back, very popular in France in the 1640s and 1650s and in England in the 1660s. (Pepys XI)

387. Mr Bryan Rogers 30 Novemb[e]r 1661

S[i]r,
The above written was intended you by the last post since which I have received Mr Amb[rose] Jennens' Letter of the 25th Curr[en]t, according to which I have enquired after yo[u]r shipp *Providence,* and have advice from one Robert Williams That departed Barbados 7 weekes agoe and left yo[u]r shipp in safety their, haveing taken in good part of her loading, might come home in Company of 2 English shipps, the one of 20, the other of 24 Gunns. Pray God send her safe. I shall give you advice what passeth and ready to serve you. This Mr Williams saith hee put into the Post house a Pacquett for you w[hi]ch was not addressed to mee. I suppose because yo[u]r servant aboard thought the shipp *Phoenix,* by which the letters came, might have putt into yo[u]r port or Plymouth.

388. Mr Bernard Sparke London Ditto

Yours of 27th Curr[en]t I have received, and Forwarded the incloseds for Amsterdam. S[i]r, According to yo[u]r desire I have enquired and am informed that some private p[er]sons are endeavouring to procure a Pattent from the King for the whole Guiny Trade But that as yett is not granted. So much I advised Mr Thierry. I shall take further notice how this Businesse goes forward, and hereafter acquaint both yo[u]r selfe, and him att large. Peece Fruite is in very little esteeme, not worth 18s p[er] c[w]t. Wine low too and generally a dead trade. This is the last day that the Common Wealth mony is Curr[en]t, the losse will

Bee about 5 p[er] c[en]t, but wee heare that there's a Proclamation intended that the Customes, Exchequer and other offices, relateing to His Maj[es]tie will yett accept of itt in [word x out] payment.

389. Mr Walwyn Gascoigne London 2 Decemb[e]r 1661

I p[re]sume S[i]r John Bankes gave you timely advice t[ha]t the bill you drew on mee for $391.10 in £92.3s.4 payable to him selfe, was accepted. It fell due on the 30th past, upon w[hi]ch Day, himselfe being out of Towne, I entreated his servant to receive the Sume due on the Bill w[hi]ch hee said was willing to doe, But that hee had not my accepted Bill, But that S[i]r John had given itt to another p[er]son, upon acc[omp]ts betwixt them. This Gentleman (it suiteing best w[i]th his occations) Discompts my bill w[i]th a Goldsmith. S[i]r John Bankes serv[an]t goes to the Goldsmith makes tender of the mony I had formerly tendred to him in satisfaction of the Bill, but the Goldsmith refuseth itt. So by consent of S[i]r Johns serv[an]t and my selfe the mony was sealed up and deposited in a third p[er]sons hand. Thus the case stands upon the scruple, I suppose, arriseth, because the mony tendred was new money, w[hi]ch after that day was not Curr[en]t according to the King's proclamation.[1] What I did was by advice of a Publique notary, and their Cannot follow any p[re]judice to yo[u]rselves, S[i]r John or my selfe, but onely upon the goldsmith. The losse will be inconsiderable for wee heare the King will receive [inserted] all that sort of money into [word x o] his treasury. Herew[i]th you have Bill of Lading for some Pewter etc. on the *Leister* for acc[omp]t of Sig[nor]e Baldinotti, arriveing pray take all necessary Care and follow his order for the Costs & Charges. I have past my Bill on him for $ [blank] if hee should not be punctuall in discharging itt Pray let itt by yo[u]r meanes finde due honour on behalfe of the Drawer, though I hope there will bee noe such occasion and I shall see you reimbursed. My bill is pay[able?] to Mr Edw[ar]d Mico or order so I suppose you may learne who itts assigned to.

1. The Commonwealth money (called harp and cross money because it had the English cross and the Irish harp on the reverse) was demonetised in 1661-2 (Pepys IV p 148 note).

390. Mr Arnold Breames Jun[io]r London 3[r]d Decemb[e]r 1661

Yo[u]rs of the 28th past I have received yesterday w[i]th the inclosed for Mr Bryan Rogers, w[hi]ch shall be forwarded. I pray favour mee w[i]th yo[u]r advice if you heare of the arrivall of the *Providence*, John Spry m[aste]r, from the Barbados. Shee belongs to Mr Rogers & would bee welcome news to him.

391. Mr Bryan Rogers Ditto

I am w[i]thout any of yo[u]rs unansweared w[hi]ch Causeth Breavity. This being onely to accompany the inclosed from Mr Arnold Braems.

392. Mr Thierry London 6th Decemb[e]r 1661

My last was on the 29th past at Large since w[hi]ch I have not received any of yo[u]rs. Yo[u]r sonn, Mr Jacobus, is now entred upon the Studdy of English in w[hi]ch I doubt not but hee wil make good progresse haveing the assistance of a very able master who teacheth many Languages and speakes Natural dut[c]h w[hi]ch I esteeme a great covenience for the True informeing the Learner the signifcation of words in his owne language. He practiseth daunceing too and I hope after some time hee will delight in itt. The begining of all things is Troblesome. S[i]r itt's necessary that Mr Jacobus make some Clothes suitable to the season of the yeare and the pr[e]sent Fashion. If you give mee order I shall act accordingly, or if to him selfe I shall furnish him w[i]th what money he shall have occation For, as you have already ordered.

S[i]r, Since the above I have yo[u]rs of the 9th Curr[en]t the inclosed delivered to yo[u]r Sonne from whome is answear. I p[er]ceive you approve of the Assurance I have made for yo[u]r acc[omp]t on the *Golden Fox*. God send her in Safety. I am Endeavouring to end w[i]th the N. Lyon assurers but they are slow in paying, my next shall give an acc[omp]t of what rec[eive]d. I hope Mr Breams will manadge our suit att Dover. I know not yet how to understand the acting betweene him & Mr Delavall, if I can Learne any thing by inquiry you shall be advised. I shall engage Mr Bridgewood to bee serviceable to S[i]r Arnold Brames at Lisborne in w[ha]t he may. Herew[i]th is a lett[e]r from Mr W[illia]m Jennens.

393. Mr W[illia]m Jennens London 7th Decemb[e]r 1661.

Y[ou]rs of the 3rd Curr[en]t I have received, the inclosed for Mr Thierry Forwarded. Mr Sparke is of opinion that the suit at Dover is Scarce worth Lookeing after for if [?] Succeeded as we hope, the Baile is but for £76 at which Sume the friggott was appraised onely. It would doe well as he saith if Capt[ain] Jacobsen might be again arrested, which Cannot bee w[i]thout another Monition and, quistionlesse, he will, upon the Least suspition, remove from Dunkirke. To sue the Bille given in Sweden is what I have not hitherto had thoughts but who to imploy & Trust there I know not espetially wee having had Such ill Successe if w[ha]t is there already Spent when the whole businesse appeared not w[i]th soe much Dificulty as itt [inserted] now (a x out] doth after such losse of time. However what shall be jointly concluded upon I shall follow. I am expecting Mr Thierry's Answear.

394. Mr Bernard Sparke London 7th December 1661

I have yo[u]rs of the 3rd Cur[ren]t. The inclosed for Mr Thierry forwarded. When I have his order (as being much Concerned) I shall proceed accordingly about the businesse of Jacobsen although I incline to yo[u]r opinion rather to desist than bee at the charge of prosecuting when, if all things goe as wee wish, our Security is but £75. And, if wee should Resolve to take out another monition on to Arrest Capt[ain] Jacobsen, itt odds but before this he is removed from Dunkirke having relation to the Sea. What shall hereafter be resolved on I shall act accordingly. The Turkes are well fitted but I hope the fleet now on departure for Tangier will much secure m[e]rchants' shipps. Itt [sic] though there will not be a proclamation for w[i]thout itt the new Coine is taken in all publique receipts, if any be published itt shall be sent you.

395. Mr Edw[ar]d Bridgewood London 7 Decemb[e]r 1661

We have yo[u]rs of the 28th past. The inclosed for Mr Thierry shall be forwarded. You may Continue to addresse yo[u]r letter to us for him, where they shall have safe conveyance. His businesse recommended to you wee hope by yo[u]r meanes will finde good Successe. A friend of Mr Thierry & ours, by name S[i]rArnold Breams, is Bound for yo[u]r Citty About p[ar]ticular Businesse, pray pr[e]sent our Service to him, and be his assistant in w[ha]t you may. The bill of Excha[nge] you sent us upon yo[u]r Bro[ther] Mr Alex[an]d[er] Bence, hee yet gives noe answear too, o[u]r next may advise more and what wee resolve about the Comoditys you say are in esteeme w[I]th you. Our Respects pr[e]sented to you and yo[u]r Lady.

> Yours etc
> Abrah[am] & Tho[mas] Hill

396. Mr Bryan Rogers London 7th Decemb[e]r 1661

I have not any of yo[u]rs to answear so this is Cheifly to accompany the inclosed rec[eive]d from Mr Arnold Breames. The Candles & hopps you orderd are in a readinesse but here is not yet a Conveyance. Wee have no news of the *Providence*. When any as shall advize you.

397. Mr Arnold Breames London 11th Decemb[e]r 1661

Yo[u]rs of the 8th Curr[en]t I have reeived, the inclosed For Mr Bryan Rogers I forwarded in due time. When I have answear I shall send itt you. Herew[i]th you have a Pacquett from Mr Thiery. I question not yo[u]r utmost Diligence in the most advantageous Manageing our Suite in yo[u]r Court so I have onely to entreat yo[u]r advice w[ha]t passeth.

398. Mr James Thierry London 13 Decemb[e]r 1661

Yo[u]rs of the 16/[6] Curr[en]t I have received, the inclosed to yo[u]r Sonne and Mons[ieur] Schelling are delivered the others forwarded according to direction. I have Letters from Mr Edward Bridgewood at Lisboa, who is mindfull of yo[u]r Businesse and writes you inclosed to w[hi]ch referr you. For proceeding to a new arresting of Capt[ain] Jacobsen I cannot well doe itt, till I have advice from Mr Arnold Breames if hee still remaine at Dunkirke. I suppose Mr Sparke hath written you, as his oppinon that the prosecuteing the businesse is scarce worth the Trouble & Charge that will be spent about itt, the security being so small att £75 [sic], however I shall doe my endeavour in any thing that may conduce to an ending this bad businesse. Herew[i]th you have a particular of the Assurers name on the *N. Lyon* w[i]th Note who have paid. They still promise Faire but doe not performe. I call often on them, and shall continue to doe itt till the acc[omp]t be cleared. As yet there is no pattent concerning the Guinny trade, if any is graunted shall give you advice. I am glad yo[u]r Straight Ships arrive in Safety. Of late are arrived 3 or 4 with us and have brought quantitys of galls Worth £3.6s p[er] cwt and silk, Burma Legee of Aleppo, worth 21 to 22s p[er] lb.. If these Comoditys would turne to acc[omp]t w[i]th you I should be ready to serve you. I pray God send yo[u]r shipp *Blacke-horse* in safety. Att her arrivall I shall be assisting to the Master in w[ha]t hee may have occasion. I returne you many thanks for yo[u]r kinde token w[hi]ch I shall studdy to requite. Herew[i]th is an inclosed from Mr Bryan Rogers & the price Curr[en]t.

399. Mr Bryan Rogers London 14th Decemb[e]r 1661

Yo[u]rs of the 9th Curr[en]t I have received & forwarded the incloseds. I know not if Mr Breames his losse by the West India Compa[ny] but now co[n]ceive Mr Thierry Concerned w[i]th him because I often convey Letters from each of them. I wish they may have restitution from those that have donne them wrong.

I have acquainted my Brother that Mr Pascoe hath paid you for him £16.5.4 for the Troble hee thanks you. Our assurers here are not very punctuall tis true the generality but some who have noe other imploym[en]t are very faire Conditioned because their Creditt depends upon the strict complying as they agree a losse. If Mr Devogell value him selfe upon mee. I shall observe yo[u]r order in satisfying his bill.

400. Mr Arnold Breames 14 December 1661

I have only at present to forward the inclosed to you from Mr Bryan Rogers. Pray S[i]r Let mee know if Capt[ain] Jacobsen be still resideing att Dunkirk and the needfull as to his personall Estate, and w[ha]tsoever [word x o] you conceive necessary for us to know in order to the better proceeding if wee should again resolve to bee att the Charge of another Monition out of our adm[ira]lty Court. Pray Let mee know [word x o] w[ha]t passeth w[i]th you.

401. Mr James Thierry 20th Decemb[e]r 1661

Yours of the 23/[13] Curr[en]t I have received, the incloseds were delivered to yo[u]r sonne & Mons. Schelling the others shall be forwarded W[i]th the first oportunites I have taken care to provide Mr Jacome Thierry a black Cloth suite w[hi]ch is fit for the season and a Civil Garbe and such as may become him. I shall [not ?] faile to serve him in w[ha]tsoever he may have occation. I pray God send yo[u]r shipp *Blacke Horse* in Safety. At her arrivall I shall be carefull to Assist the Master in all things and observe w[ha]t orders you please hereafter to give for the Dispose of her Cargo. Barbados Sugars are now worth 22s to 26s p[er] cwt according to there Goodness. Cotton 6 3/4 or 7d p[er] lb. In all things I shall act for yo[u]r most advantage. I am expecting Mr Braem's answear concerning Capt[ain] Jacobsen if still att Dunkirke that so wee may resolve upon arresting him againe. The suit att Dover Mr Braems promises to follow w[i]th all diligence for our most advantage. The *North Lyon* assurers doe still delay Cleereing their Losse. I call upon them daylye but am put of and finde very tedious ending such Busnisses But pray S[i]r Lett mee have M. Sellio Marsellis' order to make good to you w[ha]t I shall receive upon this accompt. I inquire about the Patent for the Guinny Trade but finde not t[ha]t any is yet granted nor sought after. What passes shall hereafter advise you. Herew[I]th is an inclosed from Mr Bernard Sparke who I suppose writes you his sence concerning the arrested friggatt att Dover w[ha]t you please Jointly to order I shall follow.

S[i]r wee are much obliged to yo[u]r good selfe and Lady for the many favours you shew to my Brother. It will be his studdy I hope to acknowledge and I hope requite. This day the Parliam[ent] adjourned till after the Holly dayes. The price Curr[ent] you have here.

402. Mr Bryan Rogers 21 Decemb[e]r 1661

S[i]r,
Yo[u]rs of the 16th Curr[en]t I have received & according to yo[u]r order I have made a policy of Assurance in yo[u]r name with generall words upon goods & merchandizes Laden aboard yo[u]r

ship *Providence*, John Sprye master, from the Barbados to the Port of London with Liberty to touch in the west Country £200. I have gotten already underwritten att £3 p[er] C[en]t the rest shall be done on Munday. I hope itt will be to yo[u]r satisfaction, the p[re]mio being at soe easy [word x o] a rate and I shall indeavour to Chuse good men. I have Likewise made a memorandum that it shall be no p[re]judice to this pollicy if you have Caused any other to be made in some other place. I hope shall give you shortly the good news of her arrivall. Sugars att p[re]sent worth from 22 to 26s p[er] c[w]t Cottons 6 3/4d a 7d p[er] lb.

At instant was w[i]th mee Edw[ar]d James who I told should have abord yo[u]r hopps and Candles when he would but hee supposeth itt may bee after the Holly dayes before hee comes to the Key.

Att the Request of a freind I am obliged to desire yo[u]r favour in suplying Coll[onel] Edm[un]d Harvy [1] at p[re]sent a prisoner in Pendennis Castle to the value of £20 for his necessary occations takeing his bill for w[ha]t hee may receive upon Mr [?] Harvy of this Citty who hath promised to Satisfye it [blot & some crossings out] if itt might not be prejudicial yo[u]r vissitting him dureing his restraint would much engage him selfe and friends, but I onely mention & doe not recommend itt not knowing the humour of yo[u]r neighbours.

I have received £14 by the bill you sent mee upon Mr John Marvin w[hi]ch I passe to yo[u]r Cr[edit]. [Herewith x o] Here inclosed you have a lett[e]r from Mr James Thierry.

1. Edmund Harvey, a regicide. Eldest son of Charles Harvey, merchant. Edmund Harvey's son, Samuel, married Bulstrode Whitelocke's daughter, he was therefore a relation by marriage to Abraham Hill. Harvey had been tried as a regicide in October 1660, but his life was spared. Whitelocke tried to get him a pardon but he was imprisoned in Pendennis till his death in 1673. He was buried in Falmouth parish church yard. (*DNB* Vol. 25 p 650)
'A draper with an unsavoury reputation' (Spalding. *Contemporaries* p 114)

403.Mr Bryan Rogers 28th Decemb[e]r 1661

Since my Last of the 21st Curr[en]t I have not re[ceive]d any of yo[u]rs which causes Brevity. This being onely for advice that according to yo[u]r order I have caused £400 St[erling] to be assured upon yo[u]r Shipp *Providence*. God send her in Safety.

APPENDIX

[The following accounts are at the end of the book with the book reversed]

1660/1661

February

Lute strings 19 boxes Re[ceive]d out of the *Alex[an]d[er]* friggat John Nash m[a]ster for acc[omp]t as underneath

D[ebto]rs

Feb[rua]ry Paid freight	£00.15.09
Paid the party that tooke them ashore	£02.05.00
Paid the m[a]ster for his assistance	£00.05.00
paid Ships Compa[ny] for theirs	£00.10.00
Paid going by water Severall times	£00.05.00
provision att 2% [£2.10.10 at side]	£ [blank]
	£04.00.00
Ballance	£124.02.00
	£128.02.00

see Letter 268

1661

Tynn 20 Slabbs Received out of the *Silence* of Falmouth Nicholas Bloy M[aste]r for accompt as Underneath

D[ebto]rs

April Paid Landing	£00.01.06
Wharfadge	£00.00.10
Cleering at Custome House	£00.01.00
The Seamen for assistance	£00.00.06
Cartage	£00.02.06
Weighing at delivery	£00.02.03
Provision at 2 p[er] C[en]t	£02.10.04
	£02.18.11
Ballance	£123.02.07
	£126.01.06

(see Letters 264 and 303)

1660/1661

Cr[edito]r

February	By Chr[istopher] Wise for 60 bundles at 2s.6d		£07.10.00
	By Severalls for	16 bundles at 5s p[er] bund[l]e	£04.00.00
Aprill	By Tho[mas] Felgate for	864 bundles att 2s per bundle	£86.08.00
May	By Rich[ard] Hunt for	151 bundles att 4s per bun[dle]	£30.04.00
		1091 -	£128.02.00
	less the Invoice 6 bundles	6	
		1097	

The ballance being one hundred Twenty four pound
Two Shillings I passe to acc[omp]t of Mr John Byam w[i]thout
my prejudice till fully imbursed.

Dated in London adi le 21 June 1661
[Signed] Tho[mas] Hill Errors Excepted

1661

Cr[edito]r

May By John Bennet for detti sould him

	C[wt]	qu.	lb		
Way	25	.3	.24		
	0	0	.26 allowance 1 lb p[er] C[w]t		
	25	2	26 @£4.18p[er] C[w]t	£126.01.06

The Ballance being one hundred twenty three pounds Two
Shillings & Seven pence, is carried to the accompt Curr[en]t of
Mr Bryan Rogers without my prejudice till fully
Imbursed.
Dated ad London the 22th June 1661
[Signed} Tho[mas] Hill Errors Excepted

1661
Tynn 37 Slabbs Received out of the *Prosperous* George Pomrey M[aste]
r for acc[omp]t as underneath
D[ebto]rs
Aprill 1661

Paid freight & Coquet money	£2.17.06
Landing & loading	£0.03.01
Wharfadge	£0.01.06
Cartage	£0.05.02
Waying att delivery	£0.03.01
Provision att 2p[er] C[en]t	£4.06.08
	£7.17.00
balance	£209.00.00
	£216.17.00

see Letter 303

1661
Tynn 18 Slabbs Received out of the *John of London* Angell Corbin
master for acc[omp]t as underneath
D[ebto]rs
April

Paid freight	£0.19.00
Landing & Loading	£0.01.06
Wharfadge	£0.00.09
Cartage	£0.02.03
Waying att delivery	£0.01.06
Provision att 2p[er] C[en]t	£1.16.00
	£3.01.00
Balance	£87.03.06
	£90.04.06

See Letter 303

Cr[edito]r

1661

Aprill   By John Daniel for 4 Slabbs to him
          Sould way[t] 5cwt.1.3 at £4.19 p[er] C[w]t   £26.02.00

May   By Edw[ard] Goodwyn for 33 Slabbs to him
          Sould way[t]   39.2.20
                            00 1.12 allowance 1 p[er] c[en]t
                            39.1.08 at £4.17 p[er] cwt   £190.15.0
                                                              £216.17.0

The ballance being Two hundred and nine pounds
is carryed to Acc[omp]t Currant of Mr Bryan Rogers
without my p[re]judice till fully imburst.
Dated in Lond[on] 22th June 1661

      [signed] Th. Hill Errors Excepted   Cr[edit]

see Letter 264

Cr[edito]r

1661

May   By Edward Goodwyn for detti to him
sould wayt   18.3.23
                19 allowance at 1 p[er] C[en]t
                20.2.11 at £4.17   £90.04.6

The ballance being Eighty Seven pounds three
Shillings Six pence is Carryed to the acc[omp]t Curr[en]t of
Mr Bryan Rogers Without my p[re]judice till
fully imburst.
Dated in London 22 June 1661

[Signed] Thomas Hill Errors Excepted

Invoice of 2 Bales Containeing 5 long, 5 short Cloathes Laden aboard the *Leister* friggatt, Capt[ain] Aron Wallis Comander, bound for Legorne, and goes [?] consigned by order and for acc[omp]t of Mr James Thierry of Amst[erdam], Merch[an]t unto Sign[ore] Giovanni Sabe & Comp[any] under marke & number as in Margent vizt: [in the margin is a mark which could be a TH and no.112] Bought of Richard Boylstone

No.		yards		
1	Poppinge	21.0.21.0)		
2	Ditto	20.2.21.0)		
3	Grasse greene	20.2.21.0) att £12.15 p[er] Cloath		£63.15.00
4	French green	20.2.21.0)		
5	Red	19.2.21.0)		
6	Plonket [?]	16.0.17.0)		
7	Ditto	16.0.15.0)		
8	Violet	16.1.16.0) att £9 p[er] Cloath		£45.00.00
9	Plonkett	16.1.16.0)		
10	Blew	16.0.16.0)		

Charges

10 Clothes Mantled at 3s p[er] Cloth	£1.10.00
Ribband att 6d p[er] half Cloth	£0.10.00
Buckram att 22d p[er] halfe Cloth	£1.16.08
Drawing att 4d p[er] cloth	£0.03.04
Hott pressing att 2s p[er] cloth	£1.00.00
Custome £1.15.5 & the Cockett 2s 6d	£1.17.11
Packing the 2 bales	£0.13.04
Cartadge to waterside	£0.01.06
Wharfadge & Searcher's Fees	£0.03.06
Shipping off	£0.01.06
Boat hire aboard	£0.01.03
	£7.19.00
Provision att 2%	£2.06.08
	£119.00.08

London 25th October 1661 Th. Hill

(see Letter 353)

[in Italian]

Invoice of 4 barrels of wrought pewter loaded for the account of Signore Jacopo Baldinotti on the ship *Leister* frigate consigned to Messrs Lytcott & Gascoigne in Livorno under the Mark and number as in the Margin [in margin is TH no 1234] vizt.

Bought from Mr Thomas Heath

4 dozen plates 'Reali' } weighing 6cwt 9 qtr. 17 lbs @ 4d the lb	£45.01.10
6 dozen half [plates] 'Reali' }	
12 dozen drinking tankards weighing 2 cwt. 3 qtr 1 lb @ 15d the lb	£14.01.03
12 bowls with their jugs [?] @ 16d the lb	£09.12.00
6 candlesticks for the table & 3 pair of candle snuffers[?]	£01.16.06
4 [hoods for the candles?]	£01.04.00
2 salt cellars	£00..06.06
1 basin	£00.04.06
1 buckle	£00.02.02

The case was loaded as above

[In margin TH]

6 pairs of shoes	£01.12.00
1 Dictionary Italian English	£00.05.00
4 small books	£00.06.00
	£75.11.09

Charges etc

Tax on the pewter of 9 cwt @ 5s the hundred is	£ 2.10.08	
4 large barrels	£ 0.08.06	
1 case with canvas	£ 0.01.06	
Boat hire, bringing aboard and other similar tasks	£ 0.04.09	
		£03.05.05

Commission at 2 per cent	
[remaining figures mostly blotted out therefore say]	[£01.11.04]
	[£80.08.06]

On the 29th October 1661 London

(see Letter 297)

INDEX

White, Robert xxiii; Thomas 61,
    75, 153, 175
Whitehall 69
Whitelock, Bulstrode xlv, xlviii,
    lii, lviii, 74 & n., 76
Whiting, Mr 58
Whitmore, Sir George 36n.
Wight, Isle of 115n, 116, 117, 121
Wild, Mr 158
Wilde, Sir William 36 & n., 134
    & n.
Williams, Robert 207
Williams, William 60, 80, 160
Willis, Edmond lxx; John lxx
Wilson, Samuel xliv, 142, 187
wine, xvii, xxxiii, xxxiv, 47, 59,
    80, 120, 137, 154, 159, 207
Wise, Christopher 217

Woodland, Devon liv
Woodrof[fe], John 1 & n., 18, 24,
    32, 35, 40, 43
wool 102
Woolwich lxiii
Wren, Christopher 100n.
Wynsveare, Thomas xxxiii

Yardly, Christopher 25
Yarmouth li, 2n., 10, 24, 25, 36,
    44, 53, 58
Yeo, John liv
York, Duke of 44 & n., 46, 108;
    Duchess of York, 108 & n.
Young, James 108

Zante xxxvi, xl, lvii, lxvii, 149

DEVON AND CORNWALL RECORD SOCIETY PUBLICATIONS

The following New Series titles are obtainable from the Administrator, Devon and Cornwall Record Society, 7 The Close, Exeter EX1 1EZ

Unless otherwise indicated, prices are: £15.00 UK, £20.00 overseas (surface mail). All prices include p/p.

At joining, new members are offered volumes of the preceding 4 years at current subscription prices rather than the listed price.

Fully-paid members are offered a discount on volumes older than 5 years if the remaining stock exceeds 20: please enquire.

ISSN/ISBN 978-0-901853-

New Series

Bath, and Rachel, Countess of Bath, of Tawstock and London, 1639–54, ed. Todd Gray, 1996 *£17.00 UK, £22.00 overseas -* **39 9**

40 *The Uffculme Wills and Inventories, 16ᵗʰ to 18ᵗʰ Centuries*, ed. Peter Wyatt, with an introduction by Robin Stanes, 1997 *£16.00 UK, £21.00 overseas -* **40 2**

41 *Cornish Rentals and Surveys of the Arundell Family of Lanherne, Fourteenth to Sixteenth Centuries*, ed. H S A Fox and O J Padel, 1998 *£20.00 UK, £25.00 overseas -* **41 0**

42 *Liberalism in West Cornwall: The 1868 Election Papers of A. Pendarves Vivian MP*, ed. Edwin Jaggard, 1999 - **42 9**

43, 45 *Devon Maps and Map-makers: Manuscript Maps before 1840*, ed. with introduction Mary R Ravenhill and Margery M Rowe, 2000 & 2002, *£30.00 UK, £37.00 overseas -* **43 7, 45 3**

44 *The Havener's Accounts of the Earldom and Duchy of Cornwall, 1287–1356*, ed. Maryanne Kowaleski, 2001, *£20.00 UK, £25.00 overseas -* **44 5**

46 *Death and Memory in Medieval Exeter*, ed. David Lepine and Nicholas Orme and D Lepine, 2003, *£20.00 UK, £25.00 overseas -* **46 1**

47 *The Survey of Cornwall by Richard Carew*, edited by John Chynoweth, Nicholas Orme & Alexandra Walsham, 2004, *£25.00 UK, £32 overseas -* **47 X**

48 *Killerton, Camborne and Westminster: The Political Correspondence of Sir Francis and Lady Acland, 1910–1929*, ed. Garry Tregidga, 2005, *£18.00 UK, £23.00 overseas -* **48 8**

49 *The Acland Family: maps and surveys 1720–1840*, ed. with an Introduction by Mary R. Ravenhill & Margery M. Rowe, 2006, *£20.00 UK, £25.00 overseas -* **49 3**

50 *Cornish Wills 1342–1540*, ed. Nicholas Orme, 2007, *£20.00 UK, £25.00 overseas -* **50 9**

Extra Series

1 *Exeter Freemen 1266–1967*, edited by Margery M Rowe and Andrew M Jackson, 1973. *£18.00 UK, £23.00 overseas -* **18 6**

Shelf list of the Society's Collections, revised June 1986. *£2.30 UK, £3.50 overseas.*
http://www.devon.gov.uk/library/locstudy/dcrs.html.

New Series out of print:
1 *Devon Monastic Lands: Calendar of Particulars for Grants 1536-1558,* ed. Youings, 1955; 3 *The Diocese of Exeter in 1821: vol. I Cornwall,* ed. Cook, 1958; 5 *The Cartulary of St Michael's Mount,* ed. Hull, 1962; 8 *The Cartulary of Canonsleigh Abbey,* calendared & ed. London, 1965; 9 *Benjamin Donn's Map of Devon 1765.* Intro. Ravenhill, 1965; 11 *Devon Inventories of the 16th & 17th Centuries,* ed. Cash, 1966; 14 *The Devonshire Lay Subsidy of 1332,* ed. Audrey M Erskine, 1969; 7, 10, 13, 16, 18 *The Register of Edmund Lacy, Bishop of Exeter 1420–1455* (five volumes), ed. Dunstan, 1963–1972

Extra Series out of print: Guide to the Parish and Non-Parochial Registers of Devon and Cornwall 1538–1837, compiled: Peskett, 1979 & supplement 1983